God and the Generations

Youth, Age and the Church Today

A Report by the Evangelical Alliance Commission on Unity and Truth among Evangelicals (ACUTE)

God and the Generations

Youth, Age and the Church Today

Edited by David Hilborn & Matt Bird

A Report by the Evangelical Alliance (UK) Commission
on Unity and Truth among Evangelicals

Working Group: Roger Hitchings, Mark Knight,
Amy Orr-Ewing, Michael Penrose, Steve Spriggs

PATERNOSTER PRESS

Published 2002 by Paternoster Press

08 07 06 05 04 03 02   7 6 5 4 3 2 1

Paternoster Press is an imprint of Authentic Media,
PO Box 300, Carlisle, Cumbria, CA3 0QS, UK
and
PO Box 1047, Waynesboro, GA 30830-2047, USA

www.paternoster-publishing.com

British Library Cataloguing in Publication Data
A catalogue record for this book is available from the British Library

ISBN 1-84227-168-7

Cover by Campsie
Typeset by WestKey Ltd, Falmouth, Cornwall
Printed in Great Britain by Cox and Wyman, Reading, Berkshire

Contents

About ACUTE

ACUTE is the Evangelical Alliance Commission on Unity and Truth among Evangelicals. Co-ordinated by the Alliance's Theological Adviser, Dr David Hilborn, it is committed to an ongoing programme of research and publication on theological issues which are of concern to evangelicals. So far, in conjunction with Paternoster Press, it has published the following reports and studies: *Faith, Hope and Homosexuality* (1998), *The Nature of Hell* (2000), *'Toronto' in Perspective* (2001), *Evangelicalism and the Orthodox Church* (2001) and *One Body in Christ: The History and Significance of the Evangelical Alliance* (Ian Randall and David Hilborn, 2001). In addition to this current book, ACUTE will be publishing a report entitled *Faith, Health and Prosperity* in 2003.

For further details and information, contact ACUTE, Evangelical Alliance, 186 Kennington Park Road, London SE11 4BT.

Email – acute@eauk.org
Web – www.eauk.org

Preface

One of my greatest passions is to invest in emerging generations of leaders, to transform society. As an activist, I have approached this by mentoring, training and resourcing emerging leaders, and by encouraging denominations and organisations to do the same. As this work has developed, however, I have become increasingly aware of the need for more considered theological reflection on the significance of generational distinctions and interrelationships, both within the church and across society as a whole. I was therefore delighted when the Evangelical Alliance Commission on Unity and Truth among Evangelicals (ACUTE), under the guidance of its Co-ordinator David Hilborn, agreed to take up my suggestion that it might pursue such reflection through a special working group and a written report.

The working group first met in January 2000 and gathered on several further occasions throughout the year. At each meeting, two preliminary papers were submitted and then discussed by the group as a whole. Refinements were made in the light of these discussions and then, from January 2001, David Hilborn and I set about editing the papers into a draft report. This draft was subsequently peer-reviewed by a wider circle of readers, and by members of ACUTE, and their suggestions and corrections were taken into account in the preparation of the final text.

The following study seeks to address questions of age, cultural segmentation, family, leadership succession, ecclesiology and mission at a hermeneutical level not usually found in evangelical literature on generational issues. My hope is that it will prompt both practitioners and reflectors to think more deeply about generationally-defined ministry, and that it will lead to the more considered discussion and debate which is now needed in this area. In keeping with this, I am thrilled that Steve Spriggs, who serves as the Research Associate of Joshua Generation, the charity I lead, will be continuing to develop the work this book has begun, as he pursues doctoral research on Christian leadership and succession at King's College, London.

I would like to thank David Hilborn for first listening sympathetically to my idea for this book over lunch. His friendship, support and work throughout the project have been greatly appreciated. I am also grateful that ACUTE has backed this research, despite the fact that in many ways it has not been typical of its usual output. Most especially, I would like to thank the members of the working group – Roger Hitchings, Mark Knight, Amy Orr-Ewing, Michael Penrose and Steve Spriggs – for all the time and effort they have given to this project. Adam Sparks supplied helpful background material, for which we are very grateful. Thanks are also due to Mark Bonnington, Chris Bourne, Graeme Codrington, Graham Cray and Steve Moore for acting as peer reviewers.

We do not expect that the analyses and arguments we have presented here will win universal assent on every point. We do believe, however, that they seek seriously to address issues which deserve closer scrutiny. We trust that the report will be read in this light, and we look forward to receiving feedback on it.

Matt Bird,
Chair of Evangelical Alliance 'God and The Generations'
Working Group and Director of Joshua Generation

mattbird@joshgen.org

Foreword

At numerous points in my ministry, I have encouraged churches, Christian organisations and individuals to address the needs of the 'emerging generation', the 'younger generation' and the 'older generation'. At other times I have found myself calling for greater intergenerational co-operation, for generational balance on councils and committees, and for cross-generational mentoring, training and support. Then again, as a son and father, I have often contemplated my own generational identity within the family context.

I have long realised that such concerns are thoroughly biblical. After all, it is difficult to read Scripture in any depth without encountering generational language. Yet like most Christians, and many evangelicals in particular, I have talked of generations intuitively and instinctively rather than exegetically and theologically. I have known, of course, that age is a major part of the equation, but have sensed that worldview, lifestyle and historical experience also bear on the matter. Quite how all these things interact has, however, been unclear. Over the past few years, plenty of books have appeared on the characteristics of various generational groups, and quite a few have offered helpful advice on reaching such groups with the Gospel. Still, though, these have tended to borrow models from non-theological sources, rather than relating what the Bible has to say about generations to the generational distinctions so often made in society today.

Here, however, is a book which skilfully applies close exposition of the generational language of Scripture to contemporary
culture, church life and mission. I am delighted that the Alliance's
theological commission, ACUTE, has produced it. ACUTE is
often asked to deal with established doctrinal debates, and to
review, explain and mediate between positions which have been
well developed among evangelicals. Here, however, it has under-
taken a good deal of genuinely original, interdisciplinary research,
and has come up with a text which promises to lead Christian
thinking about contemporary culture, and Christian mission to
that culture, in significant ways. The working group are to be
commended for their attention to detail. As joint editors, David
Hilborn and Matt Bird deserve thanks for having produced a
scholarly yet readable book – one which admirably bears out the
Alliance's commitment to be a servant of the church and a movement for change in society. I hope that it will be widely read, and
look forward to the discussions and debates which it will no
doubt provoke!

Joel Edwards
General Director,
The Evangelical Alliance UK
Easter 2002

1

Generations in Cultural and Theological Perspective

Introduction

Generations are much discussed, defined and differentiated in Western Christianity today. Particularly during the last three decades or so, it has become common for missiologists, church growth theorists, sociologists of religion and pastoral leaders to segment both society and church into groups defined in one way or another as 'generations'. What is more, this trend appears to have been especially prevalent among evangelicals. In the following study, we seek to highlight the importance of such generation-based analysis for contemporary Christian life and mission. Also, however, we offer a constructive critique of existing work in this field. This critique suggests that evangelicals in particular have failed sufficiently to address the cultural and philosophical assumptions underlying the generational models they have borrowed. It also suggests that they have not adequately placed these models in hermeneutical and theological perspective.

Having highlighted these gaps, we seek to bridge them by (i) offering a more detailed biblical account of generational structures, (ii) relating this account to contemporary social science thinking on generations, and (iii) applying insights gained through (i) and (ii) to key issues in family life, church organisation, Christian mission and the providence of God.

The Rise of Generational Thinking in the Western Church

The 'generation gap problem'

From the late 1960s, the evangelical missionary anthropologists Donald McGavran and Charles Kraft began to address what they perceived to be a sharpening of the distinctions between different generational groups within the USA, and to chart the implications of this for the life and outreach of the church. Indeed, Kraft went so far as to diagnose a 'generation gap problem', and to warn that growing 'intergenerational antipathy' was presenting the Christian community in North America with a grave challenge.[1] A similar, early expression of such concern from the UK appeared in a cover article for the March 1967 issue of the Evangelical Alliance-backed magazine, *Crusade*. Entitled 'The Drifting Generation', this feature charted the disaffection of many young people at the time with their elders, and with the institutions represented by those elders.[2] In the same period, evangelical cultural commentators like the Briton Os Guinness and the American Francis Schaeffer published extended analyses of a new and distinct 'youth culture', which they challenged the church to address in relevant and constructive ways.[3]

Guinness defined this emergent culture as a loose affiliation of beatniks, existentialists, angry young men, hippies and political revolutionaries – a culture which, for all its diversity, was remarkably united in its alienation from the church. Indeed, as Guinness described it, the younger generation of the late 1960s looked at the church and typically levelled a 'catalogue of criticisms' against it, from poverty of leadership through vacuousness in public statements, to an inveterately 'bourgeois' sensibility.[4] Most pervasive of all, however, was its association of the church with a separate, older generation – that is, with a sterile version of 'middle age', and even with 'obsolescence'.[5]

There have been many scholarly reflections on this association, but as the Scottish historian Callum Brown has noted, it was popular culture, and pop music in particular, which most powerfully crystallised it.[6] As Brown recounts, the new pirate radio stations, and the pop records they broadcast between 1964–7, effectively 'displaced the printed word as the key method by which young people formed their own discursive world'. Of all the groups who shaped this fresh discursive world, it was the Beatles who brought the apparent decrepitude of the church most influentially to light. Famously, John Lennon told the London *Evening Standard* in the summer of 1966 that his group had become 'more popular than Jesus', while Paul McCartney's chart-topping song of the same year, *Eleanor Rigby*, hauntingly portrayed 'Father MacKenzie/ Writing the words of a sermon that no-one will hear'.[7]

Against this background, it is telling that the first recorded use of Charles Kraft's favoured term 'generation gap' dates from 1967[8] – the year when popular music, radical politics, drugs, hippiedom, fashion and general permissiveness coalesced to establish the identity of a distinct 'youth generation' set very consciously over against the generation of its parents.

Now of course, the mere coinage of the term 'generation gap' in the late sixties does not mean that intergenerational tension *as such* only began to emerge at that point. After all, the Greek poet Hesiod had warned as early as the eighth century BC that society could have no future if it depended on 'the frivolous youth of today, for certainly all youth are reckless beyond words'. The philosopher Aristotle apparently drank hemlock after being blamed for encouraging 'corrupt youth'. In 1114 Peter the Hermit voiced a familiar perception of intergenerational relationships when he complained, 'Youth has no regard for old age and the wisdom of the centuries is looked down upon both as stupid and foolishness. The young men are indolent; the young women are indecent and indecorous in their speech, behaviour and dress.' And Shakespeare's Shepherd in *The Winter's Tale* complained that the young do nothing except 'getting wenches with child, wronging the ancientry, stealing, fighting'.[9] Yet while Jonathon Green is right to warn against viewing cultural change in neat chronological divisions, and while, as we shall see, the isolation of a distinct *economic* class of 'teenagers' had begun somewhat earlier, the generation of young people that arose in the sixties does appear to have represented a new departure:[10]

> It is as if there arose a gradual, ever-intensifying sense of one's own potential. And as the state of mind known as 'the Sixties' came up to speed, fuelled by that triumvirate of "dope, sex and rock 'n' roll", plus the non-specific and never so popular concept of "revolution", there developed an "alternative" society ... [This society] had its own media – newspapers, magazines, film, theatre and even fledgling videos. Much of the rock industry was targeted straight at it. It had advice centres and self-help groups. There was the world of drug selling for those who fancied an alternative brand of "venture capitalism" and for those more respectful of the law, a whole range of craft and cottage industries. It had restaurants, food shops, clubs and outfitters. And at its tribal gatherings, the great rock festivals, tens of thousands claimed allegiance to its ranks ... [T]he hippie hardcore were in their early twenties and the feel was student rather than schoolchild – but the prevailing ethos was undeniably geared towards the desire to oust the adult world.[11]

While the rise of this youth 'counter-culture' was often perceived as a threat to the authority and moral leadership of the church, one Christian group in particular sought to address it more positively. Indeed, the efforts of this group would have a major effect on the development of generationally-based ministry in the Western church.

Christian responses to the problem

One of the earliest, most radical and most foundational Christian responses to the 'generation gap problem' came in the form of the so-called 'Jesus Movement', which also emerged around 1967, in California – the same time and place in which the new younger generation described by Os Guinness was finding its most ideal-ised expression, through what was popularly dubbed the 'Summer of Love'.[12] The Jesus Movement, indeed, would become the first internationally significant Christian community to define and distinguish itself specifically in relation to a discrete youth culture. Granted, there had been ministries focused on young people before – the YMCA, Scripture Union, Inter-Varsity Fellowship, Crusaders, Pathfinders, the Christian Youth Club movement and the like – but these had existed as 'auxilia-ries' to the mainstream church, and had not attempted to establish fresh models of being church in their own right. By contrast, as Pete Ward has recounted, the urban coffee bars and nightclubs, the 'gospel rock' music and 'hip' spiritual argot, the 'underground' magazines and left-field fashions of the Jesus Movement were instrumental in prompting Western churches generally, and evan-gelical churches in particular, to recognise that 'youth genera-tions' might need not only to be evangelised, but also to express faith, in ways quite distinct from those which had hitherto been associated with 'children' and 'adults'.[13]

Even where the precise dress codes, artistic sensibilities and evangelistic methods adopted by the Jesus Movement were deemed too outlandish, the Movement itself seems to have spurred a new stream of writing, debate and action on genera-tional divisions – a stream which has continued to flow through the Western church down to the present. In the UK, the course of this stream has taken in, among other things, the birth of the Greenbelt Arts Festival in the early 1970s, Kenneth Leech's high-lighting of 'youth spirituality' in the mid-1970s, the radical younger leadership of the House Church movement in the same period, Tony Jasper's and others' work on the church and 'pop' culture in the mid-1980s, the birth and development of the 'alternative worship' movement from the late 1980s, and the upsurge of intentional 'youth churches' in the early 1990s.[14]

The emergent 'generational consciousness' which prompted these responses has since grown significantly. Indeed, it has been reflected in an ever more complex stratification of Western society into groups based on age and/or genealogy, and on perceived corollaries of attitude, behaviour, experience and social function. As the new youth counter-culture arose in the 1960s, sociologists and others began to link it with the so-called 'baby boom' which had ensued when servicemen had returned home after World War II and had belatedly started families. The analysts in question surmised that bulges in the birth rate like this were always likely to leave an imprint on society, and suggested that as the 'Baby Boomers' reached adulthood in relatively large numbers, they were beginning to define themselves very consciously as a 'post-war' generation, intent on relinquishing the austerity and conformism of their parents in favour of a more libertarian outlook.[15]

The distinctiveness and self-awareness of this 'Boomer generation' in turn threw the profile of their grandparents' and parents' sets into sharper relief, and these sets retrospectively acquired their own labels and generic identities. So in the USA, those born before, during and just after the First World War became the faithful and patriotic 'G.I. generation', while the Boomers' parents and their peers were tagged as typically stolid 'Silents' or 'Builders'.[16] By the same token, as Boomers themselves have used the pill, planned families and reduced the birth rate, and as sixties idealism has given way to a more knowing and cynical mood, so their own children have acquired a separate designation as 'Baby Busters' or 'Generation Xers'.[17] Now, as even some Xers are approaching middle age, certain commentators are beginning to anatomise yet another, emerging generation – a generation most often referred to as 'the Millennials'.[18]

We shall examine the definition of these different generational groups much more fully in chapters 6–10. At this stage, however, it is important to note that although 'generational consciousness' has been present in Christian thinking from the days of Kraft, McGavran, Guinness and Schaeffer in the late sixties, the last decade or so has seen a considerable intensification of generationally-based Christian study. Indeed, during the last ten years it has become standard practice for those who write on youth ministry, evangelism and ecclesial demographics to relate their work to generational sub-groups within society, and then to suggest often markedly different plans for attracting such groups to, and keeping them within, the church. We shall deal with such work more fully as our own study develops, but it is worth noting here the sheer proliferation of generationally-oriented Christian titles which have been issued in the period mentioned.

Year by year, books published in this field have included: from 1993, Wade Clark Roof's *A Generation of Seekers: The Spiritual Journeys of the Baby Boom Generation*; from 1994, George Barna's *Baby Busters: The Disillusioned Generation*, William Mahedy and Janet Bernardi's *A Generation Alone: Xers Making a Place in the World* and Mark DeVries' *Family-Based Youth Ministry: Reaching the Been-There, Done-That Generation*; from 1995, Barna's *Generation Next: What You Need to Know About Today's Youth*; from 1996, Kevin Ford's *Jesus for a New Generation* and Tim Celek and Dieter Zander's *Inside the Soul of New Generation*; from 1997, Jimmy Long's *Generating Hope* and Mike Starkey's *God, Sex and Generation X*; from 1998, Tom Beaudoin's *Virtual Faith: The Irreverent Spirituality of Generation X* and Todd Hahn and David Verhaagen's *Gen Xers After God*; from 1999 Roof's *Spiritual Marketplace: Baby Boomers and the Remaking of American Religion*, Wendy Murray Zoba's *Generation 2K: What Parents and Others Need to Know About the Millennials* and Dawson McAllister's *Saving the Millennial Generation*; and most recently, Steve Rabey's *In Search of Authentic Faith: How Emerging Generations are Transforming the Church* (2001).[19]

In addition to these and many other books, a great deal of Christian writing in this area has been posted on the Internet. Inevitably, the quality of this work varies even more than that published in book form, but Graeme Codrington and Andres Tapia have produced notable online studies.[20]

Problems with existing responses

All the texts mentioned above have their merits. Yet it is noticeable that despite their often penetrating insights into cultural change, they typically rely on *general* or *non-theological* accounts of such change where 'generations' are concerned. Indeed, in surveying these and numerous other evangelical resources on generational issues, the authors of this report were struck by how readily 'secular' sociological, cultural and anthropological accounts of such issues were accepted, virtually without question, and by how seldom critique or revision of them was offered from a *biblical* or *doctrinal* perspective.

Lifting non-theological models of generation 'off the peg' like this might not matter so much if any concept of 'generation' were alien to the biblical narrative. However, as we shall show in the next chapter, this is far from being the case. The word 'generation' and its variants occur frequently in Scripture, and yet in source after source that we have reviewed on the subject of generations and the church today, little or no attempt is made to place such terms in specific biblical–theological context. Even Graeme Codrington, Steve Rabey, William Mahedy and Janet Bernardi, and Tom Beaudoin, who offer among the most detailed accounts of generation-based issues in the Christian literature we have mentioned, nonetheless seem willing to appropriate the generational taxonomies of scholars whose work is, to all intents and purposes, uninformed by theological concerns. In particular, they echo the majority of studies cited above in their adoption of the generational schemas presented by the leading market researchers

Neil Howe and William Strauss in their best-selling 1991 text *Generations: The History of America's Future*, and in several related books since.[21]

Granted, Howe and Strauss present a very detailed model, but as we shall demonstrate in chapter 5, it is both culturally limited to the North American context, and seriously over-programmatic in its approach. More problematically still, it is a model designed at least partly to identify different 'target markets' in the highly competitive US retail sector. Howe in particular has worked closely with Ann Fishman, Founder and President of the successful 'Generational Targeted Marketing Corporation', while Fishman in turn bases much of her lucrative analysis and consultancy on Howe and Strauss' approach.[22]

We shall see below that this link between marketing and generational stratification is neither new nor purely incidental. Yet leaving aside for the moment arguments about Christianity and consumer capitalism, it should at least be realised that although religious awakenings and 'spiritual moments' are afforded some place in their historical analysis, Howe and Strauss' focus is hardly theological in nature. Indeed, given the context and purpose of their work, it ought surely to be subject to more rigorous theological scrutiny than it has hitherto received.

Granted, Codrington acknowledges and seeks to rectify Howe and Strauss' limitations from his perspective as a South African Youth Ministry analyst – but he does so largely by fusing their schema with other social science and pragmatic church growth models.[23] Thus, despite the thoroughness of his own socio-cultural exposition, his work is not distinguished by very much overt biblical-theological reflection. Generation-specific youth ministry is presented by Codrington as a positive aspect of 'incarnational' church life, reflecting Jesus' own physical, intellectual, spiritual and social development after the pattern of Luke 2:52 and 1 Thessalonians 1:5. It is also said to facilitate the discernment of young people's diverse giftings, in line with 1 Corinthians 12 and Ephesians 4:11–16. It is cast as a way of efficiently 'equipping' them 'for the work of ministry' referred to in 1 Timothy 2:2. In addition, says Codrington, it can help them discover Jesus as Truth (Jn. 14:6). But these are quite general purposes which could easily apply to other kinds of Christian work with other groups. What Codrington does not do is relate 'generation' as it is understood in the various contemporary paradigms he uses, to 'generation' as it is specifically understood in the Scriptures.[24] Rabey makes a little more effort in this direction – but not much more. Indeed, in a 218-page book, he devotes just a page and a half to the subject of 'Generations in the Bible'.[25] Having observed that there are 'half a dozen Hebrew, Greek and Aramaic terms' which translate as 'generation' in Scripture, he vows to 'spare' the reader 'the detailed debates over etymology' which have attached to such terms. He does imply that the biblical concept of 'generation' can have both genealogical and wider cultural import, and he proffers what we will come to see as a somewhat overstated view that 'most scholars' set the interval between one generation and another in the Bible at 'roughly forty years'. But these are passing comments in a text driven far more by general sociological, demographic and journalistic sources.[26] As for Mahedy and Bernardi, they do offer a brief critique of Howe and Strauss' grid, but again, this rests on social scientific rather than theological grounds.[27] Meanwhile, Beaudoin suggests that Howe and Strauss' model emphasises generational chronology too much at the expense of generational attitudes, and supplies provocative theological reflection on his own particular generational group. Once more, however, he hardly touches on biblical definitions of 'generation' *per se*.[28]

In addition to all this, it should be stressed that even on its own terms, Howe and Strauss' analysis is decidedly second-hand, having been adapted from a considerable body of more specialised academic work in the social sciences. In fact, Howe and Strauss quite self-consciously present a popularised hybrid of more foundational studies done by others.[29] Yet again, with the exception of Codrington, the formative work on which Howe and Strauss rely is scarcely mentioned by those Christian authors who have appropriated their account of generations.[30]

Special reference ought also to be made here to the work done on generations by George Barna. Unlike Howe and Strauss', Barna's research institute is explicitly Christian and exists primarily to help churches towards growth. Indeed, data from his books *Baby Busters* and *Generation Next* are adduced by several of the Christian authors we have mentioned.[31] Despite this, it must be stressed that Barna's work is very deliberately empirical and pragmatic in approach. Insofar as he makes generational distinctions, they are inferred almost wholly from the social and religious attitudes expressed by respondents to his many questionnaires and surveys, rather than from in-depth biblical interpretation of culture. Furthermore, Barna's studiedly inductive approach is, if anything, even more brazenly wedded to the marketing ethic than the religiously non-aligned work of Howe and Strauss. In his 1988 book *Marketing the Church*, he quite openly states that 'the major problem plaguing the church is its failure to embrace a marketing orientation in what has become a marketing-driven environment'. Readers are duly urged to abandon 'traditional thinking about church growth' and to re-imagine their congregation 'not as a religious meeting place, but as a service agency – an entity that exists to satisfy people's needs', and as 'a business ... involved in the business of ministry'. In this scenario, the Bible is re-cast as 'one of the world's great marketing texts' and the apostolic mission of the church as 'an informed, capable distribution system'.[32] As with Howe and Strauss, this is not the place to pursue an in-depth critique of Barna's socio-economic and political philosophy. Even so, it is clear that beyond the highly contentious implication that truth is what works, and that numerical success correlates to Gospel authenticity, Barna offers little serious systematic theological exposition of what generations might be, or what generational distinctions might mean.

Charting a Way Forward

It is clear, then, that there is a double deficit to be addressed with regard to 'God and the Generations'. Christian focus on generational issues may have intensified in recent times, but as things stand, it still lacks (i) adequate theological framing, and (ii) proper socio-historical and scholarly contextualisation. In this book, we seek to advance understanding on both fronts, and to relate the one to the other. As such, our task may accurately be described as a hermeneutical one – that is, to effect in regard to the subject of generations what Hans-Georg Gadamer seminally defined as a fusion of the 'horizons' of interpretation – that is, the horizon of the biblical text on one hand, and the horizon of our current-day cultural, pastoral and missionary milieu on the other.[33] First, then, we turn to the witness of Scripture on this issue. Having done so, we will be in a position to assess the continuities and discontinuities between that biblical witness and various current social scientific models of 'generation', and will be able to go on from there to apply the insights we gain to generational issues as they arise in the home, in the church, in society, and in the mission of God.

2

Generations in the Bible

We have shown that while many Christians today possess an intuitive sense of generational variation in contemporary culture, and while some may teach and write about such variation, more work is needed on the relation of this sort of generational discourse to what the Bible has to say about 'generations'. Even as we attempt to do some of that work here, however, we need to beware of what John Lyons has called the 'etymological fallacy'.[1] As we shall see, the word from which we derive our term 'generation' appears often in Scripture; likewise, many other terms regularly translated as 'generation' also appear there. Yet in and of itself, this should not lead us to suppose that exact, direct correspondences can be drawn between the meanings borne by such terms in their ancient, biblical context and the meanings assigned to 'generation' and its variants by demographers, social scientists and cultural theorists today.

With this proviso in mind, it will nevertheless become clear that certain broad, thematic affinities do exist between key concepts of generation expressed 'then' and 'now'. Here, we shall review such concepts as they appear in the biblical text; in the next two chapters we shall relate these to modern-day understandings of generation.

Genealogical Definitions

The first major thread of generational discourse which appears in Scripture relates to genealogy – the continuation of the family line by procreation, from parents through children to grandchildren and so on. This successive process is often linked to inheritance, and to the making of covenants.

In Genesis 12:7 God resolves to give Canaan to Abram's 'offspring' or 'seed'. Contextually, the reference here is clearly to the patriarch's blood family. This point is reinforced at 15:2, where the childless Abram proposes to hand his estate to a non-relative, Eliezer of Damascus, but is told by God, "This man will not be your heir, but a son *coming from your own body* will be your heir" (15:4; our emphasis). Subsequently (Gen. 15:13), Abram is told that before the promised land is taken his natural descendants will be exiled and enslaved in a foreign land for 'four hundred years' – a period which is then equated with 'four generations' (Gen. 15:16). The key Hebrew word here is *dôr*, which is most commonly related in the Pentateuch to the age of a father when his first son is born – in this case one hundred years, since Abraham is a hundred years old when Sarah gives birth to Isaac (Gen. 21:5). *dôr* then recurs three times in chapter 17, as God emphasises that this covenant will be everlasting, and will thus incorporate 'the generations to come' (Gen. 17:7, 9, 12). As these generations follow one another, it appears that the longevity enjoyed by the patriarchs is reduced, with 'old age' considered typically to begin at sixty, and with the average lifespan being set between seventy and eighty years (Lev. 27:1–8; Ps. 90:10). So, too, the standard 'generational interval' between father and first son reduces accordingly.

Meanwhile, the Abrahamic land-covenant is realised in the time of Joshua (Josh. 1:2–9; 21:43), and is reiterated during the reign of Solomon (1 Kgs. 20–21). The link between racial descent and covenant fulfilment is therefore obviously a strong one.

Indeed, subsequent generations of Jews in the Old Testament continue to define their identity in relation to Abraham's seed, and this periodically becomes a pretext for prohibitions on intermarriage (Deut. 23: 2–3; Ezra 9). It also becomes a primary motivation in the construction of genealogical tables: as E.A. Speiser points out, most such tables of descendants and ancestors in the Old Testament are designed to establish 'the superior strain of the line through which the biblical way of life was transmitted from generation to generation'. Or as Speiser also writes, they are meant to show that 'the integrity of the mission was to be safeguarded in transmission, the purity of the content protected by the quality of the container'.[2]

Despite all this, the narrative of Israel's history confirms that the process of genealogical 'generation' among the people of God is not, in fact, entirely mono-racial. Abram's name-change to 'Abraham' suggests a shift from immediate physical fatherhood to something more cosmic: he is to be father not only to Isaac, but also to 'many nations' (Gen. 17:5). In the New Testament, Matthew radically emphasises this point in his genealogy of Jesus, which is traced back through King David to Tamar the Canaanite, Rahab the Jerichoite, Ruth the Moabitess and Bathsheba the Hittite (Mt. 1:3–6). Admittedly, Matthew's purpose here is quite distinct from the normal aim of Hebrew genealogies, in that he is seeking to validate the church's mission to the Gentiles. Still, there is no doubting the significance of the 'alien' figures he mentions for the heritage and development of Israel.[3] While Matthew undoubtedly structures Jesus' birth line in this way for theological and sociological reasons, he nonetheless maintains a basically genealogical understanding of generations here. Indeed, as he uses it in this context, the Greek word *genea* is equivalent to the use of *dôr* which we have been describing. The incorporation of Gentiles from the past may anticipate a much broader opening up of the covenant to all who will follow Christ regardless of lineage, but at this point, it is still an incorporation defined in terms of procreation and kinship.

As we shall see, the New Testament subsequently downplays this genealogical approach in favour of covenant and inheritance models based on faith. However, insofar as it maintains a genealogically specific understanding of generation, succession and covenant, it may arguably be said to do so with regard to the children of believers. On the Day of Pentecost, Peter tells the crowd that the promised gift of the Holy Spirit is not only for those present who repent and believe, but also for their offspring (Acts 2:39). Admittedly, such sons and daughters must still be 'called', but the extent to which they can be regarded as members of the church before professing faith in Christ has been a focus of considerable debate throughout Christian history – not least between paedo-baptists and believers' baptists.

Apologists for infant baptism have characteristically stressed that, at certain points in the narrative of the Acts and epistles (Acts 16:15, 33; 18:8; 1 Cor. 1:16, cf. 1 Cor. 7:14; Mk. 10:13–16), households including children appear to have been baptised *together*. They have also emphasised the parallels drawn between baptism and circumcision by Paul in Colossians 2:8–15, and have inferred that since infants were circumcised in Israel, they may also be baptised into the church. By contrast, Baptists have contended that this is a presumption which flies in the face of the apostolic imperative to renounce sin and confess Christ as a *prerequisite* to baptism. Having said all this, even baptistic Christians have tended to concede that God has a special relationship with the children of believing parents – albeit one which tends to be expressed in terms of partial or potential, rather than full or actual, covenant incorporation.[4]

For all these distinctions and qualifications, it is worth emphasising that whatever particular relationship the children of Christian parents may have with God, it cannot be construed as *purely* genealogical. Baptism may in some sense be analogous with circumcision, but even when applied to infants it is *distinguished* from circumcision inasmuch as it depends essentially not on a physical bond to a tribe or race, but on an inward work of divine grace. In its own turn, the faith of Christian parents may be modelled to their offspring, but it can neither be automatically bequeathed to, nor automatically 'inherited' by, such offspring: rather, it is a free gift of God to each individual in each generation. We shall return to this point below.

Natal Definitions

As well as signifying the process of biological succession through various 'generations' of the family tree, the Greek word *genesis* can occasionally denote a particular birth at a particular time. It is used in this sense in the Greek version of the Hebrew Bible, the Septuagint, at Exodus 28:10, to translate the word *tôl̥dôt*, which here clearly means 'birth date'. The two stones to be set on the shoulder pieces of the ephod are, says the text, to bear six names each of the 'sons of Israel', those names being arranged 'in the order of their birth'. Likewise, at Matthew 1:18 and Luke 1:14, *genesis* clearly refers to the specific nativity of Jesus.

Periodical Definitions

In addition to its genealogical meaning, *dôr* can simply refer to all the people who have lived, or are living, in a particular period of time. Thus Exodus 1:6 records the death of the 'whole generation' which had been contemporary with Joseph, while Judges 2:10 describes all those who had lived in the same era as Joshua as having been 'gathered to their ancestors'. Likewise, when Jesus refers to 'this generation' in Matthew 11:16, 23:36, Mark 8:12, Luke 11:51 and 17:25, it is likely that he is denoting, most basically, the mass of the population which is alive during his own lifetime.

Epochal Definitions

As well as denoting 'generational succession' in the Old Testament, the Hebrew term *dôr* is also sometimes used to portray a characteristic time or 'epoch'. Rather than simply marking a chronological phase, this usage is qualitative: the phase in question is cast as possessing a distinctive 'mood' or spiritual ethos. At Isaiah 51:9, for example, *dôr* evokes an exemplary period of past vision and godly insight ('awake ... as in generations of old'). Similarly, at Exodus 3:15 and (in its Aramaic parallel) at Daniel 4:3, it depicts a future golden age of God's reign and rule – a dominion which is set to last 'from generation to generation'.

By contrast, however, on the lips of Jesus, the Greek term *genea* almost always carries a negative socio-historical connotation. Indeed, insofar as his 'generation' can be said to define a contemporary epoch, it is one distinguished by faithlessness and sin (Mt. 12:39, 45; 17:17; Mk. 8:38; Lk. 11:29). We shall return to these more pejorative designations below.

Eventual Definitions[5]

At one critical point in Jesus' ministry, the term *genea* is linked not so much with a historical period or epoch, as with an apparently more specific, imminent event – the parousia, or apocalypse. 'Truly I tell you', says Jesus, 'This generation will not pass away until all these things have taken place' (Mk. 13:30, cf. Mt. 24:34; Lk. 21:32). Obviously, the fact that this parousia has been delayed well beyond the first century presents a complex exegetical challenge – a challenge which has prompted scholars either to dismiss Jesus' words as mistaken, or to offer various more figurative definitions of *genea* in this case. Among these definitions, perhaps the most plausible are those which link the 'end' referred to by Jesus with the fall of the Jewish Temple in AD 70 – a very specific historical occurrence which did effectively mark the 'close of an age' for Israel, and which did clearly occur within the lifetime of Jesus' own contemporaries.[6]

A more oblique linkage of generational distinctions with historical events may be apparent in relation to the exodus, and to Israel's wilderness wanderings under Moses. Insofar as these formative episodes occupied forty years, some commentators have construed that this span of time was subsequently taken as a round number indicating the length of a generation.[7]

Attitudinal Definitions

So far, it has become plain that the concept of 'generation' in the Old Testament is significantly, but by no means entirely, linked to the family bloodline. We have also detected hints that in the New Testament, there is a shift of emphasis away from genealogy towards other criteria. Chief among these criteria are those based on what might be termed 'attitude', 'affect' and 'behaviour'. These three facets of generational identity are closely linked, but we shall deal with attitude first.

Despite all that we have said about the racially delineating function of Israel's genealogies, the ethnic specificity of circumcision, the bans on intermarriage and so on, a closer look at the Old Testament reveals signs of a more global vision. We have already mentioned the multi-national scope of God's covenant with Abraham in Genesis 17. A glimpse of how this promise might be realised appears with the legal protocol which allows 'the third generation' of children born to Edomites and Egyptians to be admitted to the assembly in Deuteronomy 23:8. Greater weight is lent to it with Isaiah's eschatological prophecies of Gentiles being drawn to the Messiah alongside Jews (Is. 11:10; 42:6; 49:6).

Once Jesus is born, these foretastes of inclusiveness are fulfilled. For all Matthew's and Luke's desire to establish Jesus' genealogy as the Messiah of Israel, he is portrayed as being ultimately 'without descent' – conceived of the Holy Spirit and born of a virgin

(Lk. 1:26–37). In this sense, according to the writer of the epistle to the Hebrews, he belongs in the priestly order of Melchizedek, since Melchizedek is similarly 'without father and mother, without genealogy, without beginning of days or end of life' (Heb. 7:3ff., cf. Gen. 14:18–20).

All this has implications, not only for Jesus' identity, but also for the identity of his followers. For Johannine theology in particular, it is those who believe Christ who gain the right to become 'children of God', not those who claim their lineage from a particular father of Israel. Such children, indeed, are 'born not of natural descent, nor of human decision or a husband's will, but of God' (Jn. 1:12–13, cf. 8:39–41; 1 Jn. 3:1–2, 3:10; 5:19). Jesus emphasises all this vividly in his dialogue with Nicodemus: ' "I tell you the truth, no-one can enter the kingdom of God unless he is born of water and the Spirit. Flesh gives birth to flesh, but the Spirit gives birth to spirit. You should not be surprised at my saying, 'You must be born again.' ..." ' (Jn. 3:5).

When confronted with teachers of the Law who boast of their Abrahamic descent, Jesus shifts the emphasis from physical ancestry to respect for Abraham's moral example (Jn. 8:39). He then proceeds to represent Abraham as a forerunner of his own ministry (8:56), and concludes by associating himself with the divine Name over and above his physical derivation from Abraham ('before Abraham was, I am!' – Jn. 8:58).

In the Synoptic Gospels, while the race or 'house' of Israel remains primary in the overall *sequence* of Jesus' mission (Mt. 10:6, cf. Rom. 1:16, 2:9–10), he clearly ministers to Gentiles (Mt. 8:5–13; Mk. 5:1–20; 7:24–30), and perceives himself as going to the cross for Jew and Gentile alike (Mk. 10:45).

These moves beyond 'generationally successive' models of salvation are systematised vividly in the writings of Paul. In Romans 4 and Galatians 3–4, Abraham is reinterpreted as a cardinal reference-point for faith, rather than for genealogical legitimacy. In this sense, his 'seed' is not the plural tribes of Israel, but the singular Messiah, Jesus Christ, whose death redeems *any* or *all* who believe (Gal. 3:13–16). On this understanding, it becomes possible for both Jews *and* Gentiles to become 'sons of God through faith', and thereby to enter into the true 'offspring' and 'inheritance' of Abraham (Gal. 3:26–29). Faith itself is consequent upon repentance, which is a wholesale turning of the heart and mind towards God – an attitudinal paradigm shift of the most profound sort (Rom. 2:4, cf. Mk. 1:15). Genetic and racial pedigree matters little in comparison to this, even if there is a case to be made for Jews retaining their distinctive ethnic identity under the new covenant, and for their occupying a distinctive role *as Jews* in the events of the last days (Rom. 9–11).[8]

Given Jesus' emphasis on a new 'family of God' defined by faith rather than biology, it is not surprising that he also applies generational concepts to instances of faith*lessness*. He would have known that *dôr* had sometimes been qualified in the Hebrew Scriptures by epithets like 'evil', 'crooked', 'perverse' and 'rebellious' (Deut. 1:35; 32:5, 20; Ps. 78:8). He would also have known that other 'generations' had occasionally been described as 'righteous' (Ps. 14:5; 112:2). On his lips, however, the moral assessment of his contemporaries is consistently harsh: they are an 'unbelieving' (Mk. 9:19), 'perverse' (Mt. 17:17), 'adulterous' (Mk. 8:38) and 'wicked' (Mt. 12:39; Lk. 11:29) generation. Later, Peter describes the same set as 'corrupt' (Acts 2:40), and Paul as 'crooked' (Phil. 2:15). Again, this has nothing to do with genealogical legitimacy or illegitimacy: it is a consequence of having chosen to reject God.

Affectual Definitions

Of course, even as we realise the volitional aspects of being incorporated into the new covenant 'family of faith', we should recognise that the process of becoming a 'child of God' is an act of divine grace and mercy before it is a personal choice. It is an 'affect' upon us before it is an attitude expressed by us. The generationally-related language of being 'born again' (Jn. 3:7; 1 Pet. 1:23), 'adopted' (Rom. 8:23; Eph. 1:5) and becoming 'heirs' with Christ (Gal. 4:7) all points to the initiative being God's rather than ours.

The same applies to election. Under the old covenant, God freely chose Israel from among the nations to be his blessed race. In the new covenant, the people of God are a 'chosen generation' (*genos eklekton*, 1 Pet. 2:9). In each case, the grace and sovereignty of God are paramount, but thanks to Christ, Peter can present God's electing power as extending explicitly to people of every race, tribe and tongue.

Generational identity is also seen to be received rather than self-defined when God passes blessings down a family line. We have already traced this process as it relates to inheritance and covenant in the Old Testament. It is also applied to the legacy of the Mosaic Law, which is frequently defined as 'a lasting ordinance for the generations' (Lev. 3:17, 10:9, 23:14, 21, 31; Num. 15:14–15, 18:23). It is evident, too, in 2 Kings 10:30, when God promises the army commander Jehu that his sons 'of the fourth generation' will sit on the throne of Israel. Granted, this promise is a reward for Jehu's resistance of Baal worship, but when it is delivered some years later, there is no doubt that it is by the express plan and purpose of God (2 Kgs. 15:12). Similarly, in Psalms 103:17–18 and 112:2, the righteousness of God may fall specifically on those who 'fear' him and who keep his covenant and law, but his promise to extend that righteousness to 'their children's children' indicates much more than religious moralism.

While this principle of 'generational blessing' is significant in the Old Testament, it must also be acknowledged that what passes down the generations is sometimes not a blessing, but a punishment. On various occasions in the Pentateuch God vows to chasten sinners to their 'third and fourth generations' (Ex. 20:5; 34:7; Num. 14:18; Deut. 5:9). Furthermore, at Deuteronomy 23:2, His sanction extends to no fewer than ten generations of children born to those who intermarry. The precise mechanics of such generational punishment have been a focus of considerable debate: for some, the transmission of the punishment in question has been envisaged in fairly literal, congenital terms. Pennant Jones, for example, argues that if harmful traits like alcoholism and violence can be passed on genetically, then so can more obviously spiritual blights.[9] Furthermore, like Peter Horrobin, he suggests that research on one's own family tree can help to identify 'ungodly soul-ties' with the sins of one's forbears, so that these sins can then be 'confessed' and healed through the power of the Holy Spirit.[10] Others, however, have preferred a more sociological or behaviourist gloss on the phrase 'third and fourth generation', pointing out that contemporary sources often use it as a synonym for the whole age span of a household. Certainly, the 'household' was the basic unit of ancient Near-Eastern society, and would typically have comprised great-grandparents, grandparents, parents and children (Num. 16:31, Josh. 7:24; Ps. 109:12).[11] In this reading, the family unit as a whole is seen to suffer 'by association' with the failings of its heads and elders, but there is no necessary link to biological transmission.

Behavioural Definitions

Implicit within both attitudinal and affectual generational definition is what might be called a behavioural dimension. God's curse in Exodus 20:5 and Deuteronomy 5:9 falls on succeeding generations of those who actively 'hate' him, and the generational punishments mentioned above are usually associated with one wicked action or another – whether with idolatry (Deut. 5:9; Judg. 2:10–11), rebellion (Ps. 78:8) or the rejection of prophecy (Jer. 7:27–29). Similarly, when Jesus speaks of his own generation as 'crooked', 'perverse' and 'adulterous', he clearly has in mind more than a defective outlook, ideology or inherited predisposition: he is also concerned about the sinful *deeds* of his contemporaries. Indeed,

having lamented this same generation's shortcomings in
Matthew 11:16–19, he pointedly concludes that 'wisdom is
vindicated by her actions'. So, for instance, it is too ready to
chase miraculous signs (Mt. 12:39); it fails to heal the sick
(Mt. 17:14–17; Mk. 9:19); it denies its prophetic heritage
(Lk. 11:49–51), and it expresses shame at Gospel teaching
(Mk. 8:38).

Functional Definitions

The generational distinctions which we have been examining
in Scripture possess more than merely spiritual and theological
significance; they also bear important social functions. In particular,
the generational corollaries of 'youth' and 'age' are subject to heavy
cultural encoding, and in both Old and New Testaments it is
routinely expected that social relationships, structures and institutions will reflect the different age-groups which together comprise
the people of God (cf. Lev. 19:32; 1 Tim. 5:1–2).

Youth and age

The Bible typically presents long life as a blessing of God,
especially insofar as it is associated with personal development
and growth through successive stages of maturity (cf. Ps.
92:12–14; 128:5–6; Is. 65:20; 2 Cor. 4:16). Examples of good
old age permeate the whole biblical record: Jacob, Barzillai,
Simeon and Anna stand as but the most obvious exemplars of
this. However, it must also be stressed that to be young and
zealous, to have strength and energy, to find oneself at the
commencement of life and to harbour godly aspirations for the
future, are all cast in a virtuous light as well (Prov. 1:4;
Zec. 9:16–17; Tit. 2:6). Moreover, the physical decline which
can accompany old age is often held up as a spur to the young

– to prompt them to make the most of their strength and health while they possess them (e.g. Ecc. 12:1–7; 11:9–12:1; Ps. 7 1:17). It is made clear that much will be learnt in youth which cannot be gained at a later stage (Ps. 37:25). Indeed, it is accepted that through application, or through gifting and calling, youth may in certain circumstances excel age and command a respect more usually accorded to the elderly (Ps. 119:99–100; Lk. 2:46–47; 1 Tim. 4:12–14). On the whole, however, each generational group is associated with specific types of service, and if the young come to usurp the roles of the old as a matter of course, it is assumed that God will be displeased (Joel 2:28; 1 Tim. 5:1–3; Tit. 2:1–8; 1 Jn. 2:12–15; Is. 3:4–5).

As for the young themselves, those who show Godly sensitivity and who learn from their elders, are applauded. Joseph, Joshua, Elisha and Timothy are clear cases in point. Samuel, Saul, David, Solomon and Daniel each also pursued a godly youth. By contrast, presumptuousness and folly in younger years are severely condemned by God, as both Absalom and Rehoboam learn to their cost. Beyond these distinctions, the example of John Mark is also worthy of note. Rather than serving as the model either of an ideal young person or an arrogant upstart, John Mark proves to be both a blessing *and* a problem for Paul (Acts 15:37–38; 2 Tim. 4:11). In fact, his story illustrates in its own right the honesty and comprehensiveness of the Bible with respect to the younger generation. Youthful impetuousness is viewed in John Mark's case as a sign of immaturity – but one which time and sound teaching will ultimately resolve. The same can be said, of course, of the disciples of Jesus himself. Their inability to grasp the meaning of what Jesus was teaching them about himself is regularly stressed in the Gospels. Yet this did not disqualify them from the momentous tasks they were to perform after the Day of Pentecost.

Youth, age and wisdom

When Proverbs 20:29 declares that 'The glory of young men is
their strength, and grey hair the splendour of the old', it presents
not generational stereotyping, but a frank realism which is to be
found through the Scriptures as a whole. Respect for age, and
regard for the wisdom which is assumed characteristically to
come with it, is one of the foundations of biblical teaching
on generational relationships. Most obviously, it underpins the
commandment to honour one's father and mother (Ex. 20:12, cf.
Eph. 6:1–3). So, too, when the prophet Jeremiah bemoans the
tragic state of the nation, he sees the crisis epitomised in the fact
that 'elders are shown no respect' (Jer. 5:12–14). Likewise, when
Moses warns Israel about the consequences of their disobedience,
he says that God will send a fierce nation against them – a nation
which will eschew 'right' values, and which will demonstrate
such immorality by neglecting 'respect for the old and pity for
the young' (Deut. 28:50). The same expectation that age will
command honour is maintained by the former Pharisee Paul,
when he appeals to Philemon on behalf of Onesimus by invoking
his own status as an 'old man' (Phlm. 9).

Such respect is, of course, based on more than mere chronological survival. Saul, after all, became more foolish and tragic as
he grew older, and to one degree or another, Noah, Moses, Lot,
Solomon and Hezekiah all failed God in the evening of life. Such
examples bear out the implication of Proverbs 16:31 – that a grey
head in fact only becomes a 'crown of glory' when married to
righteousness (cf. Deut. 30:19–20). Even so, the link between age
and wisdom in Scripture is strong, and since wisdom is among the
most highly prized qualities in the canon, those of senior years are
accorded a particular deference. This principle is expressed with
considerable force in the book of Proverbs (Prov. 16:31; 20:29;
27:22), but it is also seen vividly in the protest of Elihu against Job
and his friends, where it is taken as read that age will confer
knowledge and insight (Job 32:6–7). In the life of the Christian

church also, wisdom is presented as the consequence of age and maturity (Phil. 3:15–16), and is commended as a goal to be set before the young (2 Tim. 2:22).

In the New Testament as well as the Old, wisdom is not the secret preserve of a privileged class, but the fruit of God's abundant faithfulness and providence. As Daniel Estes has shown, instead of being the exclusive property of the elite, wisdom in Israel was to be mediated as broadly-based instruction for the community, and especially for the young men of the community.[12] Furthermore, as he commends such principles, God is himself tellingly represented by generational appellations: he is 'the Ancient of Days' (Dan. 7:9), and our 'heavenly Father' (Mt. 5:5, 6:9, 7:11; Eph. 3:14). Significantly, too, when the glorified Christ is associated with the Ancient of Days in Revelation 1:14, he appears with white hair – a standard biblical marker of maturity, and by association, of wisdom.

Youth, age and discipleship

It follows clearly from all this that more senior members of God's covenant community have an overriding responsibility to impart knowledge and understanding to emerging generations. As teachers and sources of wisdom, the Bible makes it clear that older people ought to be an example and inspiration to those who follow behind. And just as the aged should exhibit a godliness and depth commensurate with their years and experience, so the young have a responsibility not only to honour older generations, but to copy them (Prov. 4:1–2). This imperative especially pervades the teaching of the apostle Paul (1 Cor. 4:14–17; 10:31–11:1; Phil. 3:17; 2 Thes. 3:7; 1 Tim. 4:12). What is more, the need to observe it is demonstrated starkly by the sorry fate of those who neglect to do so: thus Rehoboam (1 Kgs. 12) notoriously rejected the counsel of age and took the advice of the young, while Jesus himself pronounced judgment on the 'generation' that refused to heed the well-established wisdom of John the Baptist (Mt. 11:16–19). Indeed, such rejections of the wisdom of age are cast as nothing less than paradigms of sin (Ecc. 9:13–18).

Youth, age and intergenerational relations

Although we saw in the last chapter that that the 'generation gap problem' *per se* has played a particular role in the shaping of contemporary Western culture, our survey here has shown that at the more generally established interface of 'youth' and 'age', such tensions were apparent in biblical times. Even while recognising the potential for conflict between different generations, however, the Bible also suggests constructive ways of addressing it. Biblical distinctions between age and youth may often be quite stark, but this does not mean that they are regarded as checks on integrated community. Granted, they may serve to differentiate and facilitate appropriate forms of involvement in the life of the people of God for different generational groups; but at the same time, these groups are depicted as working in common, towards a shared goal, and as together constituting that one, multi-generational community which is God's household of faith.

Thus Paul can write variously to distinct age groups, as well to distinct social classes and subcultures, yet he consistently underlines that Christ unites all believers in a single 'family' (Gal. 6:10). Thus, too, he exhorts the Romans to 'accept one another', even as Christ has accepted them, despite their exhibiting considerable differences in terms of spiritual development and maturity (Rom. 15:7). Even to a congregation as apparently disordered as that at Corinth, Paul is able to write, 'I am glad I can have complete confidence in you' (2 Cor. 7:16) – not least because of their kindness towards his emissary, Titus, who represents the emerging generation of leadership within the church.

The multi-generational co-operation implicit in these texts is a key facet of that unity which is essential to the true nature of the church (Eph. 2:14–25; Phil. 2:1–4; Jn 17:20–23). Each local Christian community is to be multi-gifted (Rom. 12:3–8; 1 Cor. 12:27–3 1; 1 Pet. 4:10–1 1). Each is also to be a place where mutual concern and sympathy prevail between different groups of people (Rom. 15:14; Col. 3:12–17). Whatever happens within the congregation, it begins to lose its true identity once this inter-dependence, this essential oneness, is compromised by an over-emphasis on a particular sector or niche. Paul defines maturity in the church as reaching unity in the faith and in the knowledge of the Son of God. For this reason, God graces the church with appropriate ministries, and through those ministries the whole body is joined and held together by every supporting ligament, and grows and builds itself up in love as each part does its work (Eph. 1:1–16). The language of these verses makes it clear that while each generation within the church may have characteristic roles and responsibilities, these must be performed on behalf of the church as a whole. By the same token, the *failure* of different groups within the church to operate together in this is likened, aptly enough, to 'childishness' (Heb. 5:11–14).

Just as the church must be a community in which there is 'neither Jew nor Greek, slave nor free, male nor female' (Gal. 3:28) – a community free from genealogical, class and gender discrimination – so it would also seem that the church modelled in the New Testament is one which must overcome age-based prejudice, or what is now called 'ageism'. Of course, this is not a uniquely new covenant concept: the community formed at Pentecost is shaped by Joel's prophecy of the young 'seeing visions' and the old 'dreaming dreams' (Acts 2:17). Paul's protégé Timothy is duly instructed not to let anyone look down on him because of his youth (1 Tim. 4:12), while Peter appeals to old and young alike to 'clothe' themselves with 'humility towards one another' (1 Pet. 5:1–5).

Having said all this, we should not suppose that age distinctions are entirely irrelevant for the New Testament church. The category of 'elder' is retained as a key focus of leadership (Acts 15:22–23; 20:17; 1 Tim. 5:17; Tit. 1:5; Jas. 5:14), and while this may have no absolute age-threshold, it would still have been associated in both Jewish and Gentile societies at the time with those of more mature years.[13] Likewise, the distinction of 'parents' from 'children' and the 'young' from the 'old' in the Christian community may not entail rigid *religious* differentiation, but it does imply that the apostolic age was one in which broad generational types continued to be recognised (1 Cor. 13:11; 2 Cor. 12:14; Eph. 6:1–4; Col. 3:20–21).

Probably the strongest ecclesiological acknowledgement of generational *continuity* in the New Testament comes when the Ephesian elders lay hands on the emerging leader Timothy (1 Tim. 4:14). Even here, however, it is important to realise that the 'succession' is about the activity of the Holy Spirit rather than chronology: the ceremony in question is not so much a 'rite of passage' as a public endorsement of one person's anointing for service. This again suggests that the *interaction* of generationally-defined groups in Scripture is somewhat more nuanced than can be represented either in purely demographic or purely cultural terms.

Conclusion

The review of biblical material conducted in this chapter confirms that 'generation' in Scripture is a complex concept – one which is subject to a range of meanings and definitions. From what we have seen so far, there may appear to be no precise scriptural equivalent to the rarefied socio-economic categorisations of 'Builders', 'Boomers', 'Xers' and 'Millennials' which feature so heavily in today's missiologies and church growth theories. This does not, however, preclude us from drawing more general hermeneutic parallels between the biblical aspects of 'generation' which we have identified, and the understandings of 'generation' which pertain in modern-day social and cultural study. It is to this task that we address ourselves in the next two chapters.

3

Defining Generations Today I: Core Concepts

Generation and Social Differentiation

We saw in Chapter 1 that evangelicals became particularly exercised about generational issues in the 1960s. As we also suggested there, however, they were hardly alone. In fact, the growth of their concern in this area very much reflected what the sociologist Jane Pilcher has called 'the emergence of age as a basis for social differentiation' in Western cultures generally around the same time.[1] In her landmark textbook, *Age and Generation in Modern Britain* (1995), Pilcher recalls that prior to this period, such cultures had been segmented principally along lines of kinship, class, ethnicity, gender and education. However, as economic renewal took hold in America, Britain and mainland Europe after the Second World War, there arose another form of social stratification based on birth-year groupings, and more significantly, on perceived connections between those groupings and distinct attitudinal, socio-economic and lifestyle traits.[2] In order to appreciate this shift of focus more fully, it will be helpful to review its key concepts and motivations.

Generation vs Cohort

In order to make their new emphasis on age groups clear, social scientists from the mid-1960s began to make a categorical distinction between the traditional scholarly understanding of 'generation' in terms of biology, genealogy and kinship, and a model of generation defined according to age and social context. Thus, whereas social scientists had classically stratified generations in terms of 'vertical' family relationships – grandparents, parents, children, etc. – Norman B. Ryder, in a key article published in 1965, argued for a distinct model of generations which would differentiate them 'by the changing content of formal education, by peer group socialisation, and by idiosyncratic historical experience'.[3] For Ryder, this meant going so far as to adopt a separate term for the second set of criteria, even while acknowledging that everyday discourse had often intuitively used 'generation' to cover both. The term Ryder adopted was *cohort*.

'Cohort' is a word now widely used by scholars who wish to distinguish broader demographic and cultural paradigms from biological and kinship processes. Ryder argued for the necessity of this distinction on the straightforward, common sense basis that mere physical reproduction in itself 'carries no necessary implications for transformation of the population'.[4] Children are, after all, born every second of every day, and if biology and kinship alone are taken as grounds for generational segmentation, that segmentation will be quite arbitrary at the macro-social level. If, however, one takes account of the effect of common events, experiences, perceptions, circumstances, actions and identities shared by some, most or all of those born within a particular period of history, one could begin to speak meaningfully of dividing a population into 'generational' strata – or, as Ryder preferred it, into 'cohorts'.

As summarised by Pilcher, this formal, sociological distinction between 'generation' and 'cohort' can be represented as follows:

> *Generation* is a structural term in kinship studies denoting the parent-child relationship.
>
> *Cohort* is a demographic term in origin. It is used to refer to a defined population who experience the same significant event at, or within, a given period of time. Events such as birth, leaving school, or the Second World War would be examples of such significant events. [However] … the potential of cohort in relation to age is greatest where a cohort is comprised of people born in the same year (or other given time interval) who then age *together.* Such a cohort would then leave school, experience the Second World War, and enter retirement, say, at around the same chronological age.[5]

As we shall see, once the 'cohort' approach is admitted, what is popularly described as 'generation' becomes, in Michael Corsten's words, 'a concept with multiple meanings', relating to a whole range of disciplines, from history and sociology through anthropology, economics and social psychology to semiotics, cultural studies and political science.[6] For those wishing to delve more deeply into the specialised contributions of each of these disciplines to the subject of generations, Pilcher offers a very helpful bibliography.[7] Our purposes here will be served by a digest of the key ideas and dynamics identified from such disciplines as being germane to 'cohort'-style analysis, since it is this, rather than the pure 'kinship' approach, which is overwhelmingly in view in the current discussion of 'generations' in the Christian world.

Having said all this, it must be acknowledged that despite the usefulness and clarity of Ryder's formal distinction between 'generation' as kinship-related and 'cohort' as socially constructed, not only our everyday discourse, but also a large proportion of academic work in this field, still actually deploys the term 'generation' to cover both areas. As Pilcher puts it, 'generation acts as a folk model conceptualization of what are, properly, cohort processes, as in "the sixties generation" [but] this synonymous use of "generation" for "cohort" is also evident in the writings of some sociologists'.[8]

More importantly still, while the different biblical dimensions of 'generation' which we highlighted in the last chapter may also be broadly divided along the lines of Ryder's 'kinship' – 'cohort' distinction, there is no clear terminological duality which reflects that distinction in Scripture. As we noted, *genea* is used both 'genealogically' to denote blood relationships (as in Mt. 1:17) and 'periodically', to describe a set of people living at a particular time (as in Mt. 11:16). Not surprisingly in view of this, the current Christian literature on generations which we surveyed earlier in some cases deploys the 'cohort' – 'generation' contrast, and in others uses the two terms interchangeably.

In this study, while recognising the undoubted theoretical validity of the term 'cohort', and occasionally using it for clarity, we have chosen more generally to reflect the reality of Scripture, and of the wider debate within and beyond the church, and have used the term 'generation' in both its genealogical *and* demographic senses. However, this most certainly does not mean that we have been content to acquiesce in the ambiguities and confusions inherent in the word. Far from it: we have already shown that Scripture itself requires a more nuanced interpretative grid, and that beyond a merely bipartite separation of biology from social construction, social construction *itself* entails a range of different dynamics – dynamics which in their turn often overlap and intersect in the establishment of generational identity. It will be useful at this point to remind ourselves of those dynamics.

Stratification Variables in Generational Definition

The simple generation/cohort or kinship generation/social generation distinction has already been superseded in our analysis

of Scripture by various more specific qualifications to the core
term 'generation'. These qualifications relate closely to what the
sociologists Howard Schuman and Jaqueline Scott call the key
'stratification variables' of generational definition.[9] To recap, they
are as follows:

Modes	Criteria
1. *Genealogical*	kinship
2. *Natal*	birth year or birth-year period
3. *Periodical*	time span lived through
4. *Epochal*	dominant ethos 'spirit' of the age lived through
5. *Eventual*	key historical event or events experienced
6. *Attitudinal*	defining spiritual, philosophical or ideological orientation
7. *Affectual*	dominant spiritual, emotional or psychological experience
8. *Behavioural*	dominant activity and behaviour
9. *Functional*	social, cultural and institutional significance

We shall relate these nine biblical aspects of 'generation' to
current socio-cultural understandings more extensively in the
next chapter. First, however, it is necessary to grasp certain even
more fundamental concepts in the study of generations today.

Life Cycle vs Life Course

The basic distinction between genealogically and culturally
defined generations is closely linked to another distinction often
made in generational analysis – that between *life cycle* and *life
course*. As James Fulcher and John Scott point out, whereas the

notion of 'life cycle' tends to be preferred by the 'hard' natural sciences as a description of the physical phases through which a body passes as it ages, the latter is applied to stages of life which are taken to be socially determined.

On the basis of this life cycle approach, biologists routinely define 'generational time' as 'the average interval between the birth of an individual and the birth of its offspring'. In other words, it is a measure related directly to kinship. In this formula, the 'mean generation time' of the Galapgos cactus finch, for example, is 6.08 years;[10] for humans living in contemporary Britain, it is approximately twenty-eight years, and rising.[11] Similar average intervals apply to the time-gap between grandparents and parents, or great-grandparents and grandparents.

Now clearly, this life cycle approach echoes the basic 'genealogical' measure of generations found in the Bible – a measure we expounded in the last chapter. But just as we saw there that assessments of generation based purely on procreation and kinship are inadequate, so this 'life cycle' model hardly suffices on its own. One obvious reason for this is that definitions of ageing vary with life expectancy, and life expectancy can differ markedly according to social conditions. Janice Monk and Cindi Katz point out, for example, that with average longevity ranging from the mid-thirties in Afghanistan to the high seventies in Britain, it cannot be presumed that various 'life stages' (whether defined by sheer physical ageing or by kinship-status) will be universally calibrated or fixed. We have already noted the variations of generational time across Scripture, but more generally it is plain that just as the process of ageing will be accelerated where diet, sanitation and healthcare are relatively poor, so the average interval between parents and their children will vary accordingly. Hence, while it may be twenty-eight years in Britain, it is considerably less in most Third World countries, where parents procreate earlier in order to produce larger families which are expected to support them in old age, and where contraception is either less freely available, or more broadly rejected on ethical and religious grounds.[12] Then again, the fact that mean generational time is currently rising in the UK might also reflect certain social trends, just as might a fall in other periods. It clearly, for instance, mirrors changing patterns of female employment, wherein more women are choosing to delay motherhood until they have established a career. [13]

Inasmuch as it takes account of such social and economic factors, the 'life course' approach commends itself to an analysis of generational issues from a Christian perspective. Pertinently, the biblical text James 3:6 speaks of the tongue not only as a potential 'world of iniquity', but also as something which can inflame the 'course of life' or the 'course of nature' (*trokon tēs geneseōs*). Although the meaning of this phrase is unclear, most commentators have interpreted it as denoting something akin to current, sociological definitions of the 'life course'. [14] In any case, it is a fundamental principle of biblical theological anthropology that human beings are created for community and social interaction, and that the specifics of our communality will vary as a positive consequence of God's having made us with diversity (cf. Acts 17:26; Rev. 5:9; 7:9). [15] Then again, it is also a New Testament imperative that where cultural difference is either used as a pretext for oppression, or reflects socio-economic injustice, it ought to be exposed and resisted (Eph. 2:11–22; Jas. 2:1–13). [16] The 'life course' approach in this regard offers a much richer tool for theological understanding and critique of issues related to age and generation than does an approach confined simply to the terms of the 'life cycle'. As such, it will be helpful at this point to look more closely at the origins and development of 'life course' thinking in the social sciences, particularly as it has related to the delineation of a distinct stratum of 'youth'.

Generational Thinking and the Significance of 'Youth'

We have already noted that the growth of interest in age and social stratification in the 1960s was driven by the 'discovery' and definition of a specific 'youth culture', and by the codifying of a discrete category of 'young people' between established, essentially 'biological' categories of 'childhood' and 'adulthood'.[17] One key facet of this codification has been an increasing focus on the phase of life known as 'adolescence'. As we saw in the last chapter, ancient cultures, such as those which comprised the biblical world, may have distinguished between 'young men' or 'young women' and 'elders', and may have accorded distinct social functions to each. It is particularly in the modern Western world, however, that these functions have been intensified through more systematic psycho-social, socio-economic and ideological categorisation. The construction of 'adolescence' provides an important early example of this process.

Generation, adolescence and the rise of the 'teenager'

Adolescence as such began to gain formal, academic recognition as a transitional stage from infancy to maturity in the late nineteenth century – not least due to the work of the psychologist G. Stanley Hall.[18] Hall, however, still defined it largely in relation to 'life cycle' concerns such as hormonal development and fertility: so children were 'pre-pubescent'; adolescents were 'pubescent' or 'post-pubescent'; adults were 'sexually mature' or 'procreative'. As Hall and his followers saw it, this 'interim' physiological condition predisposed adolescents to tempestuous moods and impulses, often directed 'upwards', against the older 'generation' of their parents. James Côté has called this the 'storm and stress' model of adolescence, and there is little doubting its entrenchment in the modern Western cultural consciousness, from James Dean's films of the mid-1950s to Harry Enfield's comic creations, Kevin and Perry, in the 1990s.[19] The problem with such a model, however, is the same basic problem that we have already identified in respect of the 'life cycle' approach – namely, its tendency to depict adolescence as a universal state of intergenerational turmoil, whereas in

fact there appear to be many non-Western cultures in which the
progression from childhood to adulthood does *not* pass through
such a marked, traumatic phase, and in which common hormonal
changes, insofar as they exist, manifest themselves in very different
ways from group to group. Indeed, Margaret Mead advanced one
of the most important early challenges to Hall's 'universalist' paradigm of adolescence in her groundbreaking study, *Coming of Age
in Samoa* (1928).[20] Although Mead's research methods have since
been criticised, her core thesis – that generational segmentation
is a *socially relative* phenomenon – would come into its own
three decades later, when the particular conditions of post-war
Western culture helped to spawn a new generational phenomenon which the Bible certainly did not recognise – 'the teenager'.

It may not have been until 1967 that a thoroughgoing,
alternative 'youth culture' emerged in the West along with the
coining of the term 'generation gap'. Yet as Jonathon Green
notes, it is possible to view this development as in some sense a
radicalisation of specific socio-economic processes begun a
decade or so before, in the USA.[21]

Echoing Mead's analysis, Green recalls that while 'adolescence'
had existed as a concept for some time beforehand, it had meant
'simply becoming an adult' – that is, a 'passage, not a status'. By
contrast, the mid-late 1950s saw the category of 'teenager'
emerge in America to confer precisely such status. As Green
presents it, in this context 'teenage' years became much more than
a mere bridge to adulthood, employment and domestic responsibility. Rather, they took on their own cachet, as years in which
'one lingered', and from which moving on was now characteristically seen as 'a regret, and no reward'. From this perspective,
Green plausibly presents the concept of the 'teenager' as
'emblematic of the modern world', – a concept which 'emerged
in America, moved gradually across the Atlantic and had reached
its fullest flower as the sixties began'. The years between thirteen
and twenty, he adds, 'had never existed in so totemic and autonomous a way' as during this period. 'Now, in the post-war decades,

teenage life began its gradual move to centre-stage' – a position it would eventually assume and retain from 1967 onwards.[22]

And yet as Green suggests, when one more closely examines the *reasons* for the emergence of the teenager as a distinct and significant social group, and when one asks why specifically that group arose in America when it did, one realises that the roots of today's generational segmentation, both beyond and within the church, may actually have as much to do with pragmatic business strategies as with any idealistic, self-defined youth 'counter-culture' birthed in 1967's 'Summer of Love', let alone with any biblical mandate.

As Green assesses them, even while they were evolving into a distinct generational group, the teenagers of the early-mid fifties still essentially aped the lifestyle of their parents. They were focused on gaining their own income and defining a social niche for themselves through specific patterns of consumption, rather than on effecting widespread cultural transformation.[23] Thus, while it may have threatened initially to challenge social conventions and set children against their parents, the 'rock 'n' roll' culture soundtracked by Elvis Presley, Chuck Berry, Jerry Lee Lewis and others in the mid-late fifties never in fact seriously disrupted the social fabric in the way that the counter-culture of the late sixties did. 'Rockers' and 'Teddy Boys' may have slashed cinema seats and Presley may have shocked certain older moral guardians with his physical gyrations,[24] but in contrast, by the end of the next decade students had brought France to the brink of socialist revolution, young people had led the way in the securing of civil rights in America, youthful attitudes to sex and drugs had liberalised remarkably, and, spurred again by the Beatles and their seminal album *Sergeant Pepper's Lonely Hearts Club Band*, the three-minute pop single had ceded prominence to the more self-consciously artistic ethos of the 'concept' LP.[25]

This broad contrast between the 'teenager' of the fifties and the 'counter-cultural youth' of the late sixties points to an important distinction in respect of generational formation. This is the distinction between generations which are viewed as *economically* constructed, and generations which are understood more clearly to have been *ideationally* or *ideologically* constructed.

As Arthur Marwick has observed, probably the most significant identification and classification of the new category of 'the teenager' in the 1950s came not from a sociologist, but from a market researcher: the young American retail analyst, Eugene Gilbert. Gilbert's landmark 1957 study, *Advertising and Marketing to Young People,* demonstrated that merchandise targeted at 13–20 year olds was becoming a rich, multi-billion dollar sector.[26] Likewise, in the following year, his declaration that 'within the past decade teenagers have become a separate and distinct group in our society' was *financially* rather than *philosophically* determined.[27]

In Gilbert's analysis, the acceleration of technological change after World War II, coupled with the surge of consumer confidence which accompanied the end of post-war austerity, led to a flood of new goods of greater brand variety than ever before. One of the prime 'target markets' for these new product ranges was the so-called 'Baby Boom Generation' – the outsized cohort of those born when servicemen flocked home from the front towards the end of the war and just after it. In 1957–8 most of this generation were still living at home, some with only pocket money to spend. Others, however, were taking part-time jobs in a full-employment marketplace, and still others were on the brink of a full-time career. The point Gilbert emphasised was that, unlike their parents and older siblings, who would have characteristically been burdened with mortgage, insurance and pension payments, such teenagers generally possessed a good percentage of disposable income to spend on the greater variety of clothes, toiletries, make-up, electrical goods, motor vehicles, magazines and records which had lately become available. As they bought such goods, these teenagers were identified by their purchases, and in turn influenced purchases made on their behalf by parents and elders. As this pattern unfolded, so they became designated not only as a 'target market', but also, in Dwight MacDonald's telling phrase of the time, 'A Caste' and 'A Culture'. [28] Indeed, by August 1959 an article in *Life* magazine was proclaiming the 'Teenage Consumer' to be 'A New $10 billion power', 16% of whose expenditure was going on the entertainment industry, with a substantial proportion of the rest devoted to fashion and grooming.

As Britain also experienced an economic upturn and demographic boom, immortalised in Prime Minister Harold MacMillan's phrase 'You've never had it so good', similar accounts began to appear here. The most influential of these was Mark Abrams' detailed study *The Teenage Consumer* (1959), which showed that between 1938 and 1958 the real earnings of young people had risen by over 50%. Not only this: the rate of increase had been double that of adults over the same time-span. Abrams was also able to demonstrate that in the late 1950s, teenagers had fast come to account for a significant proportion of total spending on leisure products and activities. Indeed, at this stage in post-war British history, Simon Frith does not exaggerate when he writes that 'young people were distinguished from other age groups not by their 'bad' behaviour, but simply in terms of their market choices.'[29]

Of course, where marketing is concerned, demand is not merely to be recognised and charted, but also to be *created*. Hence, although Gilbert was initially focussed on *describing* an emerging teenage generation of consumers, it did not take long before he was seeking to *shape* that 'consumer generation' as a highly paid consultant to various advertisers.[30] As we noted in Chapter 1, this trend continues today in the case of top generational gurus like Neil Howe, William Strauss and Ann Fischman. It can also be witnessed in commercial copywriters' direct deployment of generational language in slogans such as 'The Pepsi Generation'[31], and 'Montblanc Generation Writing Instruments'.[32]

Now surely all this should give pause for thought to Christians who assume the generational categories of today to be either anthropologically intrinsic or socially 'neutral', or who borrow current marketing-driven models of generation without examining their assumptions and purposes. The Bible does not present youth as a 'target market', and the extent to which it can be invoked more generally in support of the consumer capitalism which underlies so much current generational segmentation is, at best, arguable.[33]

Having said all this, it should nonetheless be conceded that, as happened in the later 1960s, what starts out as a market trend *can* nevertheless transmute into something far more socially and theologically profound. It is just that Christians ought to distinguish one phenomenon from the other, the better to trace any continuities and discontinuities that might pertain between them – and this has not often been done in the generation-based Christian studies we have cited.

From 'target markets' to 'generational cultures'

In the UK, the journey from the 'teenage market' of the later 1950s to the 'youth counter-culture' of the later 1960s can be followed through a number of key 'staging posts' – staging posts which, in their turn, can be seen to have had a significant impact on the church's response to generational change at the time. For example, a Ministry of Education white paper entitled *The Youth Service in England and Wales*, known as the Albemarle Report, influentially took Mark Abrams' research and sought to re-interpret it within a more explicitly socio-psychological grid. Published in 1960, the report identified much of the consumer spending of the young as 'to an unusually high degree, charged with an emotional content' – that is, as an activity which helped 'to provide an identity or give status or to assist in the sense of belonging to a group of contemporaries'. In this regard, what had arisen most obviously as an economic trend was seen to bear deeper, underlying cultural significance. It was also seen as carrying a potential transformative power with respect to the ordering of society as a whole. For the Albemarle Committee, the social cohesion fostered by the pressures of war had, thanks to the end of rationing and the onset of the 'material revolution' of the 1950s, given way not only to greater segmentation of the retail market, but also, potentially, to greater segmentation within society at large:

> [I]t may be that some of the recent changes in style properties involved in young people's lives and especially in their reactions, make them readier than usual to desert, in their free time, an environment which seems "corny" and "square" … [T]o dismiss the outside world as "square" is to some extent a natural feature of adolescence [but] today's rejections seem often to go beyond this, to have a peculiar edge and penetration.[34]

One concrete social change which resulted from the Albemarle Report's identification of an ever-more self-contained teenage subculture was an upsurge in government support and funding for dedicated youth clubs. Many of these were linked to churches: indeed, the evangelically-oriented Fellowship of Youth Club Workers grew from attracting twenty to its first meeting in 1955, to over two hundred by 1963.[35] Yet the clubs themselves maintained a degree of autonomy commensurate with Albemarle's perception of a newly distinct and confident identity among the young.[36] This autonomy was at least partly related to the 'peculiar edge' mentioned by the white paper: insofar as the emerging generation proved increasingly mysterious and threatening to the older generation of Christian leadership, youth clubs offered a means of 'containing' that threat – by simultaneously addressing it and keeping it at one remove from standard congregational life. This was particularly true of those urban, working class areas in which many of the new clubs were founded – areas whose younger populations had become disenfranchised from a church culture which one of the youth club pioneers, David Sheppard, saw them dismissing as 'posh, snobbish and educated'.[37]

To an extent, it is not difficult to see why the church displayed nervousness in the face of the youth cohort which developed so markedly in the sixties. It is clear, for instance, that the 'penetration' which Albemarle detected in this cohort at the start of the decade deepened considerably as it unfolded. The young novelist Colin MacInness had done much to capture and define this more incisive attitude in his 1962 paperback *Absolute Beginners*, which had very consciously set 'teenagers' against the 'citizens, tax payers, oldsters, conscripts, sordids and squares' of their parent's generation.[38] By the early months of 1963, MacInness's vision was being embodied to a remarkable degree in the so-called Mod movement – a mass cult of mainly young men distinguished by its attachment to well-cut clothes, amphetamines, scooters, rhythm and blues music, and a sometimes visceral rejection of their parents' lifestyles and values. As Dave Marsh puts it:

> [M]od was something more than a marketing mechanism or an excuse for teen tribalism. At least among the hardcore who developed it, mod was a philosophy, articulated in the chrome of a motor scooter's proliferated head lamps, the flare of a pair of trousers, the choice of just the right bright shade of a Fred Perry knit shirt, the length of the vent in a sports jacket. The aim was a style both flamboyant and cool – that is, proclaiming a poise that did not need to prove itself. The result was an undercurrent of tension – the violence always implicit but rarely acted out. Mod was a signal of a new kind of working-class rebellion, not only against bosses but also against the mods' own parents and elder brothers – against the entire pattern of conformism and conservatism in British life. Where tradition called for steady saving, honoring rank and tradition, a chipper attitude and an acceptance of limits, the mods' response was a penchant for consumption – snubbing one's superiors and all that was old, a cynical outlook and a refusal to stay in one's place … mods were sophisticated and slick, rebels with a cause, an assault that burrowed from within, asserting not just their own dignity but also the absolute ludicrousness of stuffy conformism … In its myriad shifts of detail – styles radically altering not just from

month to month but from week to week and even from one
end of the weekend to the other – mod contained not just an
implicit critique but an almost conscious satire of the modernist
philosophy of planned obsolescence.[39]

In 1964, Mods clashed with leather bound rock 'n' roll devotees,
or 'Rockers', at various seaside resorts around Britain, again
confirming the 'edginess' foreseen by Albemarle. The same year,
they were also mythologised in Charles Hamblett and Jane
Deverson's pulp novel *Generation X*[40] – a novel whose title would,
some fourteen years later, be borrowed by the 'punks' Billy Idol
and Tony James to describe another equally oppositional and
nonconformist youth culture, and then again, thirteen years after
that, by the Canadian writer Douglas Coupland, to define the
latest cohort of disaffected youth.[41]

   Most pertinent of all from our point of view, however, was the
fact that the Mod sensibility found its essential expression in a
song called 'My Generation'. As recorded in 1965 by The Who,
and as written by their charismatic lead guitarist Pete Townshend,
this now classic single managed in two verses to sum up the
growing segmentation of age groups we have been examining,
and to epitomise the 'intergenerational antipathy' about which
church leaders were becoming so concerned:

> People try to put us down
> Just because we get around
> Things they do look awful cold
> Hope I die before I get old.
>
> Why don't you all f-f-f-f-fade away
> Don't try to dig what we all say
> Not tryin' to cause a big sensation
> Just talkin' about my generation.[42]

This hardly looks like 'honouring' the generation of one's parents,
and many Christians predictably dismissed the new youth culture

celebrated by Townshend as anti-biblical.[43] As the sneer, rebellion and divisiveness of The Who's song infiltrated the pop charts, however, certain academics were beginning to focus more positively on the role played by 'youth generations' in the effecting of social change. As they did so, many found a helpful explanatory model for this phenomenon in a paper written by the German sociologist Karl Mannheim, and entitled 'The Problem of Generations'. Originally published, like Margaret Mead's work, in 1928, this article did not appear in English until 1952, and even then took a decade or more to establish itself in scholarly discourse as the first programmatic attempt to show how the physiological distinctions associated with age might have variable socio-cultural corollaries.[44] In particular, it anticipated the influential assertion made by Norman Ryder in 1965, that as well as general biological considerations, the definition of generations should also include attitudinal and historical factors – factors which may differ from one society or era to another.[45] Most appositely of all, though, it was Mannheim who first seriously expounded the key role of 'youth' in the effecting of socio-cultural change, and who thereby offered the main explanatory framework for the seismic shifts, tensions and fissures which would ensue in the West from 1967 onwards.[46]

Mannheim's basic thesis was that each generation receives its distinctive imprint and character from the events, experiences and attitudes absorbed in its youth. The extent to which one generation is delineated in identity from another depends, he suggested, on the novelty of such events, attitudes and experiences as compared with the events, attitudes and experiences absorbed by the foregoing generation. Thus where novel influences are rare, such as in traditional peasant societies, Mannheim showed that clearly demarcated generational groupings might not appear.[47] However, where technological, scientific and cultural change is rapid, he wrote, those groups will be relatively more differentiated, and youth will function as what Wade Clark Roof later called the 'lead cohort' in society.[48]

By a 'youth generation' Mannheim meant roughly those between the ages of seventeen and twenty-five. This span, he argued, represents the period during which people are generally most willing and able to 'assimilate new unconscious mental attitudes and habits'. Those who are younger than this may question and reflect on things in serious ways, but Mannheim argued that they are not usually in a position to 'experiment' proactively with life. As for the older generations, he noted that they tend to maintain the 'historical-social consciousness' formed during their own early adulthood. Indeed, from this perspective, Mannheim anticipated the subsequent 'generation gap problem' very clearly: 'The "up-to-dateness" of youth', he wrote, 'therefore consists in their being closer to the "present" problems ... and in the fact that they are dramatically aware of a process of destabilization and take sides on it. All this while, the older generation cling to the re-orientation that had been the drama of *their* youth.'[49]

As we shall see, this does not necessarily mean that each successive generation will be more radical or 'progressive' in its politics and values than the one that has gone before. Neither does it imply that one generational group will inevitably be at loggerheads with another – as appeared widely to be the case in the later 1960s. Indeed, Mannheim goes on to offer a potentially valuable insight from the Christian point of view when he writes of the positive 'compensating factor' of intergenerational co-operation, education and mentoring.[50] It is worth considering this point more specifically.

Intergenerational co-operation vs ageism

As Mannheim puts it, 'Not only does the teacher educate his pupil, but the pupil educates his teacher too. Generations are in a state of constant interaction.'[51] We have already noted the biblical corollaries of this intergenerational exchange in discipleship, leadership succession, household dynamics and congregational life. Moreover, we shall relate them to the church and mission of our own time and context when we come to chapters 11 and 12. At this point, however, it is worth noting that Margaret Mead suggested a helpful model for it in her much later book, *Culture and Commitment: A Study of the Generation Gap* (1970).

Mead called the type of culture in which grandparents cannot conceive of their grandchildren's future being anything much more than a reiteration of their own lives, a *post-figurative* culture. Samoa, where Mead had conducted her early fieldwork in the 1920s, was a typical instance of such a post-figurative culture, as, indeed, were the majority of ancient Near Eastern cultures which inhabited the biblical world.[52]

By contrast, where change is more prevalent and interaction more common, but where older groups still guard the limits of innovation, Mead applied the term *co-figurative*. Most current Western, capitalist cultures would fall under this heading: youth may be more obviously demarcated and innovative, but established means of socio-economic control and political policy-making still rest largely in the hands of their elders. An analogy could be made here with the situation of the early church. Although we do not know their exact birth-years, the apostles were most likely to have been close to Jesus in terms of age, and would therefore have lent the leadership of first-generation Christian communities a relatively youthful demographic profile as compared with the leadership of synagogues and other religious and social institutions of their day.

Finally, for instances in which the young not only suggest innovation, but macro-manage it, Mead coined the word *pre-figurative*.[53] While it is hard to discern a fully-fledged pre-figurative culture in the world as yet, the student protests and near-revolution which exploded on the streets of Paris 1968 offered a glimpse of one, while the dominance of the increasingly vital computer and IT sector by young adults today might help to realise one in the near future. Indeed, Ryder, perceived as far back as the mid-1960s that societies in which change is driven ever more by technological advance will tend to be 'led' by ever-younger cohorts. Addressing the situation in America at the time, he wrote:

> The principle motor of contemporary social change is techno-logical innovation. It pervades the other substructures of society and forces them into accommodation. The modern society institutionalizes this innovation and accepts it as self-justifying. To the child of such a society, technological change makes the past irrelevant. Its impact on the population is highly differential by age, and is felt most by those who are about to make their life-long choices. Technological evolution is accomplished less by retraining older cohorts than by recruiting the new one, and the age of an industry tends to be correlated with the age of its workers ... In traditional society, age is a valid surrogate for relevant experience, but when [technological] revolution occurs, age comes to signify historical location and degree of disenfran-chisement by change, rather than due prerogatives of seniority.[54]

At a light-hearted level, the phenomenon Ryder describes is encapsulated in the now familiar scenario of the eight-year-old child showing its comparatively 'technophobic' parents and grand-parents how to operate video players, DVDs and PCs. Theologically, however, there is a serious point to be made in relation to Mead's 'pre-figurative' model. On one level, the new covenant community of God can be said to have begun when Jesus reached adulthood and began his public ministry as a young man of around thirty (Lk. 3:23). Although this was in fact the same age at which priests typically began their service,[55] it was, as we have suggested, quite early in Jesus' life course to be assuming so *distinctive* and *singular* a leadership role. Granted, his age at this point corresponded with that of David when he ascended to the throne of Israel (2 Sam. 5:4). Still, however, it is hard not to infer at least some intergenerational resentment from the reaction of those established teachers of the law whom Jesus challenged so prodigiously.

In another sense, however, the inauguration of the Messianic age can be said to have occurred even earlier – at Jesus' birth. He is, after all, referred to as 'Messiah' and 'Saviour' both before and at the moment of his delivery (Lk. 2:11), and is recognised as such a few days later by the devout old man Simeon and the aged prophet Anna (Lk. 2:25–38). Moreover, whatever Isaiah himself had in mind when he prophesied of Israel 'a little child will lead them' (Is. 11:6), this text was soon read by the church as confirming the awesomeness of God's sovereignty over the salvation of humankind. That God should entrust his plan of redemption to an infant was seen as underlining not only God's power, but also the key place enjoyed by the very young in his providence – a place reiterated by Jesus himself when he later declared, 'Let the children come to me, for theirs is the kingdom of heaven' (Mt. 19:14).[56]

Even as the focus here falls on infancy, however, it needs to be stressed that this does not imply the sort of 'disenfranchisement' of older generations envisaged by Ryder in our own contemporary society. Rather, the involvement of Simeon and Anna, as well as the roles played by the young woman, Mary, and the (probably) more mature man, Joseph, represents a rich paradigm of intergenerational mutuality. What is more, this paradigm surely stands over against what we have already referred to as 'ageism'.

Ageism received its most formative definition from R.N. Butler in 1987, who described it as 'a process of systematic stereotyping of, and discrimination against, people because they are old, just as racism and sexism accomplish this for skin colour and gender.'[57] Debate has ensued as to whether ageism might also be regarded as something inflicted *by* older generations on the young, but there is widespread agreement that in the West, the sort of 'disenfranchisement' predicted by Ryder is largely one which affects older people.[58] This is evidenced not least in the lowering of average recruitment, redundancy and retirement ages – a trend which Annie and Bob Franklin relate to the more generally increased privileging and empowering of youth in the West, compared with older sectors of the population.[59]

As it has sought to address the rise of 'youth culture' since the sixties in the ways we have outlined, the church, too, has faced the challenge of meeting the ever more specific needs of the young without similarly 'disenfranchising' the old, or worse still, promulgating ageism. We shall return to this challenge in our last two chapters.

Generation and youth in the church

In the Christian context, and in the evangelical context in particular, it has long been recognised that the majority of people come to faith in their youth. Indeed, the 1998 English Church Attendance Survey confirmed the proportion of those either converting or decisively professing faith before the age of twenty to be 70%.[60] This phenomenon has, in fact, been at the heart of modern evangelicalism's emphasis on youth mission and youth work – an emphasis which David Bebbington has called its 'Grand Strategy'.[61] Yet while recognising its importance, it is also crucial for our purposes to move beyond the basic age-change correlation which has driven this strategy, to examine other aspects of 'generation' which might bear on our life and witness in the twenty-first century. In order to do this, we need to consider more detailed insights from contemporary social science and cultural theory which might help us relate the biblical dimensions of 'generation' we have identified to the missionary agenda faced by the church in the West, and more specifically, by the church in Britain.

4

Defining Generations Today II: Towards a Hermeneutic Model

From Chronology to Worldview: A Modern Development

Despite seeking to define a new approach to the interpretation of generations, Karl Mannheim himself acknowledged that certain historians and philosophers had previously sought to theorise the interaction of biological age-groupings and social development.[1] Most especially, he recognised this as a concern expressed since the eighteenth century by certain members of the 'positivist' school, such as David Hume and Auguste Comte, and, in a very different way, by some within the so-called 'romantic-historical' school, including Wilhelm Dilthey, Martin Heidegger and Wilhelm Pinder.

As Mannheim put it, the positivists were drawn to the subject of generations because it appeared amenable to their fundamental project, which was to reduce the factors determining human existence to purely quantitative terms. Mannheim wrote:

> The positivist is attracted by the problem of generations because it gives him the feeling that here he has achieved contact with some of the ultimate factors of human existence as such. There is life and death; a definite, measurable span of life; generation

follows generation at regular intervals. Here, thinks the Positivist, is the framework of human destiny in comprehensible, even measurable form.[2]

On one level, of course, we do think of generations as being 'dateable' in these ways. As we saw in the last chapter, generations in Scripture may be chronologically located, even as they more explicitly take their bearings from a particular patriarch and his 'house', or a particular historical event (Ex. 1:6; Judg. 2:11; Lk. 21:32). Today, as Pilcher notes, our common cultural discourse regularly includes phrases like 'the sixties generation' and 'the class of '84', which at least ostensibly link generational identity to birth years and time periods.[3]

Yet, for all their interest in generational themes, Mannheim criticised the positivists for drawing too neat and automatic a parallel between numerical age and what they assumed was the 'unilinear', upward curve of social progress. Driven by their thoroughgoing attachment to evolutionary thinking, the positivists closely aligned the leadership transitions which took place in politics, education, science and the arts with the biological succession of one generation to another. This, for Mannheim, imposed an artificial, merely chronological grid on key structural and intellectual changes within culture. It meant, for instance, that major social shifts were effectively compelled to occur every fifteen to thirty years or so (depending on one's definition of a generational time-span). It also meant that each younger generation was compelled to be more radical than the one before it. As Mannheim rightly pointed out, however, the witness of history was against such rigid determinism: change may in fact be more gradual, or almost imperceptible, and even when significant, may occur at intervals which are sometimes shorter, sometimes longer.[4] Similarly, although, as we have seen, Mannheim agreed that younger generations are typically the catalysts for social change, he was aware that such change may take place in a reactionary, rather than radical, direction.[5] A more recent instance of this can be seen in the group of those who reached maturity in the UK under the Prime Ministership of Margaret Thatcher, between 1979 and 1990. This group, dubbed 'Thatcher's children' by Pilcher, Stephen Wagg and numerous other commentators, is widely perceived to have been more conservative in outlook than its immediate predecessor.[6]

Even here, however, one wonders whether the sharp contrast between 'progress' and 'reaction' which is implicit in the positivist model actually does justice to the dynamics of generational change. Many have pointed out, for example, that while Thatcherism was associated with traditional morality, nationalism and cultural retrenchment, its monetarist, free-market economics, and the privatisation and deregulation which accompanied them, were both decidedly 'liberal' and 'radical'.[7]

Indeed, a comparable complexity may be traced in the records of Israel's and Judah's successive monarchs, as they are found in the Old Testament books of Kings and Chronicles. Here, we find an irregular oscillation between corruption and idolatry, reform and reaction – but the changes wrought in each case are not so easily reduced to notions of evolutionary generational 'advance' or 'regression'. When Hezekiah accedes to the throne of Judah in 2 Kings 18:1, for example, his policy of removing pagan altars and idols erected by previous generations of kings, and of imposing economic austerity in the face of military threats from Assyria, might on one reading, be construed as 'conservative'. Yet his achievement in creating a pool and conduit to bring fresh water into Jerusalem would appear by any standards to be very 'progressive' (2 Kgs. 20:20). The truth is that in theological terms, at least as much as in political terms, generational change may *simultaneously* reassert the past and look to the future. Furthermore, in either case, the orientation may be for good or ill: reclaiming corrupted virtues may lead to revival, but blindly taking refuge in tradition may encourage dead legalism; likewise, harnessing new technology and knowledge may serve the common good, while innovating without purpose will foster superficiality and short-termism. Indeed, Jesus' critiques of his own 'wicked' and 'crooked' generation are aimed both at its failure to uphold the ancient law of Moses, *and* at its refusal to acknowledge the new dispensation which He himself represents (Lk. 11:45–52; Jn. 8:39–58).

Realising complexities of this sort, Mannheim favoured the romantic-historical legacy of thinking about generations. In particular, he drew on Dilthey's proposal that time should be viewed as not merely quantitative or 'mechanical', but also 'qualitative'.[8] Whereas the positivists measured generations objectively, according to biology and chronological history alone, Dilthey had suggested that they should also be defined in terms of the 'history of ideas'. By this he meant that they should be delineated not just by 'hours, months, years [and] decades', but by the dominant perceptions, ideologies and cultural movements around which they cluster, through which they construct their identity as generations, and in terms of which they 're-enact' their own place in the world.[9] Dilthey's collective term for such perceptions, ideologies and movements was *weltanschaunng* – or 'worldview'.[10] This has since become a keyword in the analysis of contemporary culture, and now features widely in Christian theology.[11]

For Dilthey, a worldview constituted 'an overall perspective on life that sums up what we know about the world, how we value it emotionally, and how we respond to it volitionally'.[12] For Brian Walsh and Richard Middleton, both theologians of culture, worldview 'determines our values' and 'helps us interpret the world around us'. It 'sorts out what is important from what is not, what is of highest value from what is least'.[13] For Mannheim, however, a worldview-based approach offered first and foremost a welcome corrective to merely empirical accounts of 'generation'. As he put it:

> The idea that, from the point of view of the history of ideas, contemporaneity means a state of being subjected to similar influences rather than a mere chronological datum, shifts the

> discussion from a plane on which it risked degenerating into a
> kind of arithmetical mysticism to the sphere of interior time
> which can be grasped by intuitive understanding.[14]

Indeed, Mannheim's reference to 'arithmetical mysticism' here rightly suggests that purely chronological accounts of generational identity, based as they are on the inference of 'character' and 'behaviour' from particular birth dates, are not so far removed from the pseudo-science of astrology![15]

The example of 'Thatcher's children' cited above bears all this out: insofar as it is possible to speak of the 1980s as a 'generational time', it tends more readily to be viewed in ideationally rather than merely temporal terms. It is associated in cultural discourse far more with the rise of free-market economics, the collapse of communism, the decline of radical socialism and the ending of the Cold War, and with the capitalistic ideologies associated with those phenomena, than with a sheer numerical time span.[16] Indeed, in many cases generations are portrayed more distinctively according to their dominant perceived *values*, than according to the year or years of their birth. Hence, Carlton Hayes calls the generation which assumed social leadership in Europe between 1871 and 1900 a 'generation of materialism'.[17] Hence, too, Western youth of the late 1960s are regularly cast as a 'peace and love generation', defined by opposition to the Vietnam War, by free sex, drug experimentation and a relatively permissive morality,[18] while the 'chemical generation' of the early 1990s is portrayed as equally drug-focussed, but somewhat more self-consciously hedonistic in approach. In particular, the narcotics it uses are associated with the rituals and rhythms club and dance culture, rather than with the world of inner contemplation.[19]

We saw in the last chapter that generations are often characterised 'attitudinally' rather than chronologically in Scripture. Most often the attitude in question is perceived in moral rather than metaphysical terms: thus generations may be 'upright' (Ps. 112:2), or more frequently, 'stubborn', 'rebellious' and 'perverse' (Ps. 78:8; Mt. 17:17; Lk. 9:41). Yet it is clear, most especially from Jesus' denunciations of his own generation, that such moral failure is rooted in theological and philosophical bankruptcy – that is, in a defective worldview. Thus the teachers of the law, who suffer markedly from Jesus' 'generational' broadsides, are those who in fact 'know neither the Scriptures nor the power of God' (Mk. 12:24), who 'strain out a gnat but swallow a camel' (Mt. 23:24), and who set too much store by money (Lk. 16:14). As much as their actions, it is their ideology which is denounced as a pernicious 'yeast' in the dough of Israel (Mk. 8:15).

From Worldview to Lifestyle: A Postmodern Turn

While the contemporary example of the 'chemical generation' which we cited above undoubtedly implies certain worldview features, these might well be viewed as relatively weak in comparison with what could be called 'lifestyle traits'. Indeed, it needs to be recognised that ever more within Western consumer society, generations are defined by fashion, musical taste and forms of speech rather than by any one, dominant, coherent ideology.[20] The Mod movement, indeed, is a good early example of this: as quoted above, the lyrics of The Who's 'My Generation' struck a distinctly 'anti-parental' pose and articulated what the group and their followers were *against*, but Mods themselves were defined in *positive* terms much more by their general demeanour than by any grand philosophy. Indeed, this move from the deep ideological content expected of 'high' culture towards the surface styles, symbols and slogans of 'popular' culture is a key feature of the shift in Western society in the sixties from a 'modern' to a so-called 'postmodern' sensibility – a shift which has significant implications for the methodology and form of generationally-based study. As John Storey has defined it, postmodernism first, in fact, emerged 'out of a generational refusal of the categorical certainties of high modernism', such that 'the insistence on an absolute distinction between high and popular culture came to be regarded as the 'unhip' assumption of an older generation.'[21] Indeed, so embedded has this critique of the high/low divide become that the British cultural theorist Dick Hebidge can claim with some confidence that in the Western world today, 'popular culture is no longer marginal, still less subterranean. Most of the time and for most people it simply is culture'.[22]

This new emphasis on apparently more ephemeral forms of popular culture has gone hand-in-hand with what Jean-François Lyotard famously termed an 'incredulity towards metanarratives' – that is, a refusal of overarching explanations of the world and society in favour of smaller, more localised paradigms and tactics for living.[23] As we shall see, in terms of generational analysis, this has necessitated greater appreciation of the fact that 'generations' have become more diversified at the 'horizontal' level of attitude and behaviour, as well as at the 'vertical' level of historical and technological development.

The Importance of 'Social Events'

As well as developing a model of 'generation' which fuses chronology with attitude and demeanour in the way we have described, Mannheim's work was also distinguished by its emphasis on the need for a third core variable to be included in the equation. Previously neglected in generational studies, Mannheim defined this as the variable of 'social events'. These events, he argued, are the 'medium' through which 'any biological rhythm must work itself out'.[24] That is to say, the specific profile of a generational group will be shaped as much by the key historical occurrences to which it is subject, as by the actual dates between which it is born. The 'Baby Boom generation' is a classic instance of this. On one level, as we have shown, it represents the class of people born between the

mid-1940s and the early 1960s. Yet we do not tend to charac-
terise it numerically in relation to this birth-year period:
indeed, exact definitions of its beginning and end dates vary.[25]
Rather, nominally at least, we define it biologically: the 'boom'
denotes a significant rise in the birth rate during this era. Yet
neither does this alone tell the whole story, because there was a
clear *socio-historical* reason for the boom. It was caused by the
return of soldiers to domestic and civilian life after the end
of the Second World War. As they fathered children, so the
leftward side of the population graph bulged dramatically.
Indeed, it is this specific historical context which has led to
the same generation's frequently being dubbed the 'post-war
generation'.[26]

Quite often, such socio-historical occurrences will interact with the sorts of qualitative, worldview-driven generational
identities we mentioned above. The 'peace and love generation',
for example, is often referred to in the USA as the 'Woodstock
generation', after the epochal Woodstock Music and Arts Festival,
held in upstate New York in the summer of 1969.[27] This massive
'social event' attracted some 500,000 mainly young people, and
had an immediate structural impact on the surrounding area. But
it also featured many of the most revered rock musicians of the
day, spawned an influential film and soundtrack and, for many,
epitomised the progressive, libertarian, pacifist outlook associated
with youth in the later sixties. Indeed, Joni Mitchell's song
commemorating the event mythologised it in nothing less than
Edenic terms: 'We are stardust/we are golden/and we've got to
get ourselves back to the garden'.[28] Not only did Woodstock
encapsulate a set of generationally-distinctive beliefs and
attitudes; it also gained those beliefs and attitudes a significant
international profile.

Another event-specific name sometimes given to this group is
the 'Vietnam generation', in recognition of the war to which
many young American males were drafted during the same
period, and against which many of their contemporaries

protested at home. In particular, David Wyatt, and Howard Schuman and Jaqueline Scott have acknowledged the appropriateness of this name, given the massive impact of Vietnam on modern American history.[29]

We suggested earlier that Mark 13:30 and its parallels might anticipate the key 'social event' of Jerusalem's fall in AD 70, and ventured this as one explanation for Jesus' comment that his own generation would not pass away before 'all these things have taken place'. Whether or not this interpretation is valid, however, it is clear that the Bible more generally recognises the role of key social events or 'moments' in the shaping of an era, epoch or generation. Indeed, Mannheim's distinction between 'qualitative time' and 'chronological time' in this respect bears strong affinities with the distinction often made in the New Testament, between *chronos* and *kairos*, where *chronos* denotes measured time and *kairos* an especially 'momentous' time of opportunity, crisis or fulfilment.[30] Hence while *chronos* is used either to describe a point in time (Lk. 4:5) or a span of time (Acts 13:18), *kairos* conveys more qualitative times of 'testing' (Lk. 8:13), 'harvest' (Mk. 13:30), 'judgment' (1 Cor. 4:5; 1 Pet. 4:17) and redemption (1 Tim. 2:6) – times which may well define the character of the cohort which lives through them.

The Role of 'Collective Memories'

For Schuman and Scott, the Vietnam War stands as a prime example of the way a major news event can mark out a distinct generational grouping, not simply in terms of objective history, but also in terms of what Maurice Halbwachs calls *collective memories*. For Halbwachs, collective memories denote the recollections of a shared past which are retained by the groups who experienced it, and are seen as instrumental in the definition of generational groups in particular. Schuman and Scott reiterate this basic idea, but go on to make the vital point that within any population there will be not *one* but *several* generational groupings, and that each may in fact recall the same momentous events in distinct ways. For one thing, different chronologically defined birth-groups will tend to experience key historical moments differently, according to a range of factors related to age.

As Mannheim realised, perhaps the most obvious of these age-related factors is mental development and cognition. Young children's intellectual faculties will generally be less developed and sophisticated than those of adults, and they will accordingly process major social events less precisely, and often less memorably, than their elders. Those who were three years old in 1945 will clearly have less vivid personal experience of VE Day than those who were twenty-three years old at the time. Likewise, a young child is less likely to have the New York terrorist assault of 11 September 2001 etched on its mind than its parents. By the same token, in evangelical Christian circles, a person who was taken to Billy Graham's historic Harringay rallies of 1954 as an infant is unlikely to regard them as formatively as might the parent or parents who took her. Indeed, field studies by Bärbel Inhelder and Jean Piaget, Judith Gallatin, Roberta Siegel and Martin Brooks, Erik Erikson and others demonstrate that while children of primary school age may be fairly well developed in terms of language and other abilities, they have only a relatively superficial understanding of the socio-cultural world beyond their own family and close personal relationships, and therefore define themselves much less in terms of 'current affairs'.[31]

Then again, age distinctions can be socially institutionalised in such a manner that different generational groups are forced by law or government decree to experience the same event in very diverse ways. Hence during the Second World War many children would have lived through it as evacuees; as in the days of Moses (Num. 1:3), men in their twenties and thirties would have been called up to serve in the military; older people, meanwhile, would have dealt with falling bombs at home. The same event would thus have shaped the respective generational identities of these groups in different ways. As Schuman and Scott's own extensive fieldwork on collective memories of the Second World War shows, it would also have had diverse effects on their respective 'historical consciousness'.

When we look for prefigurations of all this in the Old Testament, 'collective memories' do not appear so explicitly to segment different generational groups living at the same time – although as we shall see below, such segmentation is implicit in the division of Israel into different tribes, each with their own profile and history (Gen. 49:1–28). What is clear is that collective memories play a quite critical role in defining and galvanising whole cohorts of Israel at particular moments in its development. Most frequently and most importantly of all, it is the collective memory of the Exodus which serves to sustain successive generations of Israelites – not least when those generations are assailed by hardship or oppressed by their enemies (Neh. 9:9; Ezek. 20:6–7). More generally, recollection of faithful generations gone by is encouraged as a spur to fresh commitment and hope in the present (Is. 51:9).

Social Generational Units

If it is true that 'collective memories' may differ between different generational groups living at the same time, it also needs to be recognised that that the *same* age-defined generation may respond *attitudinally* in different ways to a particular social event or epoch. Indeed, one of the greatest dangers of generationally-driven social and cultural analysis is the temptation to stereotype particular age groups according to their worldview in general, and their response to the same historical episodes in particular. Ryder calls this the error of 'generationism'.[32] As we shall see, it is precisely this sort of stereotyping which has marred so much Christian writing on generational issues, and which has led, in turn, to a surfeit of overly programmatic church growth strategies, youth ministry models and ecclesial sub-divisions in recent times. It needs to be remembered that not all 'Baby Boomers' went to Woodstock, saw the film or were influenced by its ideals. Indeed, there were at least as many young people in the USA who would have resisted such ideals – who were, in fact, part of the conservative 'silent majority' to whom the Republican Richard Nixon appealed on his way to a land-slide victory in the 1968 Presidential election. A considerable proportion of such youngsters would, indeed, have been evangelical Christians![33]

For all Mannheim's insistence on the importance of worldview and social events for the defining of generations, he understood these complications very well. Indeed, his paper goes on to acknowledge that *within* each chronologically defined generation, there may well develop separate subcul-tures, or *generation units*, which 'work up the material of their common experiences in *different specific ways*' (our emphasis).[34] According to Mannheim, this could be seen in the fact that, from around 1800, youth generations in Europe had tended to diverge into two basic political sub-groups – one 'romantic-conservative' and the other 'liberal-rationalist'. Although members of both groups might be said to belong to the same generation in terms of their birth period and contemporaneity with major historical events, they were distinguished from each other by their different beliefs, attitudes and assumptions. For Mannheim, in fact, these beliefs, attitudes and assumptions could become *more* formative for the young people in question than the historical events and social 'facts' which they held in common: the 'generation unit', in this respect, represented in his view 'a much more concrete bond than the actual generation as such'.[35]

We have already provided an example of this 'generational unit' distinction in the Mods and Rockers of the mid-sixties – two groups who were parallel in age and who lived through the same major events and developments in society at large, but who expressed their identities in contrasting – and conflicting – ways. Jane Pilcher, who borrows extensively from Mannheim but prefers to call such groups *social generational units*, bears out the same sort of divergence in relation to the 1960s as a whole: 'Not every young person', she writes, 'was part of what might be called the "actual sixties social generation": not every youthful person actively participated in the social and cultural events of the time. Mannheim's theory ... allows for the existence of opposing "social generational units", such as pro- and anti-Vietnam campaigners.'[36]

More rarefied forms of 'social generational unit' can be seen to exist not as mass subcultures, but rather as specific 'schools' of thinkers, artists or political leaders. Joseph J. Ellis, for example, calls the 'founding brothers' of modern America – men like Thomas Jefferson, John Adams, George Washington and Benjamin Franklin – the 'revolutionary generation', even though they only actually numbered a small political class.[37] Likewise, Faith Ashford refers to a 'post-Caravaggio generation' of Italian Renaissance painters, and the Courtauld Institute to 'the second generation of post-Impressionism'.[38] And more familiarly, Robert A. Lee and Steven Watson dub post-Second World War writers such as Jack Kerouac, Allen Ginsberg and William Burroughs 'the beat generation', in reference to supposed analogies between their avant-garde literary style and the rhythms of contemporary jazz music.[39]

At a more popular level, Xer and Millennial generations in particular have sub-divided significantly according to different styles of music, and the various 'cultures' and lifestyle traits associated with them. Thus, the Seattle-based grunge rock typified by bands like Nirvana and Pearl Jam did much to define the 'slacker' generational unit portrayed by Richard Linklater's 1990 film of the same name; Goths, with their dark, funereal attire and attachment to doom-laden artists like Sisters of Mercy and Marilyn Manson, hark back to Victorian morbidity and melodrama while reflecting the nihilist underbelly of postmodern culture; hip hop attracts a predominantly black youth following, but has cross-pollinated many other musical genres, as well as influencing more mainstream youth fashion, language and attitudes; garage, techno, industrial, R & B and trance are all linked with distinct, club-based sub-cultures; and all the while, older, Boomer-originated movements like heavy metal, soul and Mod continue to generate new bands, magazines and gatherings, and to attract new young followers. [40]

Whether relatively large or small, these social generational units suggest a significant refinement to existing analyses of generations in the Christian community – particularly where those analyses are driven by generalised, macro-social schemas like that offered by Howe and Strauss. First, the notion of 'social generational units' is well exemplified by that sub-classifying of Israel into 'tribes' which we touched on above (Gen. 49:1–28). [41] Not least when such tribes come into conflict with one another, and especially once they divide into the two separate kingdoms of Ephraim and Judah in 1 Kings 11–12, to speak of them all merely as 'the generation of Israel' clearly becomes inadequate. Likewise, although the church is identified by all kinds of collective epithets in the New Testament (body, household, bride of Christ, etc.), it is physically expressed through a wide diversity of congregations and denominations formed in different places, with different demographic profiles and different socio-historical backgrounds. [42]

Even today, 'tribal' language is used by some commentators to depict the wide range of traditions, denominations and streams which together comprise the church of Christ. Clive Calver and Rob Warner, in fact, go further, and use such language specifically to describe different expressions of the evangelical movement within the church. [43]

More crucially still, however, the concept of the 'social generational unit' is helpful because it is patient of the idea that commitment to the particular worldview, lifestyle and ethos of Christianity may, in the end, be more compelling than any perceived allegiance to broader social groupings. Indeed, the claim of the gospel that faith in Christ supersedes all distinctions of age, appearance, language or culture (Acts 2; Gal. 3:28) very much bears out Mannheim's point: adherence to the minority 'social unit' called the church is likely, for Christians in today's pluralistic, postmodern, post-Christian West, to outweigh adherence to any more pervasive generational paradigm in the world at large. Indeed, the fact that the church is typically *multi-generational* rather than *mono-generational* may itself be a 'counter-cultural' characteristic in this respect.

Bridging the Interpretative Gap: Biblical Modes of Generational Definition in Twenty-First Century Perspective

Having earlier defined the nine key modes of generational definition in Scripture, and having then reviewed core concepts in modern-day analysis of generations, we are now in a position to revisit the biblical categories and explore their relevance to our contemporary culture.

Genealogical

As in Scripture, so also today, we have seen that this mode of generational definition relates to essential kinship status, i.e. whether one is defined in any given context as 'grandparent', 'parent' or 'child'. In the technical sphere of demography, it also covers family and household roles derived from adoption and guardianship – but this in fact also reflects the biblical pattern, in which the adoptee was typically accorded 'the full privileges and responsibilities of one who participated in [the family relationship] by birth'.[44]

This genealogical mode of generational definition is, literally, 'relative': one can be both a parent *and* a child, a grandparent *and* a parent, depending on whether one is looking 'upwards' or 'downwards' through the family tree. In current parlance, such genealogical definition is most often mediated through phrases like 'my parents' generation' or 'my granddaughter's generation'.

Natal

Both biblically and sociologically, we have confirmed that 'generation' is expressed in respect of numerical age, birth years and periodised birth cohorts. In today's common discourse, this idea of generations is reflected in phrases like 'the thirtysomething generation'.

Periodical

We have observed that Western social scientists regularly identify generational groups according to a particular calendrically-determined time period, e.g. 'the sixties generation' or 'the millennial generation'.[45] Here, the reference is neither to birth-year nor age as such, but to the *times through which one lives,* these being represented in chronological rather than ideological terms. However, since a period such as a decade may in fact be experienced by four of five genealogically-defined generational groups simultaneously, we have acknowledged that this sort of designation tends, in practice, to relate to those who are at Mannheim's key, socially transformative stage of 'young adulthood' during the period specified, and who thus operate as the 'lead generation' in that context.

While the biblical world of the ancient Near-East tended to be somewhat more 'elder-driven' and 'post-figurative' than is Western culture today, this focus on the 'lead cohort' is paralleled by the fact that Jesus established his mission while still a reasonably young man (Lk. 3:23).[46]

Epochal

Although we have seen it usually linked to a specific time-period in Scripture, this aspect of generational definition in fact has to do more with what Mannheim calls the *zeitgeist*, and with what Pinder defines as the signature 'entelechy', or 'spirit', of an 'age'. As it happens, while Mannheim warns against too mystical an ascription of a specific ethos, sensibility or worldview to any mere time-period, there is no doubt that generational distinctions are often made along such lines, and that they do often help to sum up the prevailing attitudes and ideas of a society at a particular stage of its development, or even more commonly, of a particularly influential generational unit within that society. Hence the use of terms like the 'Baby Boom generation', which covers a twenty-odd year period, rather than a particular birth year or age level, but which also denotes something more than purely periodical: the 'boom' here implies not only a swelled birth rate but a parallel expansion of economies, opportunities and technological innovation.[47]

Eventual

As in 'pertaining to events', rather than in 'indicating finality',[48] this category has helped us to define biblical generations in relation to especially significant historical occurrences like the fall of Jerusalem. As with periodical definition, it most particularly applies to the identity of those who live through it as youths and younger adults, and as such, retain the most potent forms of 'collective memory'.[49] In the American context, Schuman and

Scott's research shows that the key generation-defining events for those alive in 1989 were World War II and the Vietnam War.[50] It is not surprising, therefore, that the terms 'G.I. generation', 'post-war Generation' and 'Vietnam generation' are in common currency in the USA[51] – although it could be argued that the extended duration of such wars, and the fact that they comprised a number of distinct events within themselves, merit their being defined as 'epochal'. 'The Woodstock generation' would also come under this heading.

This dimension would also include phrases like 'the class of '97', to denote those who together pass through a significant life-event (e.g. college graduation), but who are not necessarily all the same age when they do so.

While such event-definition will normally apply to those who directly experience the happening in question, where genera-tional units are concerned past events may acquire retrospective significance through what Schuman and Scott call 'vicarious nostalgia'.[52] We have shown how such nostalgia operates constructively in respect of the Exodus, which is taken up by later generations of Israelites as a reminder of past divine liberation, and as a prompt to future faithfulness. A similar phenomenon is seen in 'revivalist' subcultures – both sacred and secular – which characteristically define their identity in relation to past events or times, of which they may not have direct personal experience. Hence the sixties are still frequently mythologised and 'recycled' in various branches of popular culture,[53] and the historic evangelical revivals of the eighteenth century are regularly cited as precedents for contemporary evangelical movements – most recently, the so-called 'Toronto Blessing' of the mid-1990s.[54]

Attitudinal

Insofar as the attitudinal aspect of generational identity pertains to worldview and/or lifestyle, we have seen it manifested biblically

most often through denunciations of this or that generation's
ungodliness. In our own modern Western culture, however, it
does not always carry such a strong moral charge, and may
more commonly relate to characteristic ideology or aesthetics.
Furthermore, whereas scriptural references to 'generation' in this
context tend to imply whole population-groups, in our contemporary setting the size of the group in question may vary from
mass-cultural sets like 'the Peace and Love generation' and
'Generation X', through more selective subcultures like 'the
Hippie generation', to very specific and limited artistic 'schools'
such as 'the Beat generation'.

Affectual

The biblical pattern of defining certain generations according to
some dominant 'affect' or psycho-spiritual impact, from election
on the one hand to divine punishment on the other, finds several
corollaries in our own day and age. Judy Pearsall and Bill Trumble,
for instance, define those who saw large numbers of their
contemporaries killed in the First World War as the 'lost generation' – a phrase also appropriated by Howe and Strauss.[55] Then
again, the same designation is also applied more specifically to the
American writers who best captured the mood of this much
larger social group – Ernest Hemmingway, F. Scott Fitzgerald,
Malcolm Cowley, etc.[56] Similarly, Myra MacPherson calls those
closely affected by the Vietnam War the 'haunted generation',
while A.D. Horne describes them as 'the wounded generation'.[57]

Behavioural

While justification in the New Testament may be by faith
through grace (Rom. 5:2; Gal. 2:16), final judgment is several
times defined according to works (e.g. 2 Cor. 5:10; Rev. 20:12). It

is this eschatological context which lends particular force to Jesus' implicit rejection of the deeds, as well as the attitudes, of his generation in texts such as Matthew 12:39 and Mark 9:19. While far less likely to pack such an ethical and juridical punch, behavioural definitions of generations remain in use today. Thus, James R. Brett predicts an imminent 'cyber generation' whose facility with computer technology will thrust them to the fore-front of civic leadership in the mid-twenty-first century. Thus, too, the current 'chemical generation' are identified by their active intake of pharmaceuticals.[58]

Functional

While we have recognised that 'youth' and 'age' in particular become associated with various social codes and functions in Scripture, the so-called 'functionalist' approach is well established in current sociological analysis of generations. As pioneered by S.N. Eisenstadt in his 1956 book *From Generation to Generation*, this approach seeks to explain generations 'in terms of their relationships with *other* social institutions and in terms of the role they play in contributing to social *continuity*.' [59] Hence, just as 'elder' in the New Testament signifies an institutional position within the church as well as a point in the life course, so, for example, 'senior citizenship' is closely related in British society to the condition of 'retirement', and is marked for all kinds of state-sponsored benefits and concessions, from pensions to free bus passes. Similarly, 'childhood' is cast in legal terms as 'minority', and is protected as such from certain forms of prosecution, as well as being restricted from full-time employment, driving, alcohol consumption, etc.

By the same token, contemporaneous 'living' generations may be accorded a whole range of different 'institutional' functions within the community of the local church. Different services may be aimed at different age groups. Even in so-called 'family' worship, 'young people' may leave early to continue in separate 'Sunday school' classes and 'youth' groups. Likewise, children may be routinely baptised around 6 months and confirmed at or around the age of eleven. In the para-church world, different agencies may target abused children, alcoholic adults, men with mid-life crises, menopausal women, the aged, etc.

The nine modes of generational definition defined above are shown in the diagram overleaf (Fig. 1). The existence of such complex and often simultaneous dimensions of meaning suggests that in addition to biblical and socio-cultural criteria for generational definition *per se*, we also need a model which will help us understand both how different 'living generations' can be distinguished *from* one another, and how they interact *with* one another. It is with just such a model that we shall be concerned in the next chapter.

Fig.1 – Modes of generational definition

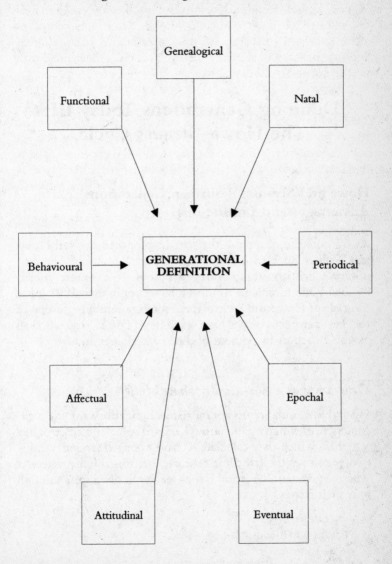

5

Defining Generations Today III:
The Howe–Strauss Cycle

Howe and Strauss' 'Fourteen Generations': Advantages and Limitations

As we noted in chapter 1, the schema proposed by Neil Howe and William Strauss is by far the most pervasive among contemporary Christian studies on generations. It therefore merits particular attention here. As most fully set out in their 1991 study, *Generations*, Howe and Strauss' methodology combines several of the key perspectives we have examined. For clarity, we shall examine each main element of this methodology in turn.

Generation as a two-decade 'phase of life'

Firstly, Howe and Strauss appropriate a straightforward 'lifecycle' paradigm, in which a generation is aligned to 'a basic phase of life' – a phase which they calculate to have averaged 'about twenty-two years over the last three centuries'. Across the lifecycle as a whole, a generational group is thus seen typically to pass through four such phases:

> youth (0–21)
> rising adulthood (22–43)

midlife (44–65)
elderhood (66–87)[1]

Howe and Strauss do not distinguish in this grid between sub-categories of 'youth' like 'childhood', 'adolescence' and 'late teenager', because at this level, they are still essentially tied to genealogy: the four phases in question relate, very roughly, to the four levels of the family tree through which individuals are most likely to pass in a lifetime (offspring, parent, grandparent, great grandparent). Although, as we have seen, Howe and Strauss are hardly driven by theology, it is worth mentioning that in an appendix note, they do relate this 'four-part generational cycle' to a pattern found in the Old Testament, from 'Exodus (ch. 1) through Judges (ch. 2)'. Specifically, they cite the fact that in Numbers 1:3 males are said to be fit for war – and thus presumably to be defined as 'adults' rather than 'youths' – 'from twenty years old and upward'.[2] More generally, one supposes that they have in mind various Pentateuchal references to God's blessing and cursing people to the 'fourth' or 'third and fourth' generation (Gen. 15:6; Ex. 20:5, 34:7; Num. 14:18; Deut. 5:9). As we saw in Chapter 2, the Old Testament picture is actually far more complex than this. Still, inasmuch as there is *a* fourfold generational pattern in Scripture, and insofar it represents *one* theological paradigm of ageing, Howe and Strauss' allusion resonates with our concerns.

The 'age-location' model

Beyond the basic life cycle categories just mentioned, Howe and Strauss go on to borrow from Mannheim, Ryder, Schuman and Scott and others as they develop what they call an 'age-location' approach to generations. Whereas a purely life cycle-based view focuses, as it were, on the main 'stations' through which human beings *as such* pass on their life journey, Howe and Strauss seek to adopt 'the perspective of *trains* rather than *stations*'.[3] This means recognising, on analogy, that several different 'trains' of different types may take different routes through the same station at different times. In other words, the basic age distinctions of the life cycle will themselves show qualitative *sub-variation* from one revolution of the cycle to the next. Hence, the typical experience and outlook of elders in the Victorian age clearly differed in key respects from the typical experience and outlook of elders in the period after the Second World War. And just as the 'environment' of stations is affected by time, and by the trains which pass through them (e.g. from steam to diesel), so 'elderhood' clearly meant somewhat different things in the two periods mentioned. In terms of generational analysis, this translates to an acknowledgement that factors other than sheer, ongoing physical ageing must be taken into account. Chief among these factors for Howe and Strauss are Schuman and Scott's key variable of 'social events', and what we have called here the 'behavioural' dimension of generational definition. As Howe and Strauss themselves put it,

> [W]e can see how events shape ... different age groups differently according to their phase of life, and how people retain those personality differences as they grow older ... There is no such thing as one universal life cycle. To the contrary, neighbouring generations can and do live very different lifecycles depending on their respective age-locations in history. While observing (or trying to predict) phase-of-life behaviour, we must remember that the age of each generation is *rising* while time moves *forward*. Thus, we can visualize age location along what we call the 'generational diagonal'. Tracing this diagonal allows us to connect the event, the age, and the behaviour of the same generation over time.[4]

This 'age-location' model thus represents an explicit move from 'lifecycle' to 'life course' thinking. More specifically, it defines generational distinctions according to a four-fold index of kinship, age, historical context and behaviour, with each factor affecting the other. Of these, the 'behavioural' factor plainly also entails what we have called an 'attitudinal' element: for Howe and Strauss, worldviews and lifestyle traits go hand-in-hand with behaviour-patterns. Through this interaction of processes, different generational groups are seen to acquire different 'characters' or 'personalities'.[5] We have already seen this exemplified by intuitive colloquial ascriptions such as 'the Peace and Love generation', 'the 'Vietnam generation' and 'Generation X', but Howe and Strauss offer a useful explanatory account of the grounds on which such ascriptions are actually made – one which for our purposes may be represented as a 'generational quadrilateral' of kinship, age, social events and worldview, where worldview (somewhat elliptically) is taken to cover both attitude and characteristic behaviour, on the basis that these are most often interdependent (see Fig. 2, below).

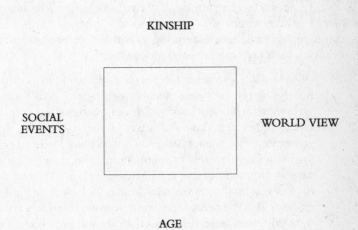

Fig. 2 – Generational 'Quadrilateral'[6]

Thus far, Howe and Strauss' 'hybrid' approach to generational segmentation offers a reasonably elegant and uncontroversial way in to the subject, and can be seen in many respects as a distillation of the nine-point model we proposed above. The final key element of their analysis, however, is both far more complex and much more contentious.

Towards a predictive model: the 'generational cycle'

While appreciating the insights of social scientists on the criteria of generational definition, Howe and Strauss argue that in and of themselves, these criteria have told us 'little about how generations shape history'. In other words, they may be help-fully *descriptive*, but they are not especially *predictive*. By contrast, Howe and Strauss are concerned to demonstrate not only how 'history produces generations', but also how *'generations produce history'* (their emphasis).[7] Central to this phenomenon, they claim, are critical, epoch-defining events, or 'constellations' of events, which they term 'social moments'.

> Because a social moment hits people in different phases of life, it helps shape and define different generations. And because generations in different phases of life can together trigger a social moment, they help shape and define history – and hence, new generations. Throughout American history, social moments have arrived at dates separated by approximately two phases of life, or roughly forty to forty-five years. Most historians look upon this rhythm as, at most, a curious coincidence. We look upon it as key evidence that a generational cycle is at work, ensuring a rather tight correspondence between constellations and events. The correspondence is not exact – but the average deviation from what the cycle would predict is only three or four years. That, we think, is a small margin of error for a theory applied over four centuries.[8]

These definitive 'social moments', say Howe and Strauss intriguingly, tend to alternate between 'spiritual awakenings' and 'secular crises'. Hence in America, the Great Awakening of 1734–43, as led by Jonathan Edwards, William Tennent and others, was followed four decades later by the American Revolution (1773–89), as pioneered by figures like George Washington, Thomas Jefferson and James Madisdon. Then, four decades after that came the so-called 'second Great Awakening' of 1822–37, also known as the 'transcendental awakening' and associated with a loose network of 'Romantic' spiritual leaders such as Ralph Waldo Emerson, Nat Turner and Charles Finney. Then, a little sooner than might have been expected by the model, came the next secular tumult – the Civil War (1857–65). This was in turn followed, from 1886–1903, by what Howe and Strauss call a 'missionary awakening' – a period of 'reform, revivalism and labour radicalism' personified by men like William Jennings Bryan, Jane Addams and W.E.B. Dubois. Another four decades on came the defining socio-political phase of the Great Depression and the Second World War (1932–45), which was for its part succeeded by what Howe and Strauss call the 'boom awakening' – an awakening which, as we have seen, began around 1967, and which they round off at 1980, when a more materialistic, 'millennial' phase is seen to arise with election of Ronald Reagan (see Fig. 3, below).[9]

SPIRITUAL AWAKENING	Great Awakening	1734–43
SECULAR CRISIS	American Revolution	1773–89
SPIRITUAL AWAKENING	Second Great Awakening	1822–37
SECULAR CRISIS	Civil War	1857–65
SPIRITUAL AWAKENING	Missionary Awakening	1886–1903
SECULAR CRISIS	Depression/World War II	1932–45
SPIRITUAL AWAKENING	Youth Counter Culture	1967–80
SECULAR CRISIS	?	1980–

Fig. 3 – Key 'social moments' in American history[10]

Each of Howe and Strauss' 'pairs' of spiritual and secular 'social moments' are taken to distinguish roughly 'one-quarter' and 'three-quarter' points of a full four-generation, eight-decade 'life cycle'. Counting forward from the generation of those who founded modern America in the eighteenth century, there have, say Howe and Strauss, been three such complete cycles – a 'revolutionary cycle' (1734–1821), a 'civil war cycle' (1822–85) and a 'great power cycle' (1886–1967). Since 1967, they suggest, we have been in a fourth, 'millennial cycle'.[11]

Having proposed this grand model, Howe and Strauss perceive further ordered patterning *within* each cycle. Specifically, they suggest that the four generations who comprise a full cycle will follow a clear attitudinal sequence: the first generation of the cycle will, they claim, be typically 'Idealist', the second 'Reactive', the third 'Civic' and the fourth 'Adaptive'. Idealists and Civics, they suggest, are characteristically 'dominant' in public life – Idealists 'through redefining the inner world of values and culture', and Civics through 'rebuilding the outer world of technology and institutions'. By contrast, Reactives and Adaptives are typically 'recessive', checking 'the excesses of their more powerful neighbours' – Reactives doing so through a contrasting pragmatism and Adaptives through assimilation and synthesis of earlier trends, and through 'amelioration' (see Fig. 4, below)

Idealists	Dominant	Redefining Values and Culture
Reactives	Recessive	Prioritising Pragmatism
Civic	Dominant	Shaping Technology and Institutions
Adaptive	Recessive	Assimilationist and Ameliorative

Fig. 4 – Generational types and characteristics in the American Cycle
(After Howe and Strauss, 1991:35)[12]

Because at any one time in history these four generational 'types' will co-exist at different stages of their *own* life cycle, Howe and Strauss suggest that the *overall* identity and ethos of a particular period will ultimately be defined by whatever 'type' happens to be passing through 'rising adulthood' at the time. In this, they echo Mannheim's view of younger people as the 'lead cohort', although their category extends to forty-three years of age whereas his had its upper limit at around twenty-five.

Although they audaciously trace their analysis as far back as 1584, Howe and Strauss track fourteen distinct generations since the period of the American Revolution in the 1770s. These are distributed across the three completed cycles we have mentioned, and the yet-to-be concluded 'millennial' cycle in which Americans find themselves now. The generations in question are shown in the table below, together with their typical 'attitude' and distinct 'personality', as embodied in the worldview, lifestyle and behaviour of the rising adults who have defined them:

GENERATION NAME	GENERATION TYPE	BIRTH YEARS	SAMPLE MEMBER
REVOLUTIONARY CYCLE			
From start of Great Awakening 1734 through American Revolution 1773–89 to eve of Second Great Awakening 1821			
Awakening	Idealist	1701–23	Benjamin Franklin
Liberty	Reactive	1724–41	George Washington
Republican	Civic	1742–66	Thomas Jefferson
Compromise	Adaptive	1767–91	Andrew Jackson
CIVIL WAR CYCLE			
From start of Second Great Awakening 1822 through Civil War 1857–1865 to eve of Missionary Awakening 1885			
Transcendental	Idealist	1792–1821	Abraham Lincoln
Gilded	Reactive	1822–42	Ulysses Grant
No obvious Civic Generation in the nineteenth century			

Progressive	Adaptive	1843–59	Theodôre Roosevelt
GREAT POWER CYCLE			
From start of Missionary Awakening 1886 through Great Depression and World War II 1932–45 to eve of Boom Awakening 1966			
Missionary	Idealist	1860–82	Franklin Roosevelt
Lost	Reactive	1883–1900	Dwight Eisenhower
G.I.	Civic	1901–24	John Kennedy
Silent	Adaptive	1925–42	Martin Luther King Jr
MILLENNIAL CYCLE			
From start of Boom Awakening 1967 and ongoing …			
Boom	Idealist	1943–60	Bill Clinton
Thirteenth (Xer)	Reactive	1961–81	Courtney Love
Millennial	Civic	1982–2003	Tara Lipinkski
Cyber★	Adaptive	2004–25	?

Fig. 5 – Generational segmentation in the USA (After Howe and
Strauss 1991:84–87, 2000:41; ★Brett, 2002)[13]

Now without doubt, the scope, detail and ambition of Howe and
Strauss' work is dazzling. As the notes and appendices of *Generations* show clearly, they have done an immense amount of research
into the primary social science sources bearing on their subject,
and they possess an encyclopaedic grasp of American history.[14]
They also write in a brisk, attractive style that uses statistics and
theoretical concepts without getting weighed down by them.
Furthermore, it is easy to see how their paradigm of alternating
'spiritual awakenings' and 'secular crises' has appealed to so many
Christian writers, and to evangelicals in particular: awakenings
and revivals are, after all, of the essence of evangelical identity,
and on one level it is gratifying to see two non-theologians still
prepared to take such phenomena seriously.

Yet having said all this, there are significant caveats and
warnings to be heeded by anyone looking to apply Howe and
Strauss' analytical method. Furthermore, these caveats and

warnings apply particularly in a Christian context, and most particularly from our perspective, to the context of church life and mission in Britain.

Problems with, and qualifications on, the Howe and Strauss cycle

1. American-centredness

First, it must be borne in mind that Howe and Strauss are focused almost exclusively on the unique history and development of the USA. By their own admission, the shapes and rhythms of this history are not so readily transferred to other cultures:

> America offers what may be mankind's longest and best case study of generational evolution. Since the eighteenth century, observers the world over have found this country unique for the freedom enjoyed by each successive generation to develop, and act upon, its own personality. When Alexis de Tocqueville visited America in the 1830s, he observed how generations mattered far more here than in Europe, how in America "each generation is a new people". Tocqueville may have overstated the case ... [:] generational change in the Old World played a key role in triggering the Colonial cycle in the New World – back when most settlers still believed themselves, culturally and socially, part of Europe. Since then, generations in America have often shared a similar mind-set, a sort of sympathetic vibration, with their transatlantic peers. Like America, Western Europe also had its romantic radicals in the 1840s; its *Blut und Esen* realists in the 1860s; its disillusioned *génération du feu* of World War I soldiers; and its *nouvelle résistance* student movements in 1968. Tocqueville's main point, however, remains sound. Far more than the Old World – with its tradition-shaped culture, heredi-tary elites, hierarchical religion, and habits of class deference –

> America has always been unusually susceptible to generational
> flux, to the fresh influence of each new set of youth come of
> age.[15]

Granted, Howe and Strauss go on to suggest that the forces of
globalisation, and its often kindred spirit of 'Americanisation',
coupled with a growing trans-national mobility in business, the
arts and religion, are combining to blur de Tocqueville's distinction. We ourselves have already shown how American marketing
theory after the Second World War led British businesses, social
institutions and churches to present 'teenagers' as a distinct group,
and how American rock 'n' roll influenced the popular culture of
the UK. Indeed, the so-called 'Americanisation thesis' is well
established in the academic study of popular culture, centred as it
is on the world dominance of Hollywood, and of USA-based
recording companies, cable television networks, publishing firms
and other multi-nationals.[16] More recently, Howe and Strauss cite
instances of generations born 'new' in post-Cold War Eastern
Europe, in Russia, and in post-Maoist China.[17] Granted, too,
evangelical religion in Britain has often 'taken its cue' from
developments in American evangelicalism – whether through
influential visits by evangelists like D.L. Moody and Billy Graham,
through the influx of Pentecostal spirituality, through the adoption of 'church growth' strategies forged across the Atlantic, or
through the writings of apologists and theologians like Francis
Schaeffer and Carl Henry.[18] More sinisterly, Stephen Brower, Paul
Gifford and Susan Rose have demonstrated at length how the
socio-economic might of the United States has at times led to the
global exportation of an 'American Gospel', rather than the
authentic Gospel of orthodox Christianity.[19] Yet in spite of all this,
it is clear that a historic segmenting of generations and generational cycles would still look significantly different for Britain and
Europe than it does for Howe and Strauss' America.

Our defining Civil War was in the seventeenth, not the nineteenth century. We had a 'revolution' of sorts in 1688, but it

replaced one sort of monarchy with another, whereas the events of 1776 led to America's becoming the first modern republic. Our key period of imperial expansion was colonial and occurred in the nineteenth century, whereas America's has been economic and has lasted from the 1950s until the present. The Wesley–Whitefield revival of the 1730s was at least as epoch-defining for Britain as the revivals that took place at a similar time in America, but we underwent no 'Second Great Awakening' to compare with theirs. For us, the First World War must surely count as a major 'social moment', but it does not figure in Howe and Strauss' grid. In the UK, the 1950s were characterised at least as much by frugality as by technological advance, and the more immediate blights of the Second World War were not shaken off until much later, in the mid-sixties. Then, ironically, the 'export trade' in popular culture began to flow for a while in the opposite direction, as a so-called 'British invasion' of beat groups, 'swinging London' fashions and UK-produced movies began to drive the consciousness of American youth. Even so, Woodstock in 1969 did not have an obvious counterpart here: there were mass rock festivals on the Isle of Wight at the turn of the decade, but no one talks of a 'Shanklin generation'! In the UK, the end of the 'peace and love' era was marked aggressively and decisively by the advent of punk rock in 1976–7, but on the whole, the youth of America did not experience the Sex Pistols, the Clash and their ilk so profoundly. No doubt the near-simultaneous rise of Ronald Reagan and Margaret Thatcher in 1979–80 signalled an end to Baby Boomer idealism on both sides of the Atlantic, but unlike in Britain, Americans did not see this played out in the stark, straight fights between socialist and free-market ideologies which marked the miners' strike of 1984, the legislative blunting of union power, the sale of council houses and the deregulation of nationalised utilities.

Perhaps most importantly of all, however, and despite our own rich stock of intergenerational antipathies, teenage rebellions, youth cultures, hippie happenings and post-sixties cynicism,

Britons still basically bear out de Tocqueville's distinction: we simply do not define ourselves, or segment our culture, so ostensibly in generational terms. Indeed, research done for this book, and reflected in our bibliography, shows that the overwhelming proportion of studies on generational issues derives from the United States. This, we suspect, is not only because cultural-generational distinctions are actually more sharp and pervasive in the USA, but also because, as Howe and Strauss admit, Americans seem so much more historically conditioned, and intrinsically disposed, towards distinguishing themselves from their immediate forbears.

2. *Over-determination and sacred-secular dualism*

Another qualification that needs to be placed on Howe and Strauss' model is that in seeking so deliberately to be predictive as well as descriptive, it appears at times to be over-determined. It is hard to believe that even with its intense generational self-consciousness, America actually does conform as rigidly as Howe and Strauss' suggest, to an eight-decade, four generation cycle delineated by so neat an oscillation between 'spiritual awakenings' and 'secular crises', or between 'dominant' and 'recessive' cohorts. At the very least, this elaborately symmetrical schema betrays signs of a retrospective, and somewhat anachronistic, ordering of history and demography. For one thing, Howe and Strauss' identification of 'social moments' is rather too conveniently spaced out to be taken at face value. As it is, they are forced to admit a great 'anomaly' in the cycle with regard to the American Civil War, which not only shortens their standard cyclical interval from eight to six decades, but also compels the acknowledgement of a 'missing' civic generation in the nineteenth century.[20]

More seriously, however, one wonders at the criteria deployed in the selection of 'social moments' themselves – namely, whether the moments are chosen purely for their relative 'momentousness', or whether some are highlighted more because they fit with

Strauss and Howe's model than because they in fact most clearly define the forty-year period in which they fall. For example, whereas Howe and Strauss cast the second Great Awakening as the key 'moment' of the early-mid nineteenth century, there is a strong case for contending that the 'secular' Industrial Revolution, whose transport systems, mining companies, factories and mass produced goods did so much to cohere America as a nation at the same time, was ultimately more formative. The 'transcendental' religious and literary movements associated with the second Great Awakening no doubt had a revivifying effect on church attendance, as well as inspiring a significant overseas mission movement.[21] Yet as David Bosch points out, its galvanising force was much less apparent in historic, mainline denominations formed from European roots, than among newer, more indigenous evangelical groups, societies and sects. Furthermore, as with Awakenings and revivals generally, the Second Great Awakening's impact on society as a whole was relatively short-lived, and was already waning significantly by the 1830s.[22]

More questionable still is Howe and Strauss' labelling of the period 1886–1903 as a moment of 'missionary awakening'. On closer inspection, it transpires that 'missionary' here is being used in an extremely loose way – not to define any overarching evangelistic or homiletic phenomenon, but rather disparate instances of '"reform", "revivalism" and "labour radicalism"', many of which could be described at least as much in 'secular' as in 'spiritual' terms. No doubt the employment laws, protest movements, industrial action, union-formation and race-awareness which Howe and Strauss adduce as distinctive for this period were backed by certain American churches; but in this case, their 'sacred-profane' dualism looks somewhat contrived.[23]

The same problem attaches to Howe and Strauss' third supposed 'awakening' of the post-Revolutionary era – the so-called 'Boom Awakening', as dated by them between 1967 and 1980. Certainly on one level, the rising 'Woodstock generation' adults of this time-span are often linked to the dawn of a transcendent 'age of Aquarius' – or what Martin Marty, writing at the beginning of the period, called 'a new language of the spirit'. Whereas religious discourse in the post-war period had been dominated either by the activist tones of Billy Graham-style evangelism or the politicised rhetoric of the liberal 'social gospel', Marty noted a turn from such outer-directedness to a fresh exploration of the inner self, in which mostly younger people were inclined to 'speak in tongues', 'enter Trappist monasteries', 'build on Jungian archetypes', 'go to southern California and join a cult' and 'borrow from cosmic syntheses'. He also detected the emerging quest for self-realisation which was being expressed through the use of psychedelic drugs like LSD.[24]

Now the social history of the late sixties is undoubtedly marked by these and other 'spiritual' departures – departures which, as Jonathon Green remarks, were notable both for their eclecticism and their general abandonment of conventional church solutions.[25] In Bernice Martin's words, there arose at the time 'a kind of do-it-yourself kit of spiritual self-development (or prophylactic against anomie) passed around by word of mouth and the odd paperback book' – a kit containing 'generalised dabbling in the literature and history of the occult, mandalas ... tarot cards, astrological prediction, yoga, techniques of mystical ecstasy (with or without drugs) in meditation and expanded consciousness'.[26] Important as they were, however, the rigidity of Howe and Strauss' model means that these developments are highlighted while other equally significant but less obviously 'spiritual' moments from the same time are seriously underplayed.

Too often, the 'peace and love' paradigm promulgated by Howe and Strauss obscures the fact that the late 1960s had a much grittier side. It should not be forgotten that in Europe, spiritual exploration in these years ran alongside sometimes violent mass political protest, and that what Ian MacDonald has called a 'revolution in the head'[27] was often matched by revolution in the streets. In 1963, a radical cohort of French and Italian students led a series of 'sit-ins' designed to underline a perceived lack of democracy in their universities. The following year at Berkeley in California, a 'free speech' movement arose with similar aims. Around the same time, civil rights marches began, focussed initially on the issue of racial segregation in the southern states of America, and culminating in the famous 'March on Washington', led by Martin Luther King Jr. And as we mentioned earlier, by May 1968, students, workers and a whole spectrum of radicals were tearing up paving stones in Paris and threatening full-blooded socialist revolution in Western Europe.[28]

As Martin Luther King so eloquently demonstrated, such campaigns could claim a spiritual impetus. But on the whole, this was not their distinguishing feature. Indeed, particularly in Europe, their genius was more typically a mixture of post-Enlightenment rationalism, agnostic existentialism, atheistic Marxism, and secular humanism.[29] Even in America, where so much of the new, 'Aquarian' spirituality of the time was being birthed, there is a strong case for holding that the dominant 'social moment' of the age was not Woodstock, but the considerably darker reality of the Vietnam War, and the mass protest it provoked.

Beginning at the University of Michigan in 1965, the anti-Vietnam War movement built into a broad left-liberal coalition of great strength, hitting a peak in October 1967, when over 100,000 pacifists, students, militants and other concerned citizens marched on the Pentagon.[30] The intensity of this activism was carried through to London the following year, as thousands descended on the American Embassy in Grosvenor Square, and to Chicago, as the Democratic Party Convention became a platform for further protest. Both events were marked by angry confrontations with the authorities, as were several later anti-Vietnam rallies.[31]

Given the tumult of these events, James Brett is surely justified in asking why the 'Vietnam experience' does not feature more prominently in Howe and Strauss' schema.[32] The answer, it would seem, is that it does not fit the model, which at this point needs a 'spiritual turn', not a tragic military entanglement in South-East Asia. Indeed, one is tempted to ask, in spite of their concession on the Civil War, just how momentous any other 'untimely' event would have to be before they would allow it to disrupt their grand plan. In this case at least, they appear to have been prepared to ignore the extensive empirical research of Schuman and Scott, which plainly identifies Vietnam as the strongest 'collective memory' of the baby boom generation in the USA.[33]

Now it could, of course, be argued that the 'new consciousness' of peace associated with the 'boom awakening' in America was a more prominent spur to political action than in Europe, where the materialist philosophies of the Enlightenment had more obviously usurped religion. Certainly, the protests in the USA were less specifically imbued with this ethos, and after all, many of those who attended Woodstock and similar 'blissed-out' gatherings also protested the war. By the same token, one might argue that Vietnam itself had a profound, if negative, spiritual effect on America – an effect brilliantly evoked in Francis Ford Coppola's 1979 film *Apocalypse Now*, not least thanks to its paralleling of the war with the disturbing psycho-religious themes of Joseph Conrad's novel *Heart of Darkness*. But such crosscurrents only serve to underline the false dualism which lies at the centre of Howe and Strauss' theory. Their analysis depends on a stark polarisation between 'real world threats triggering disciplined collective action' (secular crises) and 'sudden value changes and a society-wide effort to recapture a feeling of spiritual authenticity' (spiritual awakenings).[34] As the situation in America during the late sixties demonstrates, however, both trends can occur *simultaneously*, and to a significant degree *interdependently*.

This insight bears a good deal of theological significance. While it is superficially flattering that Howe and Strauss lend such credence to 'spiritual' developments within culture, the truth is that these developments are rarely as episodic as they suggest. Rather, they are better represented as being *continuously* intertwined with 'external', socio-political events, and with the identity of the generations who experience them. Particularly from a Christian point of view, while revivals have their place, they cannot be a substitute for *ongoing* engagement with the world. Likewise, just as individual people are an integration of body, mind and spirit, so Christian social analysis – and not least the analysis of generations – should demonstrate a *sustained* sense of the spiritual and theological dimensions of a culture, and of its cohorts. So wars can be seen to have a spiritual aspect, even when they appear to be fought within a 'secular' context; so, too, revivals can be seen to be influenced by wider social forces, even as they themselves mould social change. So, also, it is as *Christians*, and not just as *historians*, that Christian historians have a warrant to find significance in the full range of historical events, and not just in explicitly 'spiritual moments'. As Jane Collier has put it:

> The Christian vision, the gospel, is...not just a vision of a God, but also of what we as men and women are and have to be in God's kingdom. It thus gives us not only a theology, but also an anthropology and a cosmology. Furthermore, our relationship as sons and daughters of God binds us together in the human grouping we call "church", so that we look to the gospel to discern the elements of an ecclesiology. The church in the world is a sign that the kingdom grows in the midst of everyday life, that "sacred" and "secular" are inextricable. God is one with our humanity, and the world is "charged with the grandeur of God" (Gerard Manley Hopkins). The Council of Chalcedon, which in AD 451 affirmed the simultaneous divinity and humanity of Christ, gives us a model which is normative for our understanding of the relationship between Gospel and culture; to believe, therefore, that there is a dichotomy between religion and any other aspect of our lives is effectively a Christological heresy. There is no part of our existence, no aspect, whether cultural, historical, social, political, communal or familial which is not called, through conversion, to become the stuff of which the kingdom of God is being fashioned.[35]

As this more holistic, 'incarnational' perspective is applied to generational analysis, another necessary caveat on Howe and Strauss' work becomes apparent. This relates to their comparative insensitivity to what we have already identified as 'social generational units'.

3. Lack of emphasis on 'social generational units'

We have seen that Howe and Strauss allow for variation of attitude on the axis of age. This is to say, they acknowledge diversity between the four different 'generational types' who may exist together, at different phases of the life cycle, at any one time – a diversity inscribed in their chosen terms 'Idealist', 'Reactive', 'Civic' and 'Adaptive'. We have also seen that they assign each twenty-odd year generation in history a distinctive 'personality': 'Progressives', 'Missionaries', 'Xers', etc. Yet this allowance for variation does not extend so clearly *within* generational groups themselves.

To be fair, Howe and Strauss' more recent books, *13th Gen* and *Millennials Rising* do incorporate a great deal of data on the differences of political and ethical opinion, taste and lifestyle which exist *within* single generations today. Yet ultimately these variations are not absorbed into their overall model, and they do not give anything like as much attention to the different social generational units which cluster around such variations, as to the highly generalised traits which are taken to define the generational group from which those units sub-divide. However, as we have already stressed, it may well be the social generational unit which is more formative of a person's identity than the broader age-defined cohort to which he or she belongs.

If it is true, as we have noted, that postmodernity tends to collapse distinctions of 'high' and 'low' culture, then it is also true that it is characteristically expressed in a proliferation of 'sub-cultures' and 'micro-cultures', rather than in any single, grand pattern of concepts, values and actions aligned to birth-year intervals. Howe and Strauss themselves implicitly demonstrate this 'sub-cultural pluralism'. They report, for example, that political allegiance among their 'Thirteenth', or 'Xer', generation of twenty-five to thirty-eight-year-olds today is more diverse than it was among the rising Boomer generation of the late 1960s, which identified far more strongly with liberalism.[36] They also show that the spread of 'household types' occupied by this generation is much more diverse than those in which their parents grew up – largely due to the marked increase in divorce rates over the past thirty years.[37] Indeed, in these and numerous other respects, it appears from their study that one of the most striking things which such 'Thirteeners' have in common is their very *resistance* to common, all-encompassing designations of their cohort, and to the narrow stereotyping they think such designations entail. As Howe and Strauss themselves remark, this is the 'most culturally diverse young generation in living memory'.[38] From within, it resists pat definition; from without, it appears to older generations to inhabit a world in which 'progress is personal, institutions are enemies ... and individuals are either lonely nomads or mutant musketeers belonging to small, warring tribes'.[39] In Douglas Coupland's memorable phrase, if it is united at all, it is united in precisely its refusal to become a 'target market'.

Yet, in the face of all this, Howe and Strauss still push towards a reductionist conclusion in which, for all their fragmentation, Thirteeners are packaged together as 'Reactives' and slotted into the great generational mechanism of American history, along with every other two-decade cohort before them. So they will, Howe and Strauss conclude, always have a '"bad" image'; they will typically 'exploit opportunities overlooked by established businesses'; they will 'settle into the midlife role of national anchor, calming the social mood and slowing the pace of social change'; they will characteristically 'stop some righteous old Aquarian from doing something truly catastrophic'; they will make 'caustic, independent, self-effacing elders', and so on.[40]

Here, again, we can see the problems inherent in Howe and Strauss' 'predictive' approach to generations. The tension between unitary, saleable, sound-bite definitions and more complex descriptive nuances is palpable. Even more than with the Boomer sub-units of Mods, Rockers, Hippies, student radicals, Marxists and the like, Xers appear, at best, to be a conglomeration of smaller groups which may define themselves at least as much in distinction from *one another* as in relation to their wider cohort. And even if there is a basic, shared rejection of the worldview and behaviour of the previous generation, cogent, constructive alternatives are more likely to be articulated at the level of these social generational units than at the level of their age-group as a whole. What is more, study after study has shown that these social generational units are far more likely to *sustain* such distinctive convictions and modes of action through the life course, than the macro-generational group with which they are associated. As Schuman and Scott emphasise,

> Using generation as a variable to predict future behaviour has met with mixed success in systematic, as distinct from anecdotal, reports. When samples are drawn of very specific activist groups – similar to but more narrowly defined than Mannheim's 'generational units' … they do seem to carry some continuity of thought and action (e.g. Jennings, 1987; Marwell, Aiken and Demerath, 1987). However, when cohorts are identified across a broader population, there is little evidence that past experiences have permanent ideological effects on later political attitudes or actions (e.g. Barnes, 1972; Converse, 1987; Holsti and Rosenau, 1980; Weil, 1987). Even when current political attitudes or behaviour can be traced to a particular past period, the connection often extends over the entire population, or over a subpopulation defined in other than cohort terms (e.g. by race *or religion*).[41]

As we have said, people of the same age-group may live through the same historical events in the same country, and yet interpret those events in quite different ways according to the social generational unit to which they belong. Just as some Boomers thought Woodstock degenerate and actively avoided it, some willingly served in Vietnam rather than protesting it or dodging the draft, and believe to this day that, if anything, America should have stayed and 'finished the job'.[42] By the same token, not all Generation Xers are cynical 'slackers'; some are IT entrepreneurs, and CEOs; others are evangelists![43] Furthermore, as Schuman and Scott realise, but as Howe and Strauss neglect to acknowledge sufficiently, people may well *change* their personal viewpoints and habits as they get older, despite the fact that in their generation as a whole, attitudes formed in young adulthood will tend be the most persistent.

Both of these last two points are especially significant from a Christian perspective: not only do they suggest that the church as a 'social multi-generational unit' might feel itself bound to resist macro-generational trends where it perceives them to contradict the gospel; they also allow for individual 'repentance' and 'conversion' *away* from such trends, however deeply ingrained those trends might have become through a person's life course.

4. Generational models as self-fulfilling prophecies?

Yet another theological question mark arising from Howe and Strauss' model concerns its potential to function as a 'self-fulfilling prophecy'. Howe and Strauss themselves admit that whereas their earlier categorisations are largely 'read back' onto past generations who would mostly not have recognised the titles they give them, people in the West since the baby boom have become 'generationally conscious', and thus more readily identify themselves as members of particular age, event and attitudinally-defined groups.[44] In this sense, what may have originally been intended as an objective social *description* can become a deterministic self-*prescription*. There are clear signs of such a development in Howe and Strauss' most recent text, *Millennials Rising*, which focuses on the generation of those

born since 1982.[45] Here, teens as young as sixteen years old are
quoted as using highly sophisticated 'generational' language to
define their cohort – both in and of itself and over against its
'Xer' and 'Boomer' predecessors. At this point, one may be
forgiven for asking whether the analysis is following the
culture, or whether the culture is following the analysis. Not
least, given Howe's own involvement in 'targeted marketing',
this same concern could be re-framed in terms of the familiar
advertising tension to which we alluded earlier – the tension of
reflecting versus *creating* demand.

Graeme Codrington has noted a similar tension in relation to
the appropriation and 'hyping' of generational distinctions by the
media. Here again, 'target markets' are critical: as they multiply
with deregulation and new broadcast technologies, television
channels, radio stations and magazines are all typically searching
for a specific audience sector, and this quest may be aided by their
'talking up' generational differences.[46]

At least from a Christian point of view, these qualifications on
generational theory serve as a reminder that our identity is to be
shaped by our createdness in the image of God, and by our
redemption in Christ, before it is defined in conformity to any
generational category, whether prescriptive *or* descriptive (Gen.
1:26–27; 2 Cor. 5:17). Whatever the usefulness of generational
study for practical church life and mission, it needs to be stressed
that we are who we are first and foremost insofar God has made
and remade us, not insofar as a generational futurist has told us
who we are, who we shall be or, whether implicitly or explicitly,
who we *ought* to be.

5. Lack of integration with other social variables

Finally, although Howe and Strauss are not oblivious to social
distinctions *other* than those related to generation, it should be
noted that their approach places relatively little stress on class,
economic status, education, employment, ethnicity, gender and

other related variables which ought to bear on an integral, biblical understanding of contemporary culture. Indeed, while there may well be value in studying the interconnections between chrono-logical age and epochs, events, worldviews, behaviour and so on, it ought to be noted before we go any further that poverty and deprivation may function more strongly to unite children with their parents over against a more affluent class, than birth years or genealogy may function to distinguish them generationally from each other. Codrington underlines this point by suggesting that Howe and Strauss' model should be qualified by Abraham Maslow's famous 'hierarchical theory of needs', in which human fulfilment is realised through a ranked series of necessities and desires, from the most basic physiological provision of food and water, through shelter and security, to more rarefied qualities like 'esteem' and 'self-actualisation'. As Codrington notes:

> Where the first two levels of need have not been met, the third level will not be relevant, nor will it have a defining influence in a young person's life. This explains why in lower class communities, the issues related to the generational theory may not be readily apparent.[47]

Indeed, on this same basis, there is a legitimate argument that too exclusive an emphasis on generational distinctions at the expense of socio-economic and class divisions in itself betrays an inherently middle-class, consumerist worldview.

Similarly, it ought to be borne in mind that African-Caribbeans of whatever age may be more often socially delineated as 'black' than as 'rising adults' or 'elders' who share their generational character with similarly aged members of other ethnic groups in the population at large. Likewise, mature students at university may share more socially signifi-cant bonds with their younger fellow classmates than they might with their own birth-cohort. Indeed, such examples further underscore what we have been saying about Christian commitment and church membership – namely, that they may similarly supersede generational segmentation, even if they do not nullify its effect.

With these provisos and caveats in mind, Howe and Strauss' work will still serve as a fruitful resource and reference-point for the remainder of this study. Even as we make use of it, however, it will be helpful to incorporate insights from other models – most particularly as we move now to focus on the generations which Howe and Strauss define as living today, and as we seek to understand those generations theologically within our own British context.

Living Generations I: The World War Generation (born c. 1901–24)

Apart from a few centenarians, the Howe-Strauss model that we examined in the last chapter suggests that there are five 'living generations' in existence today. In the following five chapters, we shall examine each of these generational groups in turn, and consider their transferability or otherwise to the British setting. The first such generational group is called the 'G.I. generation' by Howe and Strauss, but for reasons which will become clear, we shall refer to it as the 'World War generation'.

The oldest living cohort identified by Howe and Strauss comprises the 'Civic' generation of their so-called 'great power cycle', and consists of those born between 1901 and 1924. As we have seen, Howe and Strauss are more or less obliged by their model to locate the start of this new set at the turn of the century, but in this case at least, the timing seems culturally as well as chronologically appropriate. As the 1900s dawned, the project of 'modernity' – which since the eighteenth-century Enlightenment had shifted the focus of social authority from religious revelation to human reason, and from church to state – reached its high tide in the aesthetic movement called 'modernism'. Epitomised by the geometrical, 'rationalist' architecture of Le Corbusier and Mies van der Rohe, and by the abstract paintings of Piet Mondrian and Wassily Kandinsky, the 'modern movement' both celebrated the rise of rationalism and hinted at its potential 'soul-lessness' – a soul-lessness which was confirmed when the armies of World War I turned the technological advances of the modern age towards mass destruction at Flanders, Ypres and the Somme.[1]

It is Howe and Strauss' distinctively American perspective which leads them to name this generation as they do. Their chosen term 'G.I.' refers to the fact that having been shaped early on by the Great War, and having grown up through the Great Depression which followed it, the group in question largely came of age during another period of 'industrialised conflict' – the Second World War. This war is symbolised for Howe and Strauss by the 'Government Issue' or 'General Issue' uniforms worn by most of the males who fought in it. As Howe and Strauss recognise, the generation to which most of these men belonged was also significantly shaped by the so-called 'G.I. Bill', which enabled many who had fought in the war to attend university and college, as a means of retraining for the new socio-economic context of the late forties and early fifties.[2]

In his great, era-defining inaugural address of 1961, President John F. Kennedy eloquently described this generation, which in many ways he personified, as a generation 'born in this century, tempered by war, disciplined by a hard and bitter peace, proud of our ancient heritage, and unwilling to witness or permit the slow undoing of [the] human rights to which this nation has always been committed'.[3] This, he said, was the 'new generation of Americans' to which at that moment 'the torch' of leadership and vision 'had been passed'. As it was, the 'human rights' to which Kennedy referred would be more momentously asserted through the anti-racist movement led by the next generation's Martin Luther King Jr. (1929–68), and through the subsequent rise of feminism.

Alongside his rallying call for civil liberties, Kennedy is also remembered for his pledge that the USA would land a man on the moon by the end of the 1960s – a pledge which was fulfilled by the Apollo 11 mission on 29 July 1969. As Howe and Strauss observe, the 'space race' in fact typified the rationalistic and technological confidence of this generation. 'No sector of the population in the twentieth century', they assert, 'has felt (or been) so Promethean, so godlike in its collective, world-bending power. Nor has it been so adept in its aptitude for science and engineering'.[4] In terms of popular culture, the same worldview is apparent in the fact that the most iconic strip cartoon figures of this generation were drawn from 'future worlds' placed further along the curve of scientific advance: Superman, Batman and Flash Gordon.[5]

As had already become apparent during 1914–18 and 1939 (or 1941) to 1945, however, this technological orientation had a darker side. In addition to harnessing scientific discoveries for progressive ends in medicine, contraception, transport and the like, G.I.s also 'invented, perfected and stockpiled' the atomic bomb, whose awesome power changed global politics irreversibly, and ushered in the fears and paranoias of the Cold War.[6] Indeed, by 1962, Kennedy was managing the Cuban Missile Crisis, during which the world came to the brink of self-destruction.

While this nuclear threat prompted many 'G.I.'s' to embrace a resurgent pacifism, the more radical anti-war protests of the later 1960s would, as we have already seen, come to be linked much more with their Baby Boomer offspring. As Howe and Strauss' name for them suggests, G.I's were (and are) essentially conformist by comparison. In youth, they became the first boy scouts (1910) and girl guides (1912), and then benefited from the new playgrounds, processed 'protective' foods, vitamins, child-labour restrictions and expanded public education of Franklin D. Roosevelt's 'New Deal' America. 'All their lives', write Howe and Strauss, 'G.I.'s have placed a high priority on being "general" or "regular" (as in "he's a regular guy"), since regularity is a prerequisite for being effective "team players".' They developed this instinct young, building in high school and college a 'peer society' – a harmonious community of group-enforced virtue. Such G.I. conformity and collegialism, add Howe and Strauss, later energised America's 'V for victory wartime mood' and reached its apogee in post-war suburban-isation – a process distinguished by 'its '"wonder bread" blandness, its "spic and span" kitchens and its "borrow a mower" neighbourliness'.[7]

Insofar as they see the G.I generation manifested in the religious sphere, Howe and Strauss find its embodiment in 'America's first televangelist', Billy Graham, and in the 'futuristic' cult of Scientology founded by L. Ron Hubbard.[8] Certainly, Graham possessed a 'clean-cut' image, and developed a ministry distinguished by its readiness to harness G.I.-pioneered tech-nology to spread the gospel.[9] In addition, he bore out Howe and Strauss' depiction of Civic Generations' basic conception of God as a God of power – in this case urging unprecedented numbers of people watching at home, listening on their radios or attending his rallies in sports arenas, to acknowledge their power to change their heart towards Christ, and Christ's power to change them.[10]

Much of what Howe and Strauss write about the 1901–24 cohort of Americans could be translated to the generation of Britons born during the same time-span. They, too, were matured through economic depression, reconstruction and the Second World War. They, too, put great faith in human reason, science and technology – capacities celebrated in their epochal Festival of Britain, held on the renovated South Bank in London in 1951. Even more momentously, it is this generation which is most closely associated with the formation of the National Health Service. Having delivered a landslide victory to Clement Atlee's reforming Labour government of 1945, by 1964 it was also instrumental in electing the first Prime Minister to come from its own constituency – the forty-eight-year-old Labour leader, Harold Wilson, who took office on a promise to tap 'the white heat of the technological revolution'.[11]

Although post-war economic recovery was slower here than in America, with food rationing maintained for almost a decade longer, Wilson's predecessor, Harold MacMillan, was still able to announce in 1958 that the British economy was more healthy than ever.[12] As we shall see, some in the next generation would challenge what they perceived to be the stuffiness and conformity of fifties Britain, and many more in the generation after that would seek actively to break down its class hierarchies and traditions. For most of those born in the first two decades of the century, however, social attitudes were less alarmist, and more optimistic.

Admittedly, all this must be set against the background of Britain's gradual loss of its empire, and its consequent 'coming down in the world'. The 'new frontier' of American responsibility and influence abroad, which Kennedy had defined, was not mirrored here. A raft of countries which once belonged to the British Empire, from India to Kenya, became independent in the post-war period, while the Suez Crisis of 1956, in which Anthony Eden's Conservative government tried disastrously to intervene by force, confirmed a significant loss of global standing.[13]

Yet if such setbacks affected the religious mood, they seemed to do so only as a spur to growth. Indeed, the 1901–24 birth group spearheaded what Callum Brown has described as 'the greatest church growth that Britain had experienced since the mid-nineteenth century.' Indeed, during the late 1940s and early 1950s, the UK saw a remarkable rise in church membership, Sunday school enrolment, and Anglican and Church of Scotland confirmations.[14] As Brown demonstrates, this was largely a by-product of the austerity and socio-economic retrenchment that marked post-war reconstruction. Whereas women had often worked in factories and on the land during the conflict, traditional values of home and piety were 'suddenly back on the agenda between the war and 1960'. And as Brown avers, 'the churches benefited immediately'. As Britons sought to regain stability after the upheavals of 1939–45, it appears that for many of those who returned to them, the churches embodied the very family values and spiritual certainties which had been so seriously threatened during hostilities.[15]

Another key indication of the resurgence of Christian commitment among the generation in question was the immense success of Billy Graham's 'British Crusades' of 1954–6. People in their thirties, forties and fifties made up a substantial proportion of the millions who attended Graham's meetings in stadia like Haringay Arena in London and Tynecastle in Edinburgh. The Greater London Crusade of 1954 attracted no less than 21.2% of the city's population, while attendances in Glasgow the following year saw a staggering 73.7% of the city's residents go to at least one meeting.[16] While it is true that the greater percentage of those who 'came forward' to make commitments at these rallies were from the *next* generational group, it is a testimony to the renewed spiritual energy and commitment of their parents' cohort that it was those born during the first two decades of the century who provided most of the organisation, support and finance for the Crusades. Chief among these, indeed, were leaders and supporters of the Evangelical Alliance – men and women from the same generation that had formed para-church bodies like the Inter-Varsity Fellowship (1923), Young Life (1941) and Youth For Christ (1943), and whose collegial style there now found its fullest expression in Graham's pan-evangelical, campaigning approach.[17]

Taking all these historical, social and religious features into account, it would seem most appropriate in the British context to re-name Howe and Strauss' 'G.I. generation' the 'World War generation'. While this may seem a somewhat negative appellation, it is clear that the First and Second World Wars were the foundational influences on the dominant worldview and ethos of those born between 1901–24. Insofar as it makes sense to segment living generations by birth-years at all, this 'World War generation' is a reasonable place to start.

Fig. 6, below, summarises the main facets of the 'World War' generation, from the key 'social moments' and political events which shaped it, through its prominent worldviews, to its artistic, cultural and religious features. The focus here is on the 'rising adult' phase of this generation's development since, as we have seen, it is in this phase that the identity and outlook of a generation is most deeply formed.

Fig. 6 WORLD WAR GENERATION

A.K.A.: G.I. Generation (USA)   % of current UK Population: 5
Birth Years: 1901–24   Span of Rising Adulthood: 1922–67

KEY POLITICAL & ECONOMIC EVENTS

1914–18	First World War
1917	Bolshevik Revolution in Russia
1919	League of Nations formed
1923	Mussolini becomes leader of Italy
1924	First British Labour Government
1925	Hitler publishes *Mein Kampf*
1926	General Strike in Britain
1927	British women over 21 get vote
1929	Wall Street Crash ushers in Depression
1930	British dominions become independent
1931	Stalin steps up purges in Russia
1932	Roosevelt elected President of USA
1933	Reichstag burned down in Berlin
	Hitler becomes German Chancellor
	Roosevelt launches New Deal
1935	Chinese Communists end Long March
1936–9	Spanish Civil War
1936	Edward VIII accedes to throne, then abdicates
	Italy annexes Ethiopia
1937	Japan invades China
1938	Austria & Sudentenland annexed to Germany
	Kristallnacht – Nazi pogrom against Jews
1939	German troops take Prague
	Germany signs non-aggression pact with Russia
	Germany invades Poland
	Britain & France declare war on Germany
1939–45	Second World War
1940	Churchill PM in British coalition government
	Britain suffers Blitz
	British retreat from Dunkirk
	Royal Air Force win Battle of Britain
	Germany invades Denmark & Norway
	Germany invades Low Countries
	Nazis take Paris
	Japanese sign pact with Germany/Italy
	Leon Trotsky murdered in Mexico
	Russia invades Baltic states
	Italians retreat from Addis Ababa
1941	Japanese attack Pearl Harbor
	USA joins Allies in Europe
	Severe rationing introduced in UK
	Nazis invade Russia, but are resisted
1942	Allies victorious in North Africa
1943	Italy surrenders to Allies
	Russians win Battle of Stalingrad
1944	D-Day – Allies take Normandy Beaches
	Allies liberate Paris
	Allies enter Germany
	Butler Education Act in Britain
1945	Hitler commits suicide
	Nazis surrender
	United Nations Charter signed
	Atomic bombs dropped on Hiroshima/Nagasaki
	Nazi death camps opened

KEY ARTISTIC & CULTURAL FEATURES

1908	Boy Scouts Association formed
1910	Girl Guides Association formed
1916	Jazz sweeps through America
1920	Dada Manifesto
1922	T.S. Eliot publishes *The Waste Land*
	James Joyce publishes *Ulysses*
	BBC formed
1923	Sigmund Freud's *The Ego and the Id*
1924	First Surrealist Manifesto
1925	Paris 'Art Deco' exhibition
	Charleston dance becomes fashionable
1927	First 'talkie' film – *The Jazz Singer*
1928	Walt Disney's first *Mickey Mouse* film
1932	Aldous Huxley publishes *Brave New World*
1936	'Hitler's' Berlin Olympics: Jessie Owens' 4 golds
	Charlie Chaplin's film *Modern Times*
1941	Orson Wells' film *Citizen Kane*
1945	George Orwell publishes *Animal Farm*

1945	Labour party wins election landslide
1946	Churchill warns of 'Iron Curtain'
	First session of UN
1947	India granted independence
1948	NHS formed in Britain
	Commonwealth citizens qualify for British passports
	Berlin airlift
	State of Israel formed
	Gandhi assassinated in India
1949	Indian republic formed
	Apartheid enforced in S. Africa
	China becomes Communist republic
1950	McCarthyite anti-Communist drive in USA
	Korean War begins
1952	Accession of Elizabeth II
1953	Food rationing ends in Britain
1954	Kruschev takes over from Malenkov
1955	Warsaw Pact creates 'Soviet Bloc'
1956	Egypt nationalises Suez Canal
	Britain embarrassed in Suez crisis
	First anti-nuclear march to Aldermaston
1957	Treaty of Rome creates EEC
1958	CND launched in Britain
	Race riots in Notting Hill

1959	Fidel Castro seizes power in Cuba
1960	Sharpeville massacre in S. Africa
	J.F. Kennedy elected in USA
	Lady Chatterley trial
1961	Anti-Castro forces defeated at Bay of Pigs
1962	Cuban missile crisis
1963	Profumo scandal in Britain
	President Kennedy assassinated
1964	Nelson Mandela jailed for life in S. Africa
	Harold Wilson becomes PM in Britain
1965	US begins bombing Vietnam
	Free Speech Movement in US & Europe
	Civil Rights marches in USA
	Rhodesian UDI
1966	Mao declares 'Cultural Revolution' in China
1967	Civil war in Biafra
	Che Guevara shot
	Six-Day War in Middle East

PROMINENT WORLDVIEWS

Modernism, Scientific Progressivism, Marxism, Socialism, Freudianism, Existentialism, Capitalism

1947	Abstract Expressionist art emerges in US
1949	Arthur Miller's play *Death of a Salesman*
1951	Festival of Britain
1952	Samuel Beckett's play *Waiting for Godot*
1953	Hillary & Tensing scale Mt Everest
1955	Bill Haley records *Rock Around the Clock*
1956	Elvis Presley's *Heartbreak Hotel* – the seminal rock 'n' roll single; John Osborne's play *Look Back in Anger*
1959	William Golding publishes *Lord of the Flies*
1960	Jean Luc Godard's *A Bout de Souffle* heralds 'new wave' in cinema; Harold Pinter's play *The Caretaker*
1961	*Lady Chatterley* trial; Robbins Report leads to new universities in UK
1962	Solzhenitsyn publishes *One Day in the Life of Ivan Denisovich*
1963	Beatlemania begins
1964	Stanley Kubrick's film *Dr Strangelove* satirises Cold War paranoia
	Bob Dylan's *The Times They Are a Changin'*
1965	Radio Caroline begins regular broadcasts; Dylan turns 'electric' and pioneers 'rock' music; The Who, *My Generation*
1966	England football team win World Cup
1967	The Beatles *Sgt Pepper's Lonely Hearts Club Band*; the Summer of Love; Monterey Pop Festival; emergence of youth 'Counter Culture' and Hippies

KEY TECHNOLOGICAL & SCIENTIFIC FEATURES

1915	Einstein's Theory of General Relativity; First automatic telephone exchange in Britain
1919	Ernest Rutherford splits the atom; Alcock & Brown first to fly Atlantic non-stop
1920	Regular cross-Channel air service starts; Marconi opens first radio broadcast station
1923	Hubble proves galaxies exist beyond Milky Way
1926	John Logie Baird demonstrates television
1927	Heisenberg's 'Uncertainty Principle'
1928	Alexander Fleming discovers penicillin
1930	Amy Johnson first female to fly solo to Australia
1935	Invention of Radar in UK
1936	First TV broadcasts by BBC
1937	Alan Turing produces primitive 'computer'
1941	Whittle's jet engine successfully deployed
1942	Turing & Neumann produce first programmable computer
1947	First British nuclear reactor
1948	Transistor radio & LP record invented
1949	De Haviland produces first jet airliner
1952	First nuclear-powered electricity produced
1953	Watson, Crick & Wilkins find structure of DNA
1955	Commercial TV starts in Britain
1956	World's first large-scale nuclear power station in Cumberland
1957	*Sputnik 1* satellite launched by USSR

1959 M1 motorway opened in Britain
1961 Yuri Gagarin is first man in space; Oral contraceptive pill launched
1962 Telstar satellite links US and UK TV
1963 Thalidomide drug withdrawn; Beeching Report heralds closure of many British rail lines
1965 Russian and US astronauts walk in space
1967 First colour TV in Britain; First human heart transplant (in S. Africa)

1941 Rudolph Bultmann's essay 'Myth in the New Testament' reinterprets supernatural elements of Bible in rationalistic terms.
1945 Radical Lutheran theologian Dietrich Bonhoeffer executed by Nazis
1947 Dead Sea Scrolls discovered; Carl Henry pioneers 'neo-evangelicalism' in US in response to rise of Fundamentalism
1948 World Council of Churches formed

1964 Charismatic movement emerges in UK
1965 Jürgen Moltmann publishes *Theology of Hope*
1966 Harvey Cox's *The Secular City* questions relevance of Church in modern world; UK evangelicals split on ecumenical movement
1967 Anglican evangelicals' 'Keele Congress' commits to renew Church of England; Beatles lead Counter Culture in exploration of Eastern spiritualities; Jesus Movement begins in California

KEY RELIGIOUS FEATURES

1918 Walter Rauschenbusch pioneers 'Social Gospel'
1919 Karl Barth's *Romans* heralds 'Theology of Crisis'
1923 Inter-Varsity Fellowship founded; 'Monkey Trial' re: evolution in Tennessee
1929 Vatican City state founded
1932 Reinhold Niebuhr's *Moral Man & Immoral Society* critiques Marxism & Social Gospel
1934 Dissident German theologians publish Barmen Declaration in opposition to Hitler

1951 World Evangelical Fellowship formed
1951–7 Paul Tillich's existentialist *Systematic Theology*
1953 New scholarly interest in historical Jesus
1954 Billy Graham evangelistic campaign in UK
1956 *Christianity Today* launched in USA
1962–5 Second Vatican Council
1963 'Death of God' theology emerges; John Robinson's *Honest to God* sparks controversy in Britain

Living Generations II: Builders (born c.1925–45)

In Howe and Strauss' schema, the generation after the G.I.s is defined as 'adaptive', and is dubbed the 'Silent generation'. As our survey of this generation and its successor proceeds, we shall realise that the alternative term 'Builder' may be more appropriate in the British context. Howe and Strauss define this generation as comprising those born between 1925 and 1942 – a cohort which they regard as relatively less distinctive than either of those which surround it. Whereas the preceding G.I. generation and the following Boomers are well defined both in terms of worldview and social events (e.g. civic responsibility and world wars for the G.I.s; reform and Woodstock for the Boomers), 'Silents' are described as a 'transitional generation' – one which has made a less obvious impact on history.

In Howe and Strauss' terms, Silents are 'generational stuffings of a sandwich between the get-it-done G.I. and the self-absorbed Boom. Well into their adulthood, they looked to G.I.s for role models – and pursued what then looked to be a lifetime mission of refining and humanising the G.I.-built world. [But] come the mid-1960s, the Silent[s] … fell under the trance of their free-spirited next-juniors, the Boomers.'[1] The birth span of these Silents coincided with the lowest birth rate per decade of the twentieth century. While not necessarily accounting for their low comparative profile, this may have contributed to the fact that they are the only living American generation whom polls show would rather have occupied an age-bracket other than their own.[2] As Wade Green so memorably puts it, 'During the ferment of the 1960s, a period of the famous "generation gap", we were, as usual, the gap itself.'[3]

The name which Howe and Strauss give to this set is derived from the historian William Manchester's critique of its members as typically 'withdrawn, cautious, unimaginative, indifferent, unadventurous – and silent'. If this is somewhat sweeping and harsh, Howe and Strauss at least concur in casting them, in their rising mode after World War II, as 'sober young adults' possessing an 'outer directed' personality and 'taking cues from others'. Their parents may have moved in large numbers to the newly built suburbs of the post-War recovery, but they consolidated the trend of suburbanisation, and embodied many of the middle-class, middle-way values associated with it.[4] Moreover, they also enjoyed the steepest increase in real per-capita income and per-household wealth recorded for any American generation of the modern age.[5]

For Howe and Strauss, these formative influences combined to make Silents characteristically pragmatic rather than ideological, as they adopted 'the moral relativism of the skilled arbitrator, mediating arguments between others – and reaching out to people of all cultures, races, ages and handicaps'. On the other hand, as Silents reached mid-life in the 1970s, this same relativism appears to have had a damaging effect on family life: men and women born between the mid-1930s and the early 1940s showed the biggest ever age-bracket rise in the divorce rate, while from 1969–79 silent-led legislatures ensured that the number of states adopting 'no fault' divorce laws rocketed from zero to forty-five. Silent women were chronologically the first mature female generation to take the pill, and between the 1950s and the 1970s reported, with their male peers on both sides of the Atlantic, the highest increase in sexual intercourse of any previous generation in history.[6]

This tension between social rectitude and self-assertion is personified by the many of the key figures of the American Silent generation. As we have seen, the sexual undercurrents in the music and stage act of Elvis Presley (b. 1935) may have upset some of his elders, but unlike many of the Boomer 'rock stars' who came after him, he was consistently polite to interviewers, publicly honoured his mother, kept singing the gospel songs of his youth, joined the army and never threatened anything approaching political revolution. Likewise, Marilyn Monroe (b. 1926) may have conveyed more blatant sexuality than most screen actresses before her, and may have slept with a number of top politicians, but nevertheless chose to marry first a conventional baseball player (Joe DiMaggio) and then a playwright (Arthur Miller), while seeking to train for more serious roles through Lee Strasberg's Actor's Studio.[7] James Dean (b. 1931) may have been ready to rebel, but as the title of his second film confirmed, did not yet have a cause.[8] Martin Luther King Jr. (b. 1929) may have adopted the rhetoric of the evangelical American folk preacher, but was in fact theologically quite liberal.[9]

If rising American Silents in the fifties and early sixties exhibited a mixture of conventionality and restlessness, the same could be said of their parallel younger adult cohort in Britain. Demographically, they, too, occupied a distinct 'dip' on the population chart.[10] Socially, they also were formed in an atmosphere of post-war retrenchment, yet culturally they too contributed to the first wave of self-conscious 'teenagers' and to the first set of rock 'n' rollers. On the one hand most in this group reflected the conservatism and austerity of 'fifties Britain': whereas their more proactive 'World War' predecessors had been instrumental in ensuring the Labour landslide of 1945, the older members of this group tipped the balance towards the Tories, ensuring a solid thirteen years in government for them between 1951–64. Indeed, it is worth noting that the subsequent Conservative Prime Minister, Margaret Thatcher, was born at the beginning of this interval (1925) and that her successor John Major was born at or just after its end (1943). Some of those born in the UK during this period, however, did clearly began to reject the rather staid overall mood of their times. In his 1956 play *Look Back in Anger* the then twenty-seven-year-old John Osborne railed against the stuffiness and torpor of the age, while his fellow 'Angry Young Man' John Braine, whose 1957 novel *Room at the Top* was made into a highly controversial film, predicted the sexual liberation which was to follow in the next decade.[11] Neither asserted a particularly coherent worldview, but the seeds of more concerted rebellion were being sown. For those of a less literary bent, Britain developed home-grown pop stars like Tommy Steele, Billy Fury and Cliff Richard: again, the 'message' delivered by such performers was hardly profound – but they did help to consolidate the emergent 'youth culture' which we mentioned earlier, and thereby, to suggest the onset of greater generationally-driven cultural change.

More serious philosophical focus was evident in the antinuclear protests led by the British 'Silents' of the Campaign for Nuclear Disarmament (CND). Formed in early 1958 by representatives of this and the previous 'World War' generation, CND quickly gained mass support, especially from university students born towards the end of the 'silent' birth-interval.[12] Made famous by its marches on the Aldermaston nuclear base and elsewhere between 1958 and 1964, CND was later described by one of its then-teenage champions, David Widgery, as fostering 'premature members of the love generation, as well as cadres of forthcoming revolutionary parties'.[13] At this stage, however, it should be noted that the credo was still thoroughly non-violent – a reflection of the inherently 'reasonable' ethos of the 1925–42 set.[14]

Where the G.I. generation had Superman, American silents typically let Alfred E. Neuman's credo 'What, me worry?' get them by. Significantly, William Gaines' comic creation assumed many different forms, and wore several 'masks', just as the silent generation did and to some extent, still does. In Britain, perhaps one of the most telling popular evocations of this identity-confusion was the character typically played by the great fifties comedian, Tony Hancock (b. 1924) – a figure who fitfully affected rebellion and radicalism, but was essentially conventional in his attitudes and demeanour.[15]

As far as religion is concerned, Howe and Strauss depict adaptives, such as those in their 'Silent generation', as being most characteristically drawn to God when he is presented as a God of love. Certainly, the 1950s and '60s saw liberal theology reaching a high tide, with its emphasis on the compassion and mercy of God over divine judgement and law. A leading proponent of this theology, Canon John Collins of St. Paul's Cathedral, was a founder of CND. Two of London's most popular preachers of the time – the liberal Methodists Leslie Weatherhead and Donald Soper – were also confidently liberal. Furthermore, although the liberal Anglican theologian John Robinson (b. 1919) was himself of the 'World War generation', many of his most sympathetic readers were British Silents, and when published in 1963, his controversial book *Honest to God* sold phenomenally among this age group. Robinson's text assimilated the 'demythologising' project of Rudolph Bultmann, Paul Tillich and other proponents of the so-called 'new hermeneutic', and sought to represent God as the 'ground of our being' and 'the beyond in our midst', rather than in traditionally transcendent and interventionist terms.[16] In familiar Silent fashion, this approach may have had a radical edge, but it was still conventionally cerebral and ecclesiastical – Robinson was, after all, the Bishop of Woolwich, and his views, while not widely known before the publication of his book, had been commonplace in theological colleges and faculties for some time. More thoroughgoing religious radicalism would not arrive, as we shall see, until the next generation.

By the early sixties, when British Silents were assuming positions of power and authority within and beyond the church, the gains of the Billy Graham campaigns of the previous decade had withered,[17] and attendance at worship in the UK was once more set on a downward course – a course that has continued, more or less unabated, into the present.[18]

Although George Barna broadly accords with the generational divisions mooted by Howe and Strauss, for this cohort he prefers the more positive term 'Builders' to 'Silents', because he is keener to emphasise their leading role in the reconstruction of Western society after the war. He also shifts the interval to which they belong forwards, from 1925–27 at its beginning, and from 1942–45 at its end.[19] For our part, and with the UK specifically in mind, we shall from here on favour Barna's title and end-date as more positively reflective of the retrenchment, recovery and restoration which lay at the heart of this generation's vision and purpose as it reached rising adulthood in the years immediately following VE Day. The validity of this alternative name is further borne out by Fig. 7 (below), in which the historical, cultural and spiritual profile of this generation is summarised.

Fig. 7 BUILDER GENERATION

A.K.A Silent Generation   % of current UK population: 15
Birth Years: 1925–45   Span of Rising Adulthood: 1946–88

KEY POLITICAL & ECONOMIC EVENTS

1939–45	Second World War
1944	Labour party wins election landslide
1945	Churchill warns of 'Iron Curtain'
1947	First session of UN
1948	India granted independence
	NHS formed in Britain
	Commonwealth citizens qualify for British passports
	Berlin airlift
	State of Israel formed
	Gandhi assassinated in India
1949	Indian republic formed
	Apartheid enforced in S. Africa
	China becomes Communist republic
1950	McCarthyite anti-Communist drive in USA
	Korean War begins
1952	Accession of Elizabeth II in Britain
1953	Food rationing ends in Britain
1954	Kruschev takes over from Malenkov in USSR
1955	Warsaw Pact creates 'Soviet Bloc'
1956	Egypt nationalises Suez Canal
	Britain embarrassed in Suez crisis
1958	First anti-nuclear march to Aldermaston
	CND launched in Britain
1959	Race riots in Notting Hill London
	Fidel Castro seizes power in Cuba
1960	Sharpeville massacre in S. Africa
1961	J.F Kennedy elected in USA
	Anti-Castro forces defeated at Bay of Pigs
1962	Cuban missile crisis
1963	Profumo scandal in Britain
	President Kennedy assassinated
1964	Nelson Mandela jailed for life in S. Africa
	Harold Wilson becomes PM in Britain
	US begins bombing Vietnam
1965	Free Speech Movement starts in US & Europe
	Civil Rights marches in USA
1966	Rhodesia – UDI
	Mao declares 'Cultural Revolution' in China
1967	Civil war in Biafra
	Che Guevara shot
	Six-Day War in Middle East
1968	Viet Cong launch Tet offensive
	Martin Luther King assassinated
	Workers & students riot in Paris
	Robert Kennedy assassinated
	Richard Nixon elected US President
	First moon orbit
	Enoch Powell 'rivers of blood' speech in UK
1969	Grosvenor Sq. anti-Vietnam protest in London
	Yasser Arafat becomes PLO leader
1970	British troops sent into N. Ireland
	Edward Heath elected British PM
1973	Bangladesh civil war
1972	'Bloody Sunday' – British troops kill 13 in Belfast

ARTISTIC & CULTURAL FEATURES

1945	George Orwell publishes *Animal Farm*
1947	Abstract Expressionist art emerges in USA
1949	Arthur Miller's play *Death of a Salesman*
1951	Festival of Britain
1952	Samuel Beckett's play *Waiting for Godot*
1953	Hillary & Tensing scale Mt Everest
1955	Bill Haley records *Rock Around the Clock*
1956	Elvis Presley's *Heartbreak Hotel* – the seminal Rock 'n' roll single
	John Osborne's play *Look Back in Anger* heralds era of 'Angry Young Men'
1959	William Golding publishes *Lord of the Flies*
	Jean Luc Godard's *A Bout de Souffle* heralds 'new wave' in cinema
	Harold Pinter's play *The Caretaker*
1960	*Lady Chatterley* trial
1961	Robbins report leads to new universities
1962	Solzhenitsyn publishes *One Day in the Life of Ivan Denisovich*
1963	Beatlemania begins

1973	6-day Yom Kippur war in Middle East
	Britain joins EEC
	Vietnam peace agreement
	Watergate burglars convicted
	Three-Day week in UK
	OPEC quadruples oil prices
1974	Harold Wilson elected PM
	Cyprus invaded by Turkey
	Nixon resigns
1975	Pnomm Penn falls to Khmer Rouge
	S. Vietnam surrenders
	Lebanon civil war starts
	Franco dies in Spain. Monarchy restored
	Sex Discrimination & Equal Pay Act in Britain
1976	Jim Callaghan PM in Britain
	Soweto riots in S. Africa
	Mao dies in China
1977	Steve Biko dies in S. Africa
1978–9	'Winter of Discontent' in Britain
1979	Iranian revolution
	Camp David agreement between Israel & Egypt
	Margaret Thatcher elected PM in Britain
	Five Mile Island nuclear disaster in USA

1980	USSR invades Afghanistan in Middle East
	Majority rule in Rhodesia – now Zimbabwe
	Solidarity union formed in Poland
	Ronald Reagan elected President in USA
1981	US hostages freed from Iran
	SDP formed in Britain
	Inner city riots in British cities
1982	Falklands War
1984	Miners' Strike in Britain
1985	Mikhail Gorbachev President of USSR
1986	US/USSR Summit in Iceland
1987	Gorbachev launches Glasnost & Perestroika
	Stock market crashes around world
1988	Western hostages taken in Beirut
	George Bush elected US President
	Lockerbie plane disaster

PROMINENT WORLDVIEWS

Modernism, Scientific Progressivism, Marxism, Socialism, Freudianism, Existentialism, Capitalism

1964	Stanley Kubrick's film *Dr Strangelove* satirises Cold War paranoia; Bob Dylan's *The Times They Are a Changin'*; Radio Caroline begins regular broadcasts
1965	Bob Dylan turns 'electric' and pioneers 'rock' music
1966	England football team win World Cup
1967	The Beatles *Sgt Pepper's Lonely Hearts Club Band*; the Summer of Love; Monterey Pop Festival; emergence of youth 'Counter Culture' and Hippies
1968	Rolling Stones *Jumpin' Jack Flash*; Stanley Kubrick's film *2001*
1969	Woodstock Music festival in upstate New York; Film *Easy Rider* – Counter Culture classic; Open University established in UK
1970	*Oh! Calcutta* – full frontal nudity on London stage: end of Lord Chancellor's censorship
1971	Led Zeppelin, *Stairway to Heaven* epitomises new era of 'heavy rock'
1973	Pink Floyd's LP, *Dark Side of the Moon*
1976	National Theatre opens in London; Emergence of anti-Hippie Punk Rock
1977	Queen's Silver Jubilee in UK; Sex Pistols, *God Save the Queen*; Elvis Presley dies
1979	Film: *Apocalypse Now*: Vietnam as nightmare
1981	Disco music heralds 80s hedonism; Wedding of Prince Charles and Diana Spencer
1983	Michael Jackson, *Thriller*
1985	Live Aid famine relief concerts and records

KEY TECHNOLOGICAL & SCIENTIFIC FEATURES

1947	First British nuclear reactor
1948	Transistor radio and LP record invented
1949	De Havilland produces first jet airliner
1952	First nuclear-powered electricity produced
1953	Watson, Crick and Wilkins find structure of DNA
1955	Commercial TV starts in Britain
1956	World's first large-scale nuclear power station in Cumberland
1957	*Sputnik 1* satellite launched by USSR
1959	M1 motorway opened in Britain
1961	Yuri Gagarin is first man in space; Oral contraceptive pill launched
1962	Telstar satellite links US and UK TV; Beeching report heralds rail closures
1965	Russian and US astronauts walk in space
1967	First colour TV in Britain; First human heart transplant (in S. Africa)
1969	Apollo 11 Moon landing
1970	Damages awarded to Thalidomide victims
1974	*Mariner* satellite shows Venus and Mercury
1975	First personal computers (PCs) introduced
1976	*Viking 1* and 2 land on Mars
1978	First test tube baby born – in Britain
1981	Space Shuttle launched
1982	First permanent artificial heart fitted – in USA
1986	Space shuttle explodes

KEY RELIGIOUS FEATURES

1945   Radical Lutheran theologian Dietrich Bonhoeffer executed by Nazis

1947   Dead Sea Scrolls discovered
       Carl Henry pioneers 'Neo-Evangelicalism' in USA

1948   World Council of Churches formed

1951–7   Paul Tillich's existentialist *Systematic Theology*

1953   New scholarly interest in historical Jesus

1954   Billy Graham evangelistic campaign in UK

1960   *Christianity Today* launched in USA

1962–5   Second Vatican Council

1963   'Death of God' theology emerges
       John Robinson's *Honest to God* sparks controversy in Britain

1964   Charismatic movement emerges in UK

1965   Jürgen Moltmann publishes *Theology of Hope*

1966   Harvey Cox's *The Secular City* questions relevance of Church in modern world

1967   UK evangelicals split on ecumenical movement
       Anglican evangelicals' 'Keele Congress' commits to renew Church of England
       Beatles lead Counter Culture in exploration of Eastern spiritualities
       Jesus Movement begins in California

1968   Pope issues anti-pill *Humanae Vitae*

1970   Gustavo Gutierrez, *Theology of Liberation*
       Festival of Light seeks to combat 'moral decline'

1977   *Myth of God Incarnate* debate

1978   Election of Pope John Paul II

1979   First Spring Harvest festival held in Britain

1980   New Ecumenical Instruments in British Isles

1982   Billy Graham – Mission England

1984   Bishop of Durham questions resurrection

1985   Church of England *Faith in the City* report

Living Generations III: Boomers (born c. 1946–63)

When recounting the rise of generationally-based thinking in the West in chapter 1, we noted that the 'boomer' cohort of those born in the two decades following the Second World War was the first 'generationally conscious' population group. Indeed, as Howe and Strauss observe, this group remains probably the best known and most closely analysed generation in history.[1]

American Boomer identity is derived from the significant bulge in fertility which occurred in the US between 1946 and 1957 – a bulge which Howe and Strauss attribute to 'the coincident babymaking' of late-nesting G.I.s detained by the war, and of Silents caught up relatively early into post-war re-domestication and suburbanisation.[2] Even so, Howe and Strauss extend the beginning of this Boomer generation back to 1943, and on to 1960.[3] 1943 is chosen as a start-date partly because it was during this year that the tide of the Second World War turned decisively towards the Allies, but mainly because it was those babies born after 1 January 1943 who were later deemed eligible for the Vietnam draft – a phenomenon which we have already recognised as foundational for American Boomer identity. 1960 is chosen because it marked the election of the 'first G.I. President', John F. Kennedy, and because those born after this date are thought to have begun to shed the supposed Boomer hallmarks of 'intellectual arrogance and social immaturity'.[4]

These chronological markers are obviously less applicable to Britain, and there is a case for suggesting that a discernible Builder–Boomer shift did not begin to emerge here until a few years later. Certainly, as Jane Pilcher attests, the rise in the fertility graph did not come through strongly until the very end of the forties and the early fifties.[5] Culturally also, the poet Philip Larkin's implicit later dating of the Boomer turn in the UK may be deliberately impressionistic and tongue-in-cheek, but the iconic status it has acquired suggests a strong ring of truth:

> Sexual intercourse began in
> Nineteen sixty-three
> (Which was rather late for me) –
> Between the end of the Chatterley ban
> And the Beatles' first LP.[6]

The 'end of the Chatterley ban' here refers to the result of the Old Bailey obscenity trial launched by the Director of Public Prosecutions in October 1960, when Penguin Books decided to publish D.H. Lawrence's erotic, expletive-heavy 1928 novel, *Lady Chatterley's Lover*, in a cheap, paperback edition, so challenging the censorship which had hitherto forced its publication abroad. Arguing that circulation of the novel would encourage a growing wave of sexual permissiveness and libertinism, the prosecution counsel, Mervyn Griffiths-Jones, fatally undermined his cause when he asked the jury whether they would let their 'wives and servants' read it. Rather than clinching his case, this arrogant, class-ridden comment was perceived as belonging to a former age. Indeed, many of the seventy-odd academics, clergymen and artists whom the defence lined up to support publication made precisely this point. Certainly, it did not take the jury long to find Penguin not guilty.[7]

As Larkin realised, the looser, more egalitarian attitude evident at the Chatterley trial was epitomised by the Beatles –

a quartet of working- and lower middle-class musicians from Liverpool whose cultural impact probably summed up the Baby Boom ethos, and the 'sixties era' with which it is so inextricably linked, better than any other. From the release of their debut album *Please Please Me* in March 1963 until the dissolution of their partnership – symbolically enough – at the close of the decade, they captured and disseminated the 'spirit of the age', from the infectious release of 'Builder' shackles which can be sensed in their earlier pop songs, through the drug-influenced mysticism and eastern religious explorations of their 'psychedelic' period, to the more politically-aware material of 1968's *White Album*. Ian MacDonald captures these influences astutely:

> The Beatles' appearance in 1962–3 coincided with the fall of Conservatism in sixties Britain … Fortunately, buoyancy in the property market, aided by full employment, quickly created a youth-led consumer boom. Spearheaded by the Beatles, the two-year "British Invasion" of the American top ten established the UK as the centre of the pop world with a flowering of talent matched nowhere else before or since. As British Pop Art and Op Art became the talk of the gallery world, a new generation of fashion designers, models and photographers followed Mary Quant's lead in creating the boutique culture of swinging London to which international filmmakers flocked in the hope of siphoning off some of the associated excitement into their pictures. Long-standing class barriers collapsed overnight as northern and cockney accents penetrated the hitherto exclusively Oxbridge domains of television, advertising and public relations. Hair lengthened, skirts shortened and the sun came out over a Britain rejuvenated, alert, and determined to have the best of good times.[8]

For MacDonald, such social changes also had clear consequences for religion, theology and the church:

> As tradition became outmoded and a dispirited Christianity forfeited influence, the public focus began to shift from nostalgia and the compensation of a reward in heaven to an eager stress on the present combined with an impatient hope for a social heaven on earth in the near future.[9]

We have already highlighted how this combination of 'hedonism' and 'immediacy' marked the British Mod movement of 1963–4, and how it both fed into and gained succour from the 'drug culture' and the overwhelmingly non-Christian 'Aquarian spirituality' of the later sixties. But as we have also hinted, it became starkly apparent in the growing impatience felt by many Boomers, towards the socio-political profile of their elders.

One of the greatest influences on the 'intellectualisation' of the Beatles, and of Boomer culture as a whole, in the mid-sixties was the American singer, Bob Dylan. When he encountered The Beatles for the first time in 1965, Dylan had already sounded strong notes of intergenerational antipathy and urgent social protest – notes which had led to his being dubbed a 'spokesman' for the new cohort. Nowhere were these clearer than on his 1964 hit, 'The Times They Are A Changin':

> Come mothers and fathers throughout the land
> And don't criticize what you can't understand;
> Yours sons and your daughters are beyond your command;
> Your old road is rapidly ageing.
> So get out of the new one if you can't lend your hand,
> For the times, they are a changin'…
>
> The line it is drawn, the curse it is cast
> The slow one now will later be fast
> As the present now will later be past
> The order is rapidly fadin'
> And the first one now will later be last
> For the times they are a changin'…[10]

Dylan may have echoed a saying of Jesus here (cf. Mt. 19:30), but most of those who took his words as their own, including the Beatles, did so within a climate of what MacDonald calls 'post-Christian "nowness"'.[11] While various forms of 'social' and 'political' theology on both sides of the Atlantic sought to assimilate rather than merely resist this new mood – from Harvey Cox's 'secular gospel' to Jürgen Moltmann's 'theology of hope' – the mass rejection of mainline Christian faith and values by English Boomers in particular was seen in a near 50% decline in church recruitment between 1960 and 1970.[12]

Insofar as there was any significant *popular* Christian response to the experimentation and immediacy of the times, it is perhaps most clearly evident in the emergence of the so-called 'charismatic movement', which took root in the UK from around 1964. As a leading chronicler of this movement, Nigel Scotland, has observed:

> The 1960s … saw the emergence of the hippie culture which was a reaction to the materialism of the 'never had it so good' post-war years under Harold MacMillan … [P]eople began to take drugs in the hope of getting in touch with some deeper level of reality. Others followed the example of the Beatles and began to look East for meaning … and the practice of meditation became the focus of many hopes in a country which was losing its way spiritually. The charismatic experience which began to emerge in England in the 1960s was to some extent part of this environment. On the one hand, it was a reaction away from enlightenment thinking. On the other, it reflected the widespread quest of the time for the exotic and the culturally new. Western evangelicalism was very much a one-dimensional affair in which the middle classes, reinforced by InterVarsity paperbacks, looked for 'sound' teaching. But for most, there was little in it beyond a certain satisfaction of having been able to bend one's mind around a 'good word'. At the same time existentialist thinking which emphasised the importance of the

present moment prompted people to seek new experiences and the growing popularity of television increased their desire for deeper emotional and spiritual satisfaction.[13]

In Howe and Strauss' view, 'reactive' generations, of which the rising Boomers of the sixties were a prime example, typically respond to God in terms of 'persuasion' rather than in terms of 'truth', 'power' or 'love'. Yet while it seems clear that the introspection and sensualism which led Tom Wolffe to dub Boomers the 'me generation' challenged established notions of objective truth in religion, it is arguable that the same Boomers placed as much emphasis on 'power' and 'love' as any other generation had before them. Certainly, the exploration of Eastern spiritualities and mind-altering drugs so closely associated with hippies and others was a search for experiences more intense than those which the church was thought able to provide. Certainly, too, the Beatles would not have scored a worldwide hit with *All You Need is Love* in the summer of 1967 if this, too, had not been a dominant concern.

It probably better reflects the spiritual profile of the Boomer generation to describe it not with reductionist definitions, but rather to represent it as unprecedentedly 'eclectic' and 'pluralistic'. Once immediacy and individualism had come to the fore among the members of this generation, such diversity was inevitable, since what most quickly 'works' for one open-minded seeker may not work for another. Once self-realisation takes over from divine revelation, faith, as we noted earlier, becomes a 'DIY' process, and the objective truths of classical Christianity typically fall out of favour. This is represented in Fig. 8 (below) as one of the key 'worldview' developments associated with Boomer identity. Moreover, while the generation which *followed* the Boomers differs from them in many significant respects, this, at least, is one legacy which it appears to have been happy not only to inherit, but to extend. It is to this post-Boomer generation that we now turn.

Fig. 8 BOOMER GENERATION

% of Current UK Population: 25

Birth Years: 1946–63   Span of Rising Adulthood: 1962–2007

KEY POLITICAL & SOCIAL EVENTS

1962	Cuban missile crisis
1963	Profumo scandal in Britain
1964	Nelson Mandela jailed for life in S. Africa
	Harold Wilson becomes PM in Britain
1965	USA begins bombing Vietnam
	Free Speech Movement starts in USA & Europe
	Civil Rights marches in USA
	Rhodesia – UDI
1966	Mao declares 'Cultural Revolution' in China
1967	Civil war in Biafra
	Che Guevara shot
	Six-Day War in Middle East
1968	Viet Cong launch Tet offensive
	Martin Luther King assassinated
	Workers & students riot in Paris
	Robert Kennedy assassinated
	Richard Nixon elected USA President
	First moon orbit
1969	Enoch Powell 'rivers of blood' speech in UK
	Grosvenor Sq. anti-Vietnam protest in London
	Yasser Arafat becomes PLO leader
1972	British troops sent into N. Ireland
	'Bloody Sunday' – British troops kill 13 in Belfast
1973	6-day Yom Kippur War in Middle East
	Britain joins EEC
	Vietnam peace agreement
	Watergate burglars convicted
	Three-Day week in UK
1974	OPEC quadruples oil prices
	Harold Wilson elected PM
	Cyprus invaded by Turkey
	Richard Nixon resigns
1975	Phnom Penh falls to Khmer Rouge
	S. Vietnam surrenders
	Lebanon civil war starts
	Franco dies in Spain. Monarchy restored
1976	Sex Discrimination & Equal Pay Act in Britain
	Jim Callaghan PM in Britain
	Soweto riots in S. Africa
	Mao dies in China
1977	Steve Biko dies in S. Africa
1978-9	'Winter of Discontent' in Britain
1979	Iranian revolution
	Camp David agreement between Israel & Egypt
	Margaret Thatcher elected PM in Britain
	Five Mile Island nuclear disaster in USA
	USSR invades Afghanistan
1980	Majority rule in Rhodesia – now Zimbabwe
	Solidarity union formed in Poland
	Ronald Reagan elected President in USA
1981	USA hostages freed from Iran
	SDP formed in Britain
	Inner city riots in British cities
1982	Falklands War
1984	Miners' Strike in Britain

1985	Mikhail Gorbachev President of USSR
1986	US/USSR Summit in Iceland
1987	Gorbachev launches Glasnost & Perestroika
	Stock market crashes around world
	Western hostages taken in Beirut
1988	George Bush elected US President
	Lockerbie plane disaster
1989	Berlin Wall torn down: collapse of Communism in Europe and Russia
1990	Margaret Thatcher resigns as PM in Britain
1991	Poll tax riots in UK
	Iraq invades Kuwait
	Gulf War
1992	Coal industry privatised in UK Tories win 4th consecutive term: John Major PM
1993	Maastricht Treaty establishes European Union
1997	Labour win landslide election under Tony Blair
	Princess Diana killed: mass mourning in UK
	Hong Kong returned to China
1998	Good Friday Peace Agreement in N.Ireland
1999	Monetary Union in EU – UK opts out
	Hereditary Peers' right to sit in Lords abolished
	Devolution for Scotland & Wales
2000	Millennium celebrations around world
	Millennium Dome fails to attract support in UK
	Fuel tax protests in UK
	US Presidential election extended – George W. Bush eventually declared winner
2001	Foot & Mouth disease outbreak across Britain
	Labour maintains large majority in election
	September 11th Islamic terrorist attack flattens World Trade Centre in New York and damages Pentagon in Washington DC
	'War Against Terror' launched in Afghanistan
2002–	Introduction of Euro in EU – UK defers use
	Queen Mother dies

PROMINENT WORLDVIEWS

Modernism, Scientific Progressivism, Marxism, Socialism, Secularism, Free-Market Capitalism, Free Expression, Individualism, 'DIY' spirituality,

ARTISTIC & CULTURAL FEATURES

1962	Solzhenitsyn publishes *One Day in the Life of Ivan Denisovich*
1963	Beatlemania begins
1964	Stanley Kubrick's film *Dr Strangelove* satirises Cold War paranoia
	Bob Dylan's *The Times They Are a Changin'*
1965	Radio Caroline begins regular broadcasts
	Dylan turns 'electric' and pioneers 'rock' music
1966	England football team win World Cup
1967	The Beatles *Sgt Pepper's Lonely Hearts Club Band*; the Summer of Love; Monterey Pop Festival; emergence of youth 'Counter Culture' and Hippies
1968	Rolling Stones *Jumpin' Jack Flash* Stanley Kubrick's film *2001*
1969	Woodstock Music festival in upstate New York
	Film *Easy Rider* – Counter Culture classic

1969	Open University established in UK
	Beatles disband
1970	*Oh! Calcutta* – full frontal nudity on London stage: end of Lord Chancellor's censorship
1971	Led Zeppelin, *Stairway to Heaven* epitomises new era of 'heavy rock'
1973	Pink Floyd's LP, *Dark Side of the Moon*
1976	National Theatre opens in London
	Emergence of anti-Hippie Punk Rock
1977	Queen's Silver Jubilee in UK
	Sex Pistols, *God Save the Queen*
	Elvis Presley dies
1979	Film: *Apocalypse Now*; Vietnam as nightmare
	Disco music heralds 80s hedonism
1981	Wedding of Prince Charles & Diana Spencer
1983	Michael Jackson LP, *Thriller*
1985	Live Aid famine relief concerts and records
1987	U2 LP, *The Joshua Tree*
	TV Series *Thirtysomething* captures Boomer mid-life angst
1991	Acid House music heralds new dance culture
	Douglas Coupland publishes *Generation X*
1994	National Lottery launched in UK
1997	Radiohead LP *OK Computer* evokes post-industrial angst
	New 'BritArt' movement summed up by *Sensation* exhibition

KEY TECHNOLOGICAL & SCIENTIFIC FEATURES

1961	Oral contraceptive pill launched
1962	Telstar satellite links US and UK TV
1965	Beeching report heralds rail closures
	Russian and US astronauts walk in space
1967	First colour TV in Britain
	First human heart transplant (in S. Africa)
1969	Apollo 11 Moon landing
1970	Damages awarded to Thalidomide victims
1974	*Mariner* satellite shows Venus & Mercury
1975	First personal computers (PCs) introduced
1976	*Viking 1* and *2* land on Mars
1978	First test tube baby born – in Britain
1981	US Space Shuttle launched
	Scientists identify AIDS and HIV
1982	First permanent artificial heart fitted – in USA
1986	Space shuttle explodes
	Chernobyl nuclear disaster
	AIDS crisis threatens to become epidemic
1994	Channel Tunnel opens to traffic
	15 million connected to internet
1997	Mars landing by American Rover
	Land speed record breaks sound barrier
	Cloning of Dolly the sheep

KEY RELIGIOUS FEATURES

1947	Dead Sea Scrolls discovered
	Carl Henry pioneers 'neo-evangelicalism' in US
1948	World Council of Churches formed
1951–7	Paul Tillich's existentialist *Systematic Theology*
1953	New scholarly interest in historical Jesus
1954–6	Billy Graham evangelistic campaigns in UK

1956	*Christianity Today* launched in USA
1962–5	Second Vatican Council
1963	'Death of God' theology emerges
	John Robinson's *Honest to God* sparks controversy in Britain
1964	Charismatic movement emerges in UK
1965	Jürgen Moltmann publishes *Theology of Hope*
1966	Harvey Cox's *The Secular City* questions relevance of Church in modern world
	UK evangelicals split on ecumenical movement
1967	Anglican evangelicals' 'Keele Congress' commits to renew Church of England
	Beatles lead Counter Culture in exploration of Eastern spiritualities
	Jesus Movement begins in California
	Pope issues anti-pill *Humanae Vitae*
1970	Gustavo Gutierrez, *Theology of Liberation*
	Festival of Light seeks to combat 'moral decline'
1974	Lausanne Congress revives Evangelical social concern
1977	*Myth of God Incarnate* debate
1978	Election of Pope John Paul II
1979	First Spring Harvest festival held in Britain
	Mother Theresa awarded Nobel Peace Prize
	Mass cult suicide at Jonestown, Guyana
1980	Rise of Moral Majority & 'Religious Right' in US
	Billy Graham – Mission England
	WCC report *Baptism, Eucharist & Ministry*
1981	Bishop of Durham questions resurrection
	Desmond Tutu awarded Nobel Peace Prize
1982	Church of England *Faith in the City* report
	Desmond Tutu becomes first black bishop of Johannesburg
	Rise of ecological awareness prompts growth in New Age spirituality
1988	Lambeth Conference of Anglican bishops
1989	First woman diocesan bishop in New Zealand
1990	New ecumenical instruments in British Isles
1992	Church of England votes to ordain women
1993	Pope John Paul II's *Veritatis Splendor* reaffirms traditional Catholic teaching
1994	Toronto Blessing sweeps through charismatic and evangelical churches
1994–9	Christians prominent in Truth and Reconciliation Commission in S. Africa
1997	Mother Theresa dies
2000	Catholic and Lutheran churches make joint declaration on justification by faith

Living Generations IV: Xers (born c. 1964–81)

In Douglas Coupland's seminal 1991 novel *Generation X*, the young American narrator, Andy, recounts an argument with his forty-year-old Baby Boomer boss, Martin. In his own youth Martin had been a hippie, and appears to have espoused most of the 'Woodstock generation' values we have been discussing. By this point, however, he has transmuted into a 'yuppie' – a 'young urban professional'. In doing so, he has traded sixties idealism for financial success, having become a middle manager in an advertising agency. Despite wearing a 'salt and pepper ponytail' in deference to his past, Martin is now devoted to promoting hamburgers. As a member of the next generation, Andy despises the way Martin has 'sold out' on the high aspirations of the 1960s. He also despises what he regards as the tarnished legacy which Boomers in general have bequeathed to their children – a legacy of compromise, corruption and failed promises in a whole range of spheres – from politics to economics, from world peace to care of the earth. Indeed, partly as an expression of this resentment, Andy arranges for a health inspector to visit the agency's office, on suspicion that it might be inducing 'sick building syndrome' in those who work there. This makes Martin furious, and a heated argument ensues, which ends with Andy making what is, in effect, his resignation speech:

Hey, Martin … Put yourself in my shoes. Do you *really* think we enjoy having to work in that toxic waste dump in there … and then have to watch you chat with your yuppie buddies about your gut liposuction all day while you secrete artificially sweetened royal jelly here in Xanadu? … Or for that matter, do you really think we *enjoy* hearing about your million-dollar *home* when we're pushing *thirty*? A home you won in a genetic lottery, I might add, sheerly by dint of your having been born at the right time in history? You'd last about ten minutes if you were my age these days, Martin. And I have to endure pinheads like you rusting above me for the rest of my life, always grabbing the best piece of cake first and then putting a barbed-wire fence around the rest. You really make me sick.[1]

If Boomers were defined by the 'gap' that opened up between them and their Builder Generation elders, Coupland here dramatises a new, post-boomer gap marked by a different sort 'intergenerational antipathy'. The resentment expressed in this passage is not Bob Dylan's resentment towards elders who might block the path of social progress; it is, rather, resentment that the progressives *themselves* have abandoned their journey, and have left no decent maps for those who have come after them.

The sense of directionlessness and unease that runs through Coupland's novel has a clear historical context. As a devotee of British alternative music, Coupland borrows his title from a band linked to a punk rock movement whose figureheads, the Sex Pistols, were renowned for their hatred of hippies. Indeed, when the band Generation X released their first single, 'Your Generation', in July 1977, they may have been referencing the Boomer rebellion of The Who and their Mod audience twelve years previously, but much of their anger was directed against the disappointments of the intervening years.[2] These disappointments were considerable, and it is important to understand them if one wishes to understand Generation X, since in so many ways it is a generation shaped by its rejection of perceived boomer dysfunction. Indeed, it is this context which justifies the pre-eminence of the term 'Generation X' in the description of the cohort born roughly between 1964 and 1981. Writing in 1994, Douglas Rushkoff noted that some were calling the same cohort 'Baby Busters', in recognition that their demographic profile reflected the advent of the pill and the growth of abortion in the sixties.[3] Yet as Howe and Strauss note of this group in the USA, and Pilcher of its counterpart in Britain, whatever 'squeezing' of the birth rate occurred within it actually took place only in its last few years, and in both sheer number and proportion of the entire population, it remains relatively large.[4]

In their 1993 book on this cohort, Howe and Strauss them-selves defined it simply as the 'Thirteenth Generation', in refer-ence to their cyclical template of American history.[5] But as we have already seen, this notion does not translate to other countries and in any case, as Kevin Ford points out, carries with it the various negative 'folk' associations of the number thirteen.[6] By contrast, 'Generation X' suggests something more profound about the prevailing *zeitgeist*, and more particularly, its divergence from Boomer attitudes, lifestyles and experience.

Insofar as John F. Kennedy's presidency prepared the way for Boomer optimism as well as for the consolidation of G.I. values, his assassination in November 1963 cast a nagging shadow over sixties idealism, as did the Vietnam War which unfolded over the next few years. Just when it appeared that this shadow might lift somewhat as the counter-culture backed his brother Bobby's candidacy in 1968, he, too, was shot dead. That other beacon of hope, Martin Luther King Jr, had already been assassinated two months earlier. Faced with such blows, some Boomers turned from hippie utopianism to radical left-wing activism, but pitched battles between President de Gaulle's police and the Maoists, Marxists and workers of Paris during the same period led many to fear for where youth idealism might end up. The Beatles' John Lennon sang that he wanted to be 'counted out' of violent revo-lution,[7] but revolutionary or not, violence would increasingly put paid to the lofty visions of the Summer of Love. The Woodstock Festival of July 1969 may have been a fillip for the hippie dream, but just a few weeks later, at another rock festival at Altamont Raceway in California, Hells Angels murdered a young fan as the Rolling Stones played on stage. By the end of 1970, musical icons like Jimi Hendrix, Jim Morrison, Janis Joplin would be dead, having overdosed on the drugs which the 'psychedelic guru', Dr Timothy Leary, had so optimistically recommended as keys to inner enlightenment. By now, the Vietnam War had escalated, and many young American soldiers had returned in body bags from battles in Ia Dang Valley, Dak To, Loc Ninh, and Khe Sanh. Moreover, the expenditure on the war had begun strain the economy, and to push up taxes.[8] John Lennon was singing 'The Dream is Over', and Pete Townshend of The Who, so often dubbed a 'spokesman for his generation', would soon be urging erstwhile sixties idealists like himself to pledge, 'Won't Get Fooled Again'.[9]

As they moved towards mid-life in the seventies and entered it in the eighties, American Boomers became increasingly anxious about their past – an anxiety explored pointedly in films like *Kramer vs Kramer* (1979), *The Big Chill* (1983), *Parenthood* (1989) and *Grand Canyon* (1991), and perhaps most signally of all, in the television series *Thirtysomething* (1987–91).[10] Not least among the concerns articulated in these and other cultural expressions of middle-aged Boomer angst were fears about the welfare of the children whom Boomers had produced in their turn. As Rob Nelson and Jon Cowan have pointed out, before one considers the philosophical bent of such children – that is, of American GenXers – one should absorb certain 'harsh facts' about them. They are those, for example, who have been marked by a decline in real wages and an increase in the length of the average working week; by a rise in young adult poverty and a corresponding fall in actual income; by the threat of AIDS; by highest-ever divorce and suicide rates; by over qualification for available specialist jobs;

by spiralling violence in schools and by an ever-widening pattern of drug abuse.[11]

To many Xers, these problems are attributable at least partly to the failures of their frequently estranged Boomer parents, and in the face of such evidence, it is not hard see why Boomer disenchantment has grown with age. Recounting a recent discussion of the sixties, ageing Boomer Pete Townshend writes of realising that 'with my contemporaries I had had a chance to build and contribute to a better world', but then, on asking himself whether he had, in fact, achieved such a world, recalls confessing, 'Tragically ... I had not'.[12] More tragically still, the first Boomer President, Bill Clinton, epitomised this loss of promise when called to account over the sordid 'Lewinsky affair' towards the end of his presidency, in 1998.

In Britain, disenchantment with boomerdom has developed somewhat less dramatically, but no less profoundly. Harold Wilson's government was forced to devalue the pound in 1967 as the economy became less stable. With the surprise return of a Conservative administration in 1970, trades unions flexed their muscles through industrial action, resulting in a series of major strikes that led, in 1973, to mass blackouts and a three-day working week. In the same year, a worldwide fuel crisis severely damaged economies in Europe and America as Arab states raised the price of oil and petrol was rationed. With inflation soaring and public utilities in crisis, punk rock arrived in 1976–7 to pronounce 'Anarchy in the UK' and 'No Future for You'.[13] Unemployment, in particular, was blighting many communities. By the time of the so-called 'winter of discontent' of 1978–9, a majority of Boomers were ready to ditch whatever vestiges of sixties radicalism they had maintained, and helped to vote Margaret Thatcher into office.

As the British version of Coupland's 'Generation X' lived through these episodes in childhood, it became broadly inured to grand, socially cohesive visions. Too many of its mothers and fathers had left homes – and ideals – broken for such visions to retain their credibility.[14] Margaret Thatcher would echo as much when she declared early in her premiership that there was 'no such thing as society'. Indeed, the oldest tranche of Xers, born around 1963–4, contributed to her landslide election victory in 1983 – a victory won in the wake of a successful but problematic 'colonial' war in the Falklands. Even when Labour eventually returned to office in 1997, with the first Boomer Prime Minister, Tony Blair, at the helm, the Xers who helped deliver *his* landslide ushered in a far more pragmatic, less ideological party, operating in the guise of 'New Labour'.

Coupland characterised his own Xer cohort as preferring individualised moral codes and 'personal taboos' to all-purpose ethical or ideological systems, and reflected the 'postmodern' sensibility with which Xers would become increasingly identified. Not surprisingly given its inherent eclecticism and pluralism, this sensibility has been defined differently by different analysts. More often than not, however, it is described in a series of marked contrasts with its Baby Boom predecessor. Hence for Mike Starkey, 'Whereas boomers retain a touching faith that science and technology will solve social problems', Xers 'know they never will, and could even make problems worse.' Moreover, whereas the Boomer mentality 'encourages people to be pushy, driven, go-getting', Xers are more likely to 'shrug their shoulders' and ask 'What's the point?'[15] This more cynical, knowing attitude is characterised by Tom Beaudoin as a 'hesitation to affirm orthodoxies' and leads to a conviction that 'institutions are suspect' – not least the institutions of state and church.[16] For Graeme Codrington, this means that for Xers, individualism and self-sufficiency are prized highly, that friendship matters more than social status or function, that work is done to live rather than vice versa, that new technologies are embraced as a means of escaping 'fixed point' communication, and that 'globalisation' is viewed as an opportunity to break down traditional cultural barriers, rather than a threat to racial, national or ethnic distinctiveness.[17]

Morally, Douglas Rushkoff portrayed Xers in 1994 as those who, having been born into a society 'where traditional templates have proven themselves quaint at best, and mass-murderous at worst', feel themselves to have been 'liberated from the constraints of ethical systems'. Media-savvy, they have learned to see things from multiple points of view, and then to adopt a perspective which suits them. Spiritually and theologically, however, Rushkoff described Xers as 'somewhat cast adrift'. He added that while it 'must be nice' to have 'something external to believe in … something absolute', the absence of such a 'permanent icon' for most Xers means that they choose instead 'to experience life as play, and trust that the closer we come to our own intentions, the closer we will come to our own *best* intentions.'[18] Even so, the persistence of a yearning after something beyond this cautious, ad hoc approach to faith prompts Coupland into a startling admission:

> I think there was a trade-off somewhere along the line. I think the price we paid for our golden life was an inability to fully believe in love; instead we gained an irony that scorched everything it touched. And I wonder if this irony is the price we paid for the loss of God. But then I must remind myself we are living creatures – we have religious impulses – we *must* – and yet into what cracks do these impulses flow in a world without religion? It is something I think about every day. Sometimes I think it is the only thing I should be thinking about … Now here is my secret: … My secret is that I need God – that I am sick and can no longer make it alone. I need God to help me give, because I no longer seem capable of giving; to help me be kind, as I no longer seem capable of kindness; to help me love, as I seem beyond being able to love.[19]

Such observations by Coupland prompt Peter Bradshaw to offer an astute, pithy summation of Xers as 'people in the West growing up in a secular, affectless society, yearning to feel rapture, and looking for love in the ruins of faith'.[20] This, indeed, could be taken as a distillation of the various events, influences and personalities reviewed in the profile of GenX presented in Fig. 9, below.

Insofar as Xers seek to sustain Coupland's poignant quest for meaning, Christian commentators who have studied them in depth broadly agree on the ways in which they might best be evangelised and nurtured. So Beaudoin encourages a more 'humble' approach, focused on companionship rather than public rhetoric, on mystical openness rather than doctrinal exposition, and on liturgical experience rather than propositionalistic sermonising.[21] Codrington enjoins lifestyle, relationship and friendship-based models of evangelism which 'incarnate' the gospel in the life of the one presenting it to 'experiential' Xers. He also underlines the value of small groups, such as those which form part of the successful Alpha course. With Kevin Ford and Richard Burton he goes on to suggest that faith-sharing works best among Xers when based on questions and stories rather than mere doctrinal assertion of rationalistic apologetics. Such 'Socratic' and 'narrative' evangelism, they maintain, is nothing less than faithful to the core methods deployed by Jesus himself in his many dialogues and parables.[22]

For all their divergence in other areas, Boomers and Xers are, it seems, more alike in their uncertainties and ambiguities about God, and in their characteristic quest for direct, personal experience of the divine. The 'Aquarian' explorations of the former in the late sixties and early seventies might now seem embarrassingly naïve to the latter, but as Coupland realises, such scepticism has not done much to enhance Xers' *own* spiritual seeking. Furthermore, as another generation comes of age at the dawn of a new century, it remains to be seen whether the church decline that began with the Boomers and accelerated with the Xers, will be slowed or reversed.

Fig. 9   GENERATION X

A.K.A. Baby Busters; Thirteenth Generation (USA)   % of Current UK Population: 28

Birth Years: 1964–81   Years of Rising Adulthood: 1982–2024

KEY POLITICAL & SOCIAL EVENTS

1982	Falklands War
1984	Miners' Strike in Britain
1985	Mikhail Gorbachev President of USSR
1986	US/USSR Summit in Iceland
1987	Gorbachev launches Glasnost & Perestroika
	Stock market crashes around world
1988	Western hostages taken in Beirut
	George Bush elected US President
	Lockerbie plane disaster
1989	Berlin Wall torn down: collapse of Communism in Europe & Russia
1990	Margaret Thatcher resigns as PM in Britain
1991	Poll Tax riots in UK
	Iraq invades Kuwait. Gulf War ensues
1992	Coal industry privatised in UK
	Tories win 4th consecutive term: John Major PM
	Bill Clinton elected President in US
1993	Maastricht Treaty establishes European Union
1997	Labour win landslide election under Tony Blair
	Princess Diana killed: mass mourning in UK
	Hong Kong returned to China
	Kyoto Summit on global climate change
1998	Good Friday Peace Agreement in N. Ireland
	Bill Clinton 'Lewinsky Affair' exposed
1999	Monetary Union in EU – UK opts out
	Hereditary Peers' right to sit in Lords abolished
2000	Devolution for Scotland & Wales
	Millennium celebrations around world
	Millennium Dome fails to attract support in UK
2001	Foot & Mouth disease outbreak across Britain
	Labour maintains large majority in election
	September 11th Islamic terrorist attack flattens World Trade Centre in New York & damages Pentagon in Washington DC
2002	Introduction of Euro in EU – UK defers use
	Queen Mother dies

PROMINENT WORLDVIEWS

Postmodernism; Free-Market Capitalism; Consumerism; Pluralism; Tolerance; Individualism; Spiritual eclecticism & introversion; New Age; Eco-awareness; Communitarianism; Globalism

KEY ARTISTIC & CULTURAL FEATURES

1981	Wedding of Prince Charles & Diana Spencer
1983	Michael Jackson LP, *Thriller*
1984	Madonna LP, *Like a Virgin*

1985	Live Aid famine relief concerts and records
1987	U2 LP, *The Joshua Tree*
	TV Series *Thirtysomething* captures boomer mid-life angst
	Acid House music heralds new dance culture
1989	Madonna single & LP, *Like a Prayer*
	Simpsons TV series launched
1990	England football team lose narrowly in world cup semi-final. Sparks revival of football in UK
1991	Douglas Coupland publishes *Generation X*
	Nirvana release *Nevermind* LP – seminal 'grunge' album beloved of many GenXers
	Richard Linklater's film *Slacker*
	REM release 'Losing My Religion' single & *Out of Time* LP
	REM LP *Automatic for the People*
1994	National Lottery launched in UK
	Kurt Cobain of Nirvana commits suicide
1995	Nick Hornby book *Fever Pitch* defines 'New Lad'
1997	Radiohead LP *OK Computer* evokes post-industrial angst
1998	New 'BritArt' movement summed up by *Sensation* exhibition

KEY SCIENTIFIC & TECHNOLOGICAL FEATURES

1979	First test tube baby born – in Britain
1981	Space Shuttle launched
1982	Scientists identify AIDS and HIV
	First permanent artificial heart fitted – in USA
1986	Space shuttle explodes
	Chernobyl nuclear disaster
1987	'Wonder' anti-depressant Prozac launched
	AIDS crisis threatens to become epidemic
1994	Channel Tunnel opens to traffic
	15 million connected to internet
1997	Mars landing by American Rover
	Land speed record breaks sound barrier
	Cloning of Dolly the sheep

KEY RELIGIOUS FEATURES

1982	Billy Graham – Mission England
	WCC report *Baptism, Eucharist & Ministry*
1984	Bishop of Durham questions resurrection
	Desmond Tutu awarded Nobel Peace Prize
1985	Church of England *Faith in the City* report
	Desmond Tutu becomes first black bishop of Johannesburg
	Rise of ecological awareness prompts growth in New Age spirituality
1988	Lambeth Conference of Anglican bishops
1989	First woman diocesan bishop in New Zealand
1992	Church of England votes to ordain women
1993	Pope John Paul II's *Veritatis Splendor* reaffirms traditional Catholic teaching
1994	Toronto Blessing sweeps through charismatic and evangelical churches
1994–9	Christians prominent in Truth and Reconciliation Commission in S. Africa
1997	Mother Theresa dies
2000	Catholic and Lutheran churches make joint declaration on justification by faith

Living Generations V: Millennials (born c.1982–)

The youngest living American generation defined by Howe and Strauss consists of those born from 1982 onwards, and is called by them 'the Millennial generation'. In fact, Howe and Strauss are keen to point out that from a range of possible designations, including 'generation Y' and 'generation 2000', this was the term preferred in a 1997 television poll of the group in question.[1]

Having only just begun to reach adulthood, one might think that it would be difficult to anatomise this cohort in detail. Being futurists as well as demographers, however, Howe and Strauss attempt to do so with great tenacity. As the generation poised to become the first full 'lead cohort' of the twenty-first century, and as the new 'Civics' according to Howe and Strauss' grid, this group is set, they predict, to 'shift away from neglect and negativism, and toward protection and support'.[2] In their youth, US Millennials have experienced abortion and divorce rates ebbing, and have witnessed popular culture changing to stigmatise the laissez-faire, 'latchkey' mentality associated with Boomers – a mentality which is now presented as having deeply harmed their Xer offspring. Child abuse and child safety have emerged as primary social concerns, while books teaching domestic virtues and values are now best sellers. Today, note Howe and Strauss, American politicians are keener than ever to define adult issues (from tax cuts to deficits) in terms of their effects on children.[3]

The Millennials, it seems, are being moulded as the public-spirited, community-oriented constituency which will steer America through its next 'secular crisis' – a crisis Howe and Strauss project as occurring around 2020. Furthermore, for the first time in generational history, because of medical science extending life expectancies, this Civic generation is expected to be still active enough to reach across the generations and mentor the next Civic generation. Then again, the rapid pace of scientific and technological progress could radically affect the development of this group. As Howe and Strauss sum them up:

> To this point, boomers and GenXers have steered millennials away from the attitudes and behaviours of their own youth eras. They have done so through new family-life and workplace accommodations, parental protections, cultural screens, educational standards, and disciplinary rules that, on balance, have served this young generation well, while providing guideposts to measure future progress. Adult America has done a decent job with these kids – so far. But millennials are growing up. The oldest of them will soon be adults, moving beyond the chrysalis of child-safety devices, Zero Tolerance rules, and standardised tests. With their leading edge entering college, these young people are on the brink of becoming a highly effective social force, given the right leadership and moment.[4]

Applying these insights to the British context, one can detect some familiar themes. Without doubt, from the murder of James Bulger in February 1993 to the anti-paedophile protests of summer 2001, we have come to share the profound concern for children's welfare which Howe and Strauss associate with the new generation. Tony Blair was swept to power in 1997 having vowed to make his priorities 'education, education, education', and if women are not exactly leaving work to become housewives in significant numbers, there is a growing sense of domestic and family retrenchment. This is most widely indicated, perhaps, by the proliferation and popularity in recent years of UK television programmes devoted to such activities as cookery, DIY, gardening and grooming. Quite how such apparently parochial emphases might shape a British version of Howe and Strauss' 'Civic generation' is, however, a moot point. Besides, on this side of the Atlantic it should not be forgotten that teenage drug abuse, crime, violence and pregnancy present at least as much cause for concern as ever.

These themes certainly resonate with one of the few serious analyses of the 'Millennial generation' yet published in the United Kingdom. Madson Pirie and Robert Worcester's 1998 report for the Adam Smith Institute, entitled *The Millennial Generation*,[5] shows only 1% of those born in the late seventies and early-mid eighties expressing any desire to pursue 'civic' careers in public service or in local and national government – a figure which is significantly lower than in previous genera- tions, and which suggests that Howe and Strauss' communi- tarian predictions about American millennials are unlikely to be replicated here.[6] Indeed, Pirie and Worcester's MORI- assisted survey of 648 sixteen to twenty-one-year-olds in Sep- tember 1998 shows the new set of rising adults to be more apolitical, self-sufficient, materialistic and hedonistic in their attitudes than any generation observed before.

Although fully 61% of British Millennials in the MORI poll indicated that they would vote for Tony Blair's New Labour party and only 17% for the Conservatives, at least as noteworthy is the fact that an unprecedented 25% were either undecided (13%), or clear that they would not vote at all (12%). Consistent with this, older Millennials played their part in making the turnout at the subsequent June 2001 general election the lowest for almost a century. Indeed, despite their bias towards New Labour, a startling 71% said they believed that the way they voted would make little or no difference to their lives.[7] It is understandable, therefore, that Pirie and Worcester dub them an 'apolitical generation'.

No doubt Howe and Strauss' perception of domestic retrench-ment among American Millennials *is* reflected in the UK, even if it is clearly not complemented, as they predict for America, by civic engagement. Whereas at the end of the Builder and Boomer-led seventies, 35% of the population still lived in state-provided council housing at subsidised rents, the selling-off of such accom-modation in the 1980s has resulted in a that figure dropping by half. Furthermore, today local authorities and new towns build only one in seventy new homes in the UK, compared with nearly one in two in 1976.[8] The rise of owner-occupation indicated by these figures has clearly affected Millennials' aspirations: 65% of them expect to find somewhere suitable to live themselves rather than relying on local authorities, and 23% have already either bought, or are in the process of buying, a home of their own.[9]

As for the life envisaged in such dwellings, while it is true that singleness is on the increase among Millennials as it is among Boomers and Xers, Millennials do at least still *aspire* in significant numbers to some form of family life, with 46% expressing a strong desire to have children, and 38% listing a happy marriage and family existence as a core life aim.[10]

A similar mood of self-reliance is found in respect of employ-ment. As Pirie and Worcester confirm, the labour market has changed so much in the last two decades or so that 'the idea of a job for life belongs to the history books'. Millennials realise this, and in a denationalised, de-regulated, flexible job market, barely 10% still look to government to assist them in finding work.[11] What is more, an unprecedented 48% indicate that their ideal is self-employment rather than working for others. This figure may not be unrelated to the fact that an equally unprecedented 43% list becoming a millionaire before they reach 35 as a key career goal.[12] Indeed, a successful career is prized even more highly than a happy family life, and is revealed as the top-scoring ambition of this generation.

In addition to all this, Millennials have far greater access to higher education than ever before, with over one-third attending state-funded colleges and universities in the UK. Although they now do so on loans rather than grants, this means that they include a considerably higher proportion of students than did their Boomer and Xer parents' generation.[13] While most of them see such education primarily as a route to a good career rather than an opportunity for self-exploration, they do show a noticeably higher regard for teachers than did their forbears.[14]

Spiritually and ethically, one might infer from Howe and Strauss' analysis that 'communitarian' millennials would be more inclined to embrace Christian faith and church commitment, but hard statistical evidence for any such trend is not yet forthcoming. Indeed in the UK, infant baptisms and confirmations continue to fall significantly, and evangelical churches are merely declining more slowly overall than others.[15] In fact, just as Boomers and Xers seem to have been closer to one another in religious attitudes than in many other aspects of their 'generational personality', it may well be that Millennials will pose similar challenges to their parents and grandparents in respect of pluralism, individualism and the institutionalisation of religion. Certainly, they appear to have little time for institutions like the church, preferring a creed of 'individual determination' and 'personal integrity' to one of self-denial or corporate submission.[16] What is more, insofar as they subscribe to any common morality, it is a morality based on tolerance, with only 12% agreeing that gay and lesbian sex between adults should be illegal, and only 15% favouring stricter laws on abortion. On the whole, they are also against censorship, with just 11% supporting statutory bans on scenes of explicit sexual activity in films, and a mere 6% ready to apply the same strictures to the depiction of graphic violence.[17] If they are censorious at all, they most clearly express it in their majority support for a ban on fox-hunting, and in a general repudiation of absolutism and 'fundamentalism'.[18]

As for drugs, the depiction of Millennials (and younger Xers) as a 'chemical generation' is borne out by the fact that one in three admit to having used illegal substances, while two in five have been offered them without consuming them.[19] As Pirie and Worcester point out, this is closely bound up with the 'club scene', which has so markedly replaced the 'rock festival', the 'disco' and the 'gig' as the defining congregational context for this new cohort.

Given that Millennials are only just now entering adulthood, we have not attempted to summarise their defining 'social moments' and worldviews as we have with older living generations. However, insofar as it is possible at this early stage to define a 'mission strategy' or 'apologetic' for Millennials, it would seem to lie in appealing to the personal benefits which might accrue to an individual's well-being and sense of purpose, from putting their faith in Christ. Rather than presenting Christian virtues and values in moralistic or legal terms, it may be necessary to frame them as means to self-actualisation and lifelong security. Furthermore, without compromising the clear demands of Christ for humility and preferment of others, Millennials may well respond best to a presentation of the gospel which does not obviously reject ambition, drive and success as inimical to authentic discipleship.

From Generational Distinctions to Intergenerational Relationships

Our attempts thus far to understand how 'generations' are defined in Scripture and contemporary Western culture raise the closely related question of how we might view the *interaction* of generational groups, and more specifically, how we might regard the process of *leadership transition* from one generational group to another. These questions have particular pertinence for the church, since if it is to have any chance of bucking the decline which we have charted, it will need to handle intergenerational relationships with great care and efficiency. Indeed, unless it can improve its own handling of the succession process from one generation to another, its future will look decidedly bleak. In the last two chapters, we shall explore these issues and seek to offer positive, biblical responses.

Intergenerational Relationships in Family, Church and Society

Intergenerational Relationships and the Family

The leading sociologist of generations, John Finch, has noted that 'age and generational position are important in families almost by definition'.[1] For our part, it has already become clear that in biblical, biological and cultural terms, generational distinctions are mediated fundamentally through the family. From the most basic, genealogical duality of 'parent-child', though the structure of Israelite domestic and social life, to the apostolic depiction of the church as an all-age community of 'brothers' and 'sisters' in Christ, it is clear that one cannot deal theologically with the issue of generations without assessing how they relate to the concept of family.

When we undertake such an assessment, it very soon becomes clear that the understanding of family which we find in Scripture differs markedly from the two-generation nuclear family of parents and children now characteristic of Western society – a model which has come under increasing strain among Boomers and Xers.[2] In the Old Testament, family consisted of those who shared a common bloodline and/or a common dwelling place. It included servants, resident aliens, widows and orphans living under the protection of the head of

the household, along with his wives and children.[3] The
Israelite family was patriarchal in structure, as indicated by the
commonly used biblical term *bêt 'āb* – 'house of one's father',
and by the fact that genealogies were typically traced through
the male line. The family unit was understood to be a basic
unit of creation: from the beginning, God's purpose was
perceived as being that humanity should increase through
families and not through isolated individuals.[4] The family also
lies at the centre of God's covenant promises. Abraham is told
that in him 'all the families of the earth shall be blessed'
(Gen 12:3). The family is therefore more than a biological or
social structure in the Old Testament – it has theological
significance. Under the Abrahamic covenant the sign of
circumcision is administered to every male child within the
family (Gen. 17:11–14), so ensuring a clear genealogical continuity of religious tradition and devotion. Indeed, through
membership of a covenant family a child is directly related to
the covenant people of Israel.

   In the New Testament the family is, perhaps, less prominent.
There seem to be two patterns: one found primarily in the
Gospels, within a rural Palestinian setting, and the other
found in the epistles as an urban, Hellenistic context. In the
Gospels the family is described primarily as a 'household'
(*oikos*). This denotes a social caring structure in which
resources are shared. The central relationship is between father
and son, and this determines issues of inheritance or the
support of elderly parents. The overarching concern in family
relationships is for support and sustenance (Acts 10:22–48; 1
Cor. 1:16; 16:15; 2 Tim. 1:16; 4:19). In the New Testament
epistles, the social structure of *oikos* is defined in relation to
patterns of authority. The household is not an ideal held in
contrast to the political structures of the day, but an integral
part of the macrocosmos ruled by the Emperor. Here again,
the household includes blood relations of each generation, as
well as servants and slaves.[5]

Intergenerational Faith-Transmission and the Family

In the Old Testament the head of the household is accorded an almost priestly function. Before the establishment of the Levitical priesthood the father was responsible for offering sacrifices to God on behalf of himself and his family (Gen. 8:20, 12:7–8, 22:2–9). At the Passover the father was given the duty of explaining the defining significance of the sacred meal to his children: 'And when your children ask you, "what does this ceremony mean to you?" tell them, "It is the Passover sacrifice to the LORD who passed over the houses of the Israelites in Egypt and spared our homes"' (Ex. 12:26–7). The family was the context in which children were to learn the faith for themselves. The injunction of Deuteronomy is clear that the responsibility for passing on the faith to the next generation rests with the fathers: 'These commandments that I give you today are to be upon your hearts. Impress them on your children. Talk about them when you sit at home and when you walk along the road, when you lie down and when you get up' (Deut. 6:6–7).

The Jewish home was to be the place where children learned first-hand how to follow God. Philo writes 'Jews have been trained from a very early age', even 'from the cradle', to follow 'the one God alone and to observe the Jewish Law.'[6] Both Philo and Josephus talk of the laws and the ancestral customs having been 'engraved' on the soul of every young Jew.[7] In the Old Testament and in the Jewish home faith in God and observance of the traditions were to be embedded and ingrained into every aspect of family life.

In the New Testament there is some indication of passing on the faith within the family. We find Christian prayer over food (1 Cor. 10:30–31, Rom. 14:6) and the expectation that children will be raised as believers: 'Fathers do not exasperate your children; instead, bring them up in the training and instruction of the Lord' (Eph 6:4). The apostle Paul also addresses children directly in both Ephesians and Colossians, encouraging them as Christians to obey their parents (Col. 3:20; Eph. 6:1–2).[8] The clear expectation of the New Testament, in fact, is that whole households, including individuals from various generations, will embrace the Christian faith (Acts 16:34). In fact the implication of the phrase 'God's household, which is the church of the living God', as used by Paul in 1 Timothy 3:15, strongly implies a conception of the home as the church in microcosm. The teaching, relationships, prayer and worship that take place in the congregation should be happening on a smaller scale in the family.

The Role of the Family in Leadership Succession

Both the Old and New Testament, then, make it incumbent upon parents to bring up their children as believers and participants in the faith. Indeed, the New Testament goes so far as to say that the ability to do this should be a test of a person's suitability for church leadership. Only those who manage their own households in an exemplary fashion should be trusted to lead God's household, the church (1 Tim. 3:5).[9] Church leaders must set an example in being able to raise godly children:

> An elder must be blameless, the husband of one wife, a man whose children believe and are not open to the charge of being wild and disobedient. Since an overseer is entrusted with God's work, he must be blameless – not overbearing, not quick-tempered, not given to drunkenness, not violent, not pursuing dishonest gain (Tit. 1:6).

More specifically in relation to our subject, leaders of the church are to be those who can relate well across the 'generation gap'. This happens first and foremost in the home. If the leaders prove able to nurture and raise children as godly men and women, they may also be able to raise up new generations within the church. It is interesting in Titus 1:7 that Paul uses two relational categories – 'not being over-bearing' and 'not being quick tempered' – before moving on to drunkenness and violence. He is clearly emphasising the need for a leader to treat those from a younger generation with respect.

In this same vein, Paul notes that Timothy had the faith passed on to him by his mother and grandmother – Lois and Eunice (2 Tim. 1:5). Indeed, Timothy represents a new generation taking on church leadership having grown up in the faith, been nurtured in it at home and then mentored for church leadership by Paul. An Old Testament parallel to this is found in the example of Mordecai and Esther. Here the family relationship is again key, with a new generation being released to play a significant role for God. Mordecai has brought Esther up in the faith, and he later challenges her to make her voice heard in the nation (Esth. 2:7, 4:14). After the deliverance of Israel the feast of Purim is established so that every generation might grasp the importance of her witness: 'These days should be remembered and observed in every generation by every family, and in every province and in every city' (Esth. 9:28). Hence both Esther and Timothy become leaders themselves, having been discipled in the home by their elders. Indeed, they bear out the fact that in biblical terms, the family is to be a microcosm of what the larger church family should be. Clearly, Christian leaders in the New Testament were required to be good at relating to other believers of a different age and generation. The significance of this priority within church life cannot be underestimated if the church is to grow and a new generation of believers and leaders is to emerge. As such, we shall now examine it in more detail.

Intergenerational Succession and Leadership Transition within the Church

Whether they are in a period of growth or decline, virtually all local churches, denominations, networks or organisations are challenged at some point with the question of how their life and work will continue from one generation to the next. Very often, as we have seen, this challenge is focused in the transition of leadership.[10] In some cases, as we have also seen, a family line provides the most obvious vehicle for such transition. Yet it has become clear from our survey of the biblical material in this area that mere blood lineage is no guarantee of anointing: the eternal family to which we belong is one into which we have been adopted by grace through faith, and it is therefore incumbent upon us to look beyond mere genetic inheritance as we consider what might make for constructive intergenerational succession.

The Old Testament book of Daniel records Nebuchadnezzar conquering and plundering Jerusalem (Dan. 1:1f.). His strategy for maintaining dominance over the city was to exile key Israelite leaders to Babylon, thus leaving Israel weak and directionless. In addition, Nebuchadnezzar identified the emerging generation of leaders in Jerusalem and exiled them also, so that an effective transition of leadership was forestalled. He then trained these emerging leaders intensively for three years in his own vision and value-system, so that he could assimilate them into the government of the empire he was seeking to build. From a Judaeo-Christian perspective this might seem like a decidedly negative model of planning for the future! Yet as Christians looking to the establishment of God's eternal kingdom (Mt. 6:10, 11:2, Mk. 1:14, Lk. 4:43), to eternal life in Christ (Jn. 3:16), and to the eternal city, New Jerusalem (Rev. 21:1–5), we would do well to consider ways in which we might more constructively nurture our forthcoming generations of leaders.

Various models of leadership transition pertain within church traditions and denominations in the UK. While these models do not turn on strict generational cycles, they do mediate overall transitions of leadership through various generational strata. Both Roman Catholic and Orthodox churches assign priests to positions essentially by episcopal decree – that is, on the direction of the relevant bishop. An episcopal system also operates within the various Anglican communions of the British Isles, accompanied by a generally greater degree of consultation – with Parochial Church Councils, patrons and the congregation as a whole.[11] Despite its nonconformist identity, the Methodist church arguably vests a comparable individual authority in District Chairpersons, who annually appoint ministers to circuit churches. By contrast, the congregational model, which operates in most Baptist and many independent churches as well as in Congregationalism *per se*, typically sees potential ministers interviewed and invited to preach 'with a view' by the elders or deacons, after which their call is assessed and voted on by a full meeting of church members.[12] In Presbyterianism the same basic approach applies, but with the elders taking relatively more responsibility for the process – functioning as the congregation's executive or 'board' in respect of the appointment.[13] A corporate 'board' system as such is more common in North America.[14] Within the so-called New Churches, which have developed from the Restorationist movement of the 1970s, leaders arise from within the community, considerable emphasis being placed on their 'anointing' for the task.[15]

All these models have potential strengths and weaknesses. The episcopal approach bears out the importance of obedience in a leader's call, and allows for very direct and strategic deployment of ministerial resources across a given area. Yet even when a measure of consultation is incorporated, it can still depend too much on the knowledge and planning of one person, and can result in leaders being 'imposed' on unsympathetic congregations. The congregational approach may accord considerable power to the membership as a whole, but as well as confirming consensus, it can also militate against challenging, prophetic leadership: if they do not like what they hear, the same people who appointed the leader can vote that leader out, even if what he or she says is God's word for that community. Within Presbyterial and 'board'-driven systems, the 'executive' may apply a degree of scrutiny which the church meeting cannot, but may eventually emerge as having been out of tune with the congregation in their choice.

Meanwhile, for all its relational qualities, the New Church model can falter, either because 'promotion from within' can lead to staleness, because the perception of 'anointing' can become over-subjective, or because 'the anointing' itself is simply not apparent among those in the succeeding generational group.

Beyond churches themselves, organisations often lack the resources and momentum to invest in long-term leadership succession. Many are formed in response to concerns which are, or which turn out to have been, time or culture-specific — issues which have less resonance or urgency for the following generation. Thus, at its height in the mid-1930s, the Anglican Evangelical Group Movement enjoyed the support of some 1500 clergy for a 'liberal evangelical' agenda which included promotion of biblical criticism, evolutionary theory and the social gospel, but by the 1960s had transmuted into a broad evangelicalism which no longer deemed it necessary to distin-guish such convictions under a 'party' name. As a result, 'liberal evangelicalism' is now viewed at best as an anachronism, and at worst as a contradiction in terms, theological liberalism having subsequently taken on a character which is both more radical and more consciously set over against evangelicalism. [16] A rather different instance of the same phenomenon would be the Christian caucus of the Campaign for Nuclear Disarmament (CND) — a group which, as we have seen, enjoyed a significant support in the 1960s, and which resurged in during a new period of nuclear tension in the 1980s, but whose membership since the end of the Cold War has dipped considerably. [17]

Other bodies can depend heavily on the genius, energy or vision of one man or woman, but fail to maintain momentum when he or she dies, retires or moves on. For all his excellence as a preacher, George Whitefield did not possess the organisational skill of his counterpart John Wesley, and his legacy to succeeding generations — at least in terms of churches, colleges and socio-political influence — was consequently much less. [18] Likewise, whereas during his lifetime the brilliant but idiosyncratic

C.T. Studd had won hundreds of recruits for the China Inland Mission (CIM) through his advocacy work among students, after his death CIM struggled to attract members from the next generation of younger people because it lacked leaders with the charisma and magnetism of Studd and his fellow missionary pioneers – the so-called 'Cambridge Seven'.[19]

As for promotions from within, these can in some cases provide positive continuity, but in others, as suggested above, it may be more appropriate to recruit 'new brooms' from elsewhere. Where the promotion is internal, it is somewhat less likely to involve a generational shift, since the need for 'fresh blood' may not be so apparent. In 1983, the Evangelical Alliance took a considerable risk when it invited a relatively unknown thirty-four-year-old called Clive Calver to be its General Director. Within months, Calver had persuaded most of the Alliance's Council to resign and make way for a new 'generation' of leaders. The methods appeared drastic, but the results were remarkable, and over the next decade the Alliance saw its membership increase more than ten-fold. Once this transformation had been effected, it was felt that continuity would be more appropriate than a second massive upheaval, and in 1997 Calver's contemporary and colleague, the UK Director Joel Edwards, was asked to take the helm. Still, Edwards would be the first to admit that without the radical changes wrought under Calver, his relatively smooth transition to General Director might have been impossible – not least because there might not have been an Evangelical Alliance to direct! [20]

In a similar context, the Salvation Army mission team emerged during the 1990s under the dynamic guidance of an ex-policeman named Phil Wall. Wall left the mission team to establish a new venture in 2000, and his closest mentoree, Russell Rook, took on his role, although the age-difference between them was only a few years rather than a full generation. Again the accent in the succession was on continuity, even as this continuity was explicitly recognised as having been 'earned' through an initial willingness to embrace radical change – a willingness which might have to be applied again should the need arise.[21]

Despite these examples, the harsh reality is that large numbers of organisations and movements die with the generation which founded them. Granted, in exceptional cases the dissolution is actively willed and welcomed: the influential charismatic association, the Fountain Trust, for instance, was voluntarily wound up in 1980 by members who sensed that it had achieved its original goals and that God was now leading them to promote its agenda in new contexts.[22] Much the same approach characterised the passing of the March for Jesus movement, which marked its own end at the millennium, but which then encouraged participants to apply its principles in fresh ways in their own settings. Founded by Ichthus Christian Fellowship, Youth with a Mission, the Pioneer church network and Graham Kendrick in 1986, the march had by that point involved some 50 million people in 188 nations. These founders decided to discontinue the event not because of financial hardship or loss of numbers, but because they believed they had finished what God had asked them to do.[23]

On the whole, however, such transparently 'happy endings' are rare: the failure of so many organisations to effect leadership transition from one generation to another may be glossed as a facet of divine providence, but it ought to be remembered, nonetheless, that providence can entail severe judgement. As Jeremiah once prophesied to sinful Judah, 'The Lord has rejected and forsaken the generation that provoked his wrath' (Jer. 7:29).

The principles and examples we have been citing can be schematised into four basic models of leadership transition. The first model bears out the problem with which we have just been dealing.

Intergenerational stoppage

As we have seen, when assessing leadership transition from generation to generation, it is salutary to realise that in some cases transition does not occur at all. Indeed, what we shall call 'intergenerational stoppage' serves in this sense as an important 'control' on theories of succession.

In the history of Israel, we see such stoppage vividly exemplified in the period of the Judges. It is recorded that the Israelites served God throughout Joshua's lifetime, and throughout the lifetime of the elders who survived him. However, we then learn that

> After that generation had been gathered to their fathers, another generation grew up, who knew neither the Lord nor what he had done for Israel. Then the Israelites did evil in the eyes of the Lord. Consequently Israel suffered the Lord's judgement, delivered to them through the enemy nations around them (Judg. 2:7–11).

In fact, the same pattern is repeated among the Israelites throughout this era: 'Whenever the Lord raised up a judge for them, he was with the judge and saved them out of the hands of their enemies as long as the judge lived; for the Lord had compassion on them as they groaned under those who oppressed and afflicted them.' Yet when the judge died, 'the people returned to ways even more corrupt than those of their fathers, following other gods and serving and worshipping them. They refused to give up their evil practices and stubborn ways' (Judg. 2:18–19).

Later, Nehemiah and Ezra reflect on leadership stoppage, after the construction of the second temple. The rebuilding project has been halted so many times, declares Ezra, because 'Our kings, our leaders, our priests and *our fathers* did not follow [God's] law' (Neh. 9:34, our italics). Intergenerational stoppage in leadership is also clearly evident at the very end of the Old Testament epoch: Zechariah and Malachi represent the close of the prophetic age, after which there is an apparent dearth of oracular divine communication until the arrival of the Elijah-like figure, John the Baptist (Lk. 3:1–6).

Beyond the obvious problems which accrue from sheer rebellion against God, church history records that a number of well-intentioned movements have experienced intergenerational

leadership stoppage following the death of a founding figure
whose very giftedness has – albeit inadvertently – distracted
others from adequate preparation and planning for his or her
succession. Such was the force of Oliver Cromwell's character and
authority, for example, that his death in 1658 effectively sealed the
fate of the commonwealth. For all his tactical triumphs on the
battlefield and in the republican government, Cromwell paid
inadequate heed to his succession, and his eventual nomination of
his son Richard to lead the country into the future was a serious
mistake. The younger Cromwell could barely begin to emulate
his extraordinary father, and within two years Parliament had
moved in a sufficiently royalist direction to recall the exiled
Prince Charles (later Charles II) from the continent. No doubt
wider political forces were also at work, but the pronounce-
ment of Oliver Cromwell as Lord Protector in 1653, and the
subsequent offer to him of the crown (though refused), had
confirmed an unhealthy focus on his own personality – a focus
which would serve finally to truncate the radical constitutional
and ecclesiastical changes he had made during his lifetime.[24]

Of course, not all problems of leadership transition are as
momentous or decisive as those encountered in the Protectorate
during the late 1650s. Indeed, many Christians today might more
readily identify with the issues raised by the unexpectedly early
death of John Wimber, the founder and director of the Association of Vineyard churches. Wimber died on 17 November 1997
of a brain haemorrhage following a fall. He had overcome cancer
and coronary bypass surgery, and had made very clear the need to
pass the mantle of leadership to new, younger leaders. Indeed,
he had embarked before his death on a process of leadership
decentralisation, handing over roles and responsibilities and
releasing whole countries and regions within the network to
function autonomously while remaining in relationship. The aim
of this, he said, was to develop the Vineyard as 'a family with
purpose' – a network of churches sharing common values,
without the need for a strongly hierarchical chain of command.

Yet despite such initiatives, Wimber was only sixty-three when he died, and the fatal fall and haemorrhage could hardly have been foreseen. As such, most were caught somewhat off guard, so that his passing is still acknowledged by many within and beyond the Vineyard to have significantly disrupted and delayed the transitional process he had set in train.[25]

No doubt for a combination of the reasons we have cited, and more, the threat of intergenerational stoppage is very real within British churches today. Not only are most denominations struggling to find new young ministers:[26] the 1998 English Church Attendance Survey showed that the cohort of those in their twenties and thirties was the least well-represented sector in church congregations as a whole, when measured against the wider population of those in their age-brackets. Hence, twenty to twenty-nine-year-olds represent just 9% of total congregational attendance, but make up 13% of the English population, while thirty to forty-four-year-olds represent 17% of congregation attendance, but comprise 23% of the population. By contrast, under-nineteen-year-olds attending congregations are in direct representational proportion to the general population figures, and worshippers who are over forty-five make up a higher percentage of church congregations than they do of the total population.[27] The Evangelical Alliance's own 'Commission on Strategic Evangelism' called in 1998 for urgent help to be given to churches so that they could reach and disciple those twenty-one to forty-year-olds who are so starkly under-represented in local fellowships.[28]

Plainly, then, the statistics confirm that today more than ever, there is a pressing need to invest in emerging generations. As one response to this need, the Evangelical Alliance commissioned a 'Generation X Lifestyle Survey' in the spring of 2001. This was initially published in the Alliance's magazine *idea*, and appears here as an appendix.

Produced with the aim of furthering the church's understanding of this 'missing generation', the survey sought to provide an accurate basis for the development of appropriate ministries among its members.[29] As such, it complements the recent *Faith in Life* survey, which shows that fifteen to twenty-four-year-olds represent 6% of attendees at church services in the UK, but compromise 15% of the population, and that twenty-five to thirty-four-year-olds represent 8% of congregation attendance, but comprise 19% of the population.[30]

Intergenerational stoppage typically follows from a lack of commitment or ability to invest in emerging generations, and in models suited to the future. It may come swiftly, or after a period of relatively gradual decline. Although, as we have seen, it may be both positive and voluntary, its arrival is more commonly undesired and unwelcome. As such, it may yet be part of God's commissive will – although it seems at least as likely that it might fall within the scope of his permissive will, and thus, from the human viewpoint, be 'avoided' by effective forward planning.

Intergenerational schism

A second generationally-based facet of leadership transition is what might be called 'intergenerational schism'. This is a form of that 'intergenerational antipathy' which we have been tracking throughout this study, and involves an age-related breach in the unity of God's people – usually with implications at the denominational, national or international level.

Perhaps the most famous intergenerational schism in Scripture is that which occurs between Saul and David; the jealously of the older king towards his anointed heir turns quickly to paranoia, and then to murderous intent (1 Kgs. 18–23). Although David spares Saul's life twice when he might have killed him, Saul's death marks not so much a transition of values and policies from one generation to another, but a sharp closure of one era and a fresh departure into very different regime (2 Sam. 2:1–7). The severity of such internecine division is also emphasised when Jesus presents enmity between fathers and sons as a key portent of the apocalypse, in Mark 13:32.

While most schisms in the church's history have been occasioned by complex webs of factors, of which generational tension may be just one[31], the rise of the Restorationist movement in Britain during the 1970s provides an example of divergence which was especially strongly marked in terms of age. The charismatic renewal that emerged in the UK during the early-mid 1960s became the focus of considerable debate and disagreement. Emphasising that the 'charismata' or gifts of the Holy Spirit included love and implied visible unity, some leaders of this renewal remained faithful to their historic denominations and worked to transform them from within. Others, however, began to meet with friends in their homes and either left, or were ejected from, their existing churches. The reconfiguration of these charismatics into the so-called 'House Church movement' prompted the development of new networks – networks which looked to particular individuals – often, as we saw in chapter 1, called 'apostles' – for leadership.[32] The 'apostles' in question were mostly in their twenties and thirties at the time, and in age as well as demeanour and outlook, stood in stark contrast to the relatively staid, middle-aged churches which they and many of their supporters had left – even if the breach was hardly as tragic or aggressive as in the biblical models we have mentioned.[33]

In more recent times, as these Restorationist churches have themselves entered 'rising adulthood', and as their leaders have approached their sixties, some have sought rapprochement with historic denominational congregations. The Ichthus Christian Fellowship, for example, interacts with a number of 'link churches', who maintain their own denominational affiliation while sharing resources and personnel. New Frontiers International has entered into association with several Baptist Union congregations, who have continued as Baptists while assimilating complementary NFI training and ministry models. At its best, such co-operation has ensured a marriage of long-standing experience with the fresh energy of renewal, thus to some degree ameliorating the schism of the generation before – even if, in some cases, it has required delicate negotiation between the new Church and the denominations concerned.

This Restorationist example underlines a point often made in studies of evangelicalism – namely that it is a movement which is particularly prone to schism, but that it typically regards such schism as sometimes necessary, and even beneficial. In fact, as David Bebbington expresses it, the distinctively activist and pragmatic worldview of evangelicalism means that it might even go so far as to view past church splits as 'an excellent index of the advance of fresh ideas' – as instances of how 'new wine broke old bottles'. [34]

Now of course such academic observation should not detract from the more emotionally damaging aspects of schism – the fractured relationships, the sundered communities, and the tainted public perceptions of the church. Such costs are well acknowledged by Kenneth Hylson-Smith, even as he makes a similar point to Bebbington's:

> The whole ethos of Protestantism – its theological basis, the behavioural patterns it inculcates, its attitudinal emphasis and its authority structure – make it inherently liable to schism and fragmentation. It has a built-in tendency to be centrifugal rather than centripetal … By its very nature it encourages individuality, stresses personal faith and promotes distinctive individual or group expressions of faith and practice. Such characteristics ensure a large measure of personal and corporate creativity; but they almost guarantee divisiveness … And what is true of Protestantism as a whole is especially so for those archetypal Protestants, the evangelicals. [35]

All in all, it is probably fairest to conclude that schism in general, and intergenerational schism in particular, while indicating our fallen humanity, can sometimes nonetheless be turned to relatively constructive ends.

Not least within the restless dynamics of Protestant culture, it is always likely that zealous younger leaders will arise who will challenge the perceived status quo embodied by their elders, and that this will lead to friction, and in some instances, to a parting of the ways. Martin Robinson has perceptively observed that in the past, the passions of such emerging leaders were typically channelled into the mission field, or into para-church agencies set on drawing the church's attention to various specialist concerns.[36] He might have added that in the increasingly entrepreneurial milieu of modern-day evangelicalism, they will now be as likely to establish new churches and organisations of their own.

It is a commonplace that intergenerational tension develops in family life when a child moves into adulthood and division arises between parents who expect certain behaviour and respect, and the adolescent who seeks to assert her own independence and identity. The family in this case functions as an analogy of the broader tensions that can develop between the generations in church life. It suggests on the one hand that arrogance and self-righteousness to which emerging leaders can be prone, and on the other, the insecurity and over-protectiveness which mature leaders can sometime exude. In each case, the challenge to submit personal interests and power to God can be very great.

Intergenerational stereotypy

The third possible outcome of generational succession in the church may be termed 'intergenerational stereotypy'. This is, in effect, 'repetition without renewal' – the adoption of a previous generation's leadership model without due re-evaluation, and without appropriate adaptation to the emergent cultural context. Now as we emphasised in chapter 3, not all shifts from generation to generation need be revolutionary: in relatively stable, post-figurative cultures, it may well appropriate for the rising genera-tion to maintain the essential characteristics and methods of its forbears. Biblically, however, it is clear that where a previous generation has been defective, those who simply follow and ape it are in a real sense even more culpable than their elders. Granted, punishment may be carried to the 'third and fourth generation' of those who disobey God, and sins inherited by children may be difficult to overcome. Still, however, the historians and chroniclers of Israel appear to retain particular scorn for those kings who merely repeat and compound the mistakes made by their fathers: kings like Abijam son of Rehoboam (1 Kgs. 15:3), Nadab son of Jeroboam (1 Kgs. 15:26) and Ahab son of Omri (1 Kgs. 16:30).

In the Gospels, Jesus several times takes the religious leaders of his day to task for the sort of intergenerational stereotypy which breeds legalism and ritualism. This lies at the heart of his dialogues with them about healing (Mk. 2:6–12), fasting (Mk. 2:18–22), Sabbath-keeping (Mk. 2:23–28) and the legacy of Abraham (Jn. 8:39–59). In our own day churches, too, can lose their way, forgetting the purpose for which they exist, and resorting to the routines of the past. To ask oneself the question, 'If God withdrew from our activities, how long would it be before we noticed?' can be a sobering challenge. If our programmes become hollow and stagnant, as those of the Israelites sometimes did, we may need to take stock, repent and develop fresh models, and with them, fresh attitudes.

As a boy the great revivalist John Wesley was saved from a fire in his home and became convinced God had a purpose for his life. Later his father Samuel pushed him to follow his own career as an ordained Anglican priest. Early in that career Wesley discovered a passion for holiness, but was troubled that he could not attain it. He sailed to the USA but failed as a missionary there and returned to the England to preach, despite a growing conviction that he was not in fact saved. On 24 May 1738 he attended a Moravian meeting in London and declared in his journal 'I felt my heart strangely warmed. I felt I did trust Christ ... an assurance was given me that he had taken away my sins, even mine, and saved me from the law of sin and death.'[37]

Like Wesley, church leaders today may periodically need to question whether they are simply going through the motions, and if so, what changes might be made in order to do God's will more effectively. Thus, what begins in an admission of intergenerational stereotypy can lead into a radical reassessment and restructuring of ministry and mission. For Wesley, despite a lifelong attachment to the Church of England, it meant founding and directing a major new movement, Methodism, which inspired revival, even while prompting considerable debate and hostility.[38]

At worst, intergenerational stereotypy can stifle diversity, prophetic insight, and even revival. Ultimately, churches and movements with too 'fixed' a model of leadership risk allowing transition to become little more than cloning – and, maintaining the 'family' analogy, thereby to incur all the potential genetic defects associated with a clone. Indeed, it is no coincidence that this model of transition is the one most obviously appropriated by religious cults. While the precise definition of cults is notoriously contentious, most analysts agree that they typically subjugate the individuality of their members to structures, methods and thought-forms modelled after the personality of a dominant founder.[39] Clearly, however, this is far removed from the model of intergenerational transition encouraged in the Scriptures (cf. 1 Cor. 1:12–13)

Constructive intergenerational succession

The three paradigms of intergenerational succession examined so far have been shown to be at best ambiguous, and at worst destructive of Christian community life. Intergenerational stoppage may be a godly response to the 'seasonal' limitations of a ministry, but more often results from organisational failure. Schism may *incidentally* spur innovation, but is hardly to be commended as an intentional strategy. Stereotypy may spring from a commendable instinct for preservation, but is prone to inculcate spiritual stagnation. Clearly, however, the more attractive paradigm is that which mediates what might be called constructive intergenerational succession – a paradigm which effects continuity, but is open to such changes as may be directed by the leading of the Holy Spirit.

The history of Israel shows this kind of constructive succession to be at work in the transfer of role and responsibility from Moses to Joshua. Moses invested heavily in the next generation of leadership through his mentoring relationship with Joshua. When Moses was at the peak his powers he encouraged Joshua to lead also: he stood Joshua up in front of God's people and with Eleazar the priest laid hands on him, granting him a portion of his authority so that the people of God would follow him (Num. 27:15–23). An obvious example of effective intergenerational succession among the prophets is that which passes from Elijah to Elisha (1 Kgs. 19:15–21). Furthermore, in the New Testament it is salutary to recall that Jesus himself spent the greater percentage of his three years of ministry in shaping the characters, minds and spirits of his disciples.[40] He may have been contemporary with them in terms of sheer age, but he was clearly planning ahead for the sake of the generation which would lead the church after his death. The continuity between Paul's teaching and that of his protégés, Timothy and Titus, also plainly falls into the 'constructive succession' category (2 Tim. 2:2; Tit. 1:5; 2:1–3:15). In none of these cases is the next generation of leadership merely 'cloned'. The disciples, for instance, retain their diverse characters – for better, and sometimes, as in Peter's denials and Thomas' doubts, for worse. Certainly, the essence of what made the mentors effective is preserved, but it is not assumed that the challenges which face the succeeding generation will be identical.

No doubt John Calvin had these biblical precedents and principles clearly in mind when, towards the end of his remarkable ministry in Geneva, he began to plan carefully for his succession. In the late 1550s he developed an academy in the city to ensure that his theological ideas would be maintained and developed by a younger generation of scholars. One such was Theodore Beza, like Calvin a former law student, whose reading of the New Testament in Greek had contributed to his renunciation of Roman Catholicism. Soon after appointing Beza to a professorship at the academy, Calvin groomed him to be his principal successor, and Beza went on to lead the Swiss Calvinists, publishing several expositions of the Reformed faith.[41]

While none of these examples involve parent-child successions, it is worth balancing our earlier Oliver-Richard Cromwell warning here with a more positive and more recent familial hand over of leadership responsibilities – that which has taken place within the Double family at St. Austell Church, Cornwall. Don Double founded this church in the 1960s. Then, when he was travelling extensively during the 1980s, the congregation began to look to his son Steve for leadership. This pattern developed with Don's encouragement, so that even when he was present in church services, he would look to Steve to take the initiative. Steve was initially appointed as one of the leadership team, and latterly as the key leader when his father stepped down fully. In a recent interview Steve commented:

> Things really did seem to happen 'naturally' and it just seemed to be the right thing to happen. The existing leadership and the church allowed it to happen, although it would be wrong to say that there was 100% support for it. My father remained an active part of the church even though he was no longer part of the leadership. He has stood back, but remained supportive even when I know I have lead the church in ways he would never have done. I can think of only a small handful of times when he has come to have a wise word because he felt it necessary. Most people would say that the church today is unrecognisable from ten years ago (that is not to say it is necessarily better, it is just very different). It would also be true to say that the emphasis of the church now is much younger and many people of my

father's generation have not felt able to move with us and have gone elsewhere.[42]

A higher-profile father-son leadership transition occurred in January 2001, when the American magazine *Christianity Today* reported that fifty years after founding the Billy Graham Evangelistic Association (BGEA), the famous evangelist had 'turned over the role of chief executive officer to his son, Franklin'. [43] Although the BGEA board meeting was unanimous in this decision, it remains to be seen whether this transition proves as successful as most other elements of Billy Graham's ministry have been.

Intergenerational Succession and Mentoring

One of the most potentially rewarding means by which constructive intergenerational succession may be achieved is through mentoring. In recent years, mentoring has enjoyed something of a vogue in evangelical church life.[44] Its roots, however, go back at least to Homer's *Odyssey*. There, Odysseus entrusts the upbringing of his son, Telemachus, to his friend and adviser, Mentor. Models of mentoring vary, but key definitions refer to it as 'a relational experience in which one person empowers another by sharing God-given resources'[45] and 'a lifelong relationship, in which a mentor helps a protégé reach her or his God-given potential'.[46]

Here we shall consider the extent to which mentoring may be defined as biblical concept. We shall then seek to distinguish and evaluate different basic types of mentoring. We shall also identify those methods which might make mentoring effective. In all of this, while realising that mentoring does not always conform to the elder-protégé model, we shall be concerned principally with cross-generational versions of mentoring.

Mentoring in Scripture

'Mentoring' as such is not a word that appears in the Bible. However, other words that can be construed as synonymous with it are used. 'Disciple' is the term most commonly deployed in Scripture to translate the Greek word *mathētēs* (Mt. 5:1; 28:19) and the Hebrew words *talmîd* (1 Chr. 25:8) and *limmûd* (Is. 8:16) – each of which can mean pupil, scholar, student, adherent or follower. [47] The Old Testament does not present especially programmatic models of discipleship, but the passing on of wisdom and skill from an older expert to a younger pupil clearly formed part of Hebrew culture. Hence we can see a discipling dynamic at work between Abraham, Isaac and Jacob, between Moses and Joshua, between Ruth and Naomi, between Eli and Samuel, and between Elijah and Elisha.

Religious instruction in the Jewish culture of the ancient world was routinely given through family and rabbi to the disciple, who would devote himself to the study of Scripture, and to the traditions of the elders. As Günter Krallmann notes, 'For a *talmid*, his rabbi was not merely an intellectual and theological authority, he served as a living example, too. He influenced his student through what he said and what he did, impacted his life through teaching and conduct.'[48] In this Jewish culture the only institution available for the vocational development of most people was that of the family, in which sons would typically learn a trade through an apprenticeship with their fathers, or with other male relatives.

Jesus, of course, learnt the trade of a carpenter, almost certainly from boyhood (Mt. 13:55, Mk. 6:3). His declarations that 'the Son can do nothing by himself', that 'he can do only what he sees his Father doing, because whatever the Father does the Son also does', and that 'the Father loves the Son and shows him all he does' (Jn. 5:19–20), echo the discipling relationship he would have experienced while growing up in Joseph's workshop. So naturally, Jesus used the approach of rabbi and *talmîd* with his own disciples. He called twelve men (Mt. 10:1; Mk. 3:13–14), and these men in turn recognised him as their Teacher (Mt. 9:5). Again, while he may have been roughly the same age as, or even younger than, these men, one must presume that he was preparing them for the new 'generational time' which would ensue once he had left the earth.

The word 'disciple' was not used exclusively of the twelve, however. Indeed, there was a wider circle beyond them (Mt. 8:19–20, 10:24–25, 42). Joseph of Arimathea was described as 'a disciple of Jesus' (Mt. 27:57; Jn. 19:38), and the disciples were themselves commanded by Jesus to 'go and make disciples' (Mt. 28:19). Neither was discipleship limited to males: there was a group of women who also served as disciples of Jesus (Lk. 8:1–3), and who were the first witnesses of his empty tomb (Lk. 24:1–3; Jn. 20:1). There were other disciples, too: the 'disciples of the Pharisees' (Mt. 22:15–16, Mark 2:18), the 'disciples of John the Baptist' (Mk. 2:18) and the 'disciples of Moses' (Jn. 9:24–29). Likewise, Barnabus mentored Mark, and Paul mentored Timothy and Titus. Thus, although 'mentor' is not in itself a biblical word, the reality to which it points is it is clearly integral to the Judeo-Christian culture of biblical times. In fact, one-to-one mentoring relationships emerge as a primary method through which God chooses to raise up the next generation of leaders.

Types of Mentoring

Paul Stanley has identified seven types of mentor – discipler, guide, coach, counsellor, teacher, sponsor, contemporary and historical. These range from intentional to less intentional mentors. [49] For our purposes, however, it will suffice to consider three essential forms of mentoring.

First, we may define *retrospective mentoring*. Here, a mentoree learns from the life of a person who is dead through studying their lives using biographies, visiting places where they were born and where they worked, and by absorbing other relevant documentation. Although there is no living relationship in this model, it can be said to be cross-generational inasmuch as insights from previous times, contexts and cohorts are adduced and applied in the present situation of the mentoree.

Secondly, we may identify *coincident mentoring*, where coincident means 'contemporary with' but not 'personally known to'. Here, the mentoree learns from a person who is alive by becoming familiar with their life and work – for example through the books they have written.

Thirdly, there is what might be called *personal mentoring*. Here, a mentoree is schooled by someone they know and meet for dialogue and review, either on an occasional or on a regular basis. Using Margaret Mead's distinctions, we may recognise that such personal mentoring can be peer-based or 'co-figurative'; it may even be pre-figurative, that is, led by the younger participant. Overwhelmingly, however, it is post-figurative: in other words, a member of an older generation serves as mentor to someone from a younger generation. [50]

The Purpose of Mentoring

Throughout the New Testament, and most especially in the life of Jesus and the instruction of Paul, we see a pattern of mentoring that was foundational to the growth and establishment of the early church. One of Paul's key instructions to the congregations with which he was in contact was that they should 'imitate', or become 'imitators'. Hence the believers in Macedonia and Achaia imitated the Thessalonians (1 Thes. 1:7), and the Thessalonians imitated the Judean churches (1 Thes 2:14). The Thessalonians also imitated Paul, as did the Corinthians (1 Cor. 4:6; 11:1). And just as all believers are called to imitate their leaders (2 Thes. 3:7, 9; 1 Tim. 4:12; Tit. 2:7; 1 Pet. 5:3), so Paul imitated Christ (1 Cor. 11:1), and the Thessalonians did the same (1 Thes. 1:6). All were to imitate God (Eph. 5:1), just as, during his ministry, Jesus had perfectly imitated his Father in heaven.[51] From these patterns of imitation, and from Jesus' ministry as a whole, it is possible to construe the models of mentoring mentioned above. Today, as we reflect on the lives of biblical 'heroes' and heroines, and as we seek to learn from them, we practise what may reasonably be called retrospective mentoring. However, in the specific case of Jesus, we are concerned not only with a mentor of the past, but also with a mentor of the present. We read about Jesus' ministry as history, but his teaching is living and dynamic, not static. Paul describes Christ's involvement in the lives of Christians as current and ongoing (Col. 3:4; 2 Thes. 2:16–17; Phil. 4:13; 2 Cor. 10:8; 2 Cor. 12:9). The Lord is presently living in all believers (Gal. 2:20). As Krallmann puts it, 'The Lord Jesus as our coaching model seeks more than our mere interest in him as a historical forerunner, he in fact claims our wholehearted trust in him as present enabler.'[52]

Despite the relationship between biblical mentoring and imitation, it should not be supposed that mentorees are thereby expected to become mere carbon copies of their mentors. Rather, it is the responsibility of the mentor to empower the mentoree – to unlock his or her distinctive, God-given potential. One of the first things Jesus did during his ministry was to look ahead, and seek out twelve disciples who could continue what he was starting. He named Simon 'Cephas' (Peter), and thus designated him as the 'person of rock' who would eventually found the church. From time to time, Peter proved both cowardly and impulsive. Yet Jesus recognised his leadership qualities, and committed himself to developing Peter's character and abilities.

A key text for understanding Jesus as a mentor is John 14. Here, Jesus attributes his success in ministry to his Father, tells his followers they will do greater things than him, and introduces the unique life-mentor who will be with them always: the Holy Spirit. He is not proud or precious with his own authority, but points to the Father and to the Holy Spirit as his empowerers. Such encouragement and perspective enables the disciples (and present-day Christians) to be released into doing great things.

Christ believes in the God-given ability of his followers. As we go on to read about the birth of the early church in the Book of Acts and beyond, it becomes clear that Jesus put in place a highly effective model of mentoring – one that is as relevant now as it was in the first century. As Krallmann points out, 'Jesus made sure that the emergence and growth of the energetic global harvest force he initiated would not be stifled or even counteracted by a static recipe for the mentoring of its leaders.'[53]

Jesus' mentoring prototype was markedly informal and relational. It eschewed rigid structuring. Indeed, Krallmann presents it as a complex of eight key dynamics. First, he notes, Jesus' approach was oral rather than written. Secondly, it was mobile rather than place-bound. Thirdly, he modelled, taught and enabled practical application. Fourthly, he stressed the indispensability of divine empowerment.[54] Fifthly, he allowed his disciples to get involved with his ministry as well as observing his everyday living. Sixthly, while learning from him, they also became his friends, seeing his struggles and sharing in his sorrow (Lk. 22:39–45). Seventhly, while some limit mentoring to a curriculum-based relationship in which the mentor imparts knowledge to the mentoree, Jesus empowered his followers by also drawing God-given talents *out* of them. And eighthly, he allowed them to learn from their mistakes (Lk. 22:54–62; Jn. 21:15–19). Together, these dynamics operated to lead the disciples towards spiritual maturity.

Although their age difference is unclear, Barnabas, the 'son of encouragement' (Acts 4:36–37), mentored Paul while in the process of introducing him to the disciples in Jerusalem (Acts 9:26–28). Others kept their distance and were afraid to let Paul join them because of his previous allegiance to Pharisaism, and because of his former persecution of Christians. Despite this, Barnabas had recognised Paul's great leadership potential. If he had not done so, the church would not have grown in the way it did. In turn, Paul went on to became one of the most significant mentors in the New Testament, as he invested in the lives of Timothy, Titus and the other leaders of the churches he planted.

From Paul's example and context, it is possible to infer five core purposes in the mentoring process.

First, mentoring can be seen as motivated by *aspiration* – and specifically, the positive emulation the mentor. Paul, for example, taught the church at Corinth to imitate him even as he himself sought to imitate Christ (1 Tim 4:12, 1 Cor. 4:16, 11:1).

The second key purpose of mentoring is *accountability* – that is, being held responsible for one's own character development by a more objective evaluator (2 Tim. 3:17 and 4:2).

Mentoring's third main purpose can be defined as *association* – that is, sharing friendship and fellowship with someone of experience and insight as well as simply emulating them. (1 Cor. 15:33; 2 Cor. 6:14). The communion of saints aside, most obviously this works on the 'personal' model we have mentioned.

A fourth identifiable aim of mentoring is *autopoesis*, or self-discovery. Paul's conversion to Christ was such that his essential personality could be said have been preserved. Before he encountered the risen Jesus he was extremely zealous and advanced for his years (Gal. 1:13–14); once he was in Christ he continued to be extremely hard working and persevering (1 Cor. 11:23–29). The essential difference was that being 'in Christ', and associating with the disciples, turned him from a church persecutor into a church planter.

A fifth purpose of mentoring is *affirmation*. People tend to perform best when they know there is someone who believes in them. Classically, Paul taught his mentoree Timothy that he should not let anyone 'look down' on him because he was 'young', but that instead he should be an example to others in his speech, life and conduct (1 Tim. 4:14; 2 Tim. 1:6).

Conclusion

Leadership transition typically entails a tension between continuity and reform. Whether strongly institutionalised or relatively informal, communities depend on intergenerational relation-ships, and these can go wrong for a variety of reasons. No doubt there are those who have devoted significant time, resources and energy to succession, but who have even then experienced a painful and damaging split with those future and emerging leaders whom they have been training. This scenario is hardly likely to become less common as generational segmentation increases, and as distinctive generational self-consciousness is raised. Nonetheless, a church created by God for eternity ignores the imperative of constructive intergenerational succession at its peril. While in some cases it may be right to allow one ministry to die so that new ones may flourish, and while in God's grace renewal can stem from the deepest of schisms, most churches and organisations will surely find that to prepare diligently for, and with, the next generation of leaders is to make a vital investment for the future.

Even as we assent to this principle, the question of how best to enact it in our contemporary culture remains. Mentoring may have re-emerged in recent times as an attractive way forward, but its specific definition and enactment are still subject to testing and discussion. More generally, while the need to ensure good generational succession may be agreed, the means to that end have become a focus of considerable debate in the fields of ecclesiology and missiology. It is to this debate, and these fields, that we shall now address ourselves as we come to our final chapter.

12

Generations, Church and Mission

Generations, Church and Contemporary Culture

Writing with generational issues in mind, the Anglican theologian Graham Cray suggests that the postmodern West is marked by a 'crisis in mutual society'. Specifically, he argues, the crisis in question is one in which *inter*dependence is being exchanged for *in*dependence: 'The breakdown of bonds of commitment and mutuality at family, local and national levels' is, he argues, 'the harvest reaped from a partial understanding of what it means to be human, mistaking the individual for the personal and ignoring the relational altogether.'[1]

Cray's assessment is borne out by a recent initiative, 'The Tomorrow Project', which has considered the potential shape of British society over the next twenty years. One of the Project's reports suggests that the society which emerges over this period will be marked by increasing fragmentation and isolation: 'As made-to-measure expectations spread', it concludes, 'people will be less inclined to negotiate difficulties and conflicts in a group: "If the group does not fit me exactly, I'll move on".'[2] The Tomorrow Project text illustrates these trends particularly with reference to growing divorce rates, and, most significantly for our purposes, to growing conflict within and between different generational groups.[3]

In the West, loneliness and isolation are increasingly being acknowledged as social problems. As people live for longer, family structures are becoming 'verticalised'. This distension of relationships across the age scale, allied to increased social mobility, means that blood ties are loosening, particularly beyond the nuclear family unit of the home or single house-hold. It is anticipated that the growing elderly population will peak towards the end of the first quarter of the twenty-first century, and that there will be a corresponding 'crisis in care for old people'.[4] Another recent study has concluded that 'with the ageing of the population a much greater level of understanding [will be] important if we are to achieve harmony and balance within society'. For this reason, the Tomorrow Project report recommends that 'more inter-generational programmes in education, work, volunteering and care must be developed as a matter of urgency'.[5]

The church has enormous potential to meet this challenge by demonstrating through its own communal life the reconciling, uniting power of the Gospel. It also has a mandate prophetically and practically to resist the 'crisis in mutual society' mentioned by Cray. Indeed, as our survey of relevant biblical literature has shown, it is obliged to foster meaningful relationships and community – not least on the intergenerational front.

Having said all this, we must recognise that it is not always clear how the church's obligation to 'generational mutuality' might be fulfilled in practice. We may readily agree the church *as a whole* should be generationally diverse, but must accept that many individual congregations are effectively 'mono-generational', just as they are often mono-cultural with respect to other key categories such as income, class, ethnicity and churchmanship. What is more, as the statistics on church attendance which we have presented confirm, such mono-generationalism in the British congregational context is increasingly a mono-generationalism of the elderly – a trend which incidentally bodes ill for the future health and renewal of the Christian community.

What is more, even where specific church rolls show a significant generational mix, the different age-groupings may in fact rarely, if ever, meet one another. There may be a formal 'prayer book' rite at 8 a.m., a traditional communion at 9.30 a.m., an informal 'family' service at 10.30 a.m. and a youth meeting in the evening. While different generations may be catered for in this model, they are still liable to be catered for separately rather than together: indeed, grandparents, parents and children may each find themselves attending different services. Then again, in some circumstances, a distinct 'youth congregation' may be formed as a 'satellite' of the main congregation, the better to reach and minister to teenagers and young people.

These various forms of congregation-based generational segmentation have met with a range of responses – not least among church growth theorists and missiologists. While clearly falling short of the all-age, 'family' ideal presented in the passages of higher biblical ecclesiology which we have examined, such 'sectored' approaches are regarded by certain more pragmatic commentators as the most effective models of congregation for a fallen, fragmented, postmodern world. Hence, in an article entitled 'The Tailor-Made Church',[6] Michael Moynagh argues that for a postmodern Western society driven by consumerism, individualism, customisation and differentiation, the 'traditional church with its wide mixture of people, will seem increasingly alien to those who want to join others like them.' Moynagh continues:

> Our society is becoming ever more fragmented. Let us incarnate the church by establishing new kinds of congregations within the fragments instead of inviting people to us. Just as Christ's love is tailor-made for individuals, the church's mission should be tailor-made to the different groups in our society …We may recoil at this theologically because a fragmented church seems to fly in the face of the 'one church' ideal. However, planting churches in the fragments would proclaim that our unity is in Christ, not place.[7]

More specifically with regard to generationally-targeted mission, youth congregations and 'niche' services defined by age, John Buckeridge suggests that the challenge of bridging the gap between different demographic groups has become so great that we cannot avoid separate meetings for each:

> Growing numbers of churches appear to find the challenge of all-age meetings too tough. Coming up with a formula that addresses the needs and holds the attention of young children, teenagers, singles, marrieds, the middle aged, divorced and senior citizens – all together in one church service – is about as easy as turning the Millennium Dome into a money maker … The early church knew no barriers between races, ages, genders or background. But that was then – what about now? I believe that if niche fosters spiritual maturity and growth significantly better than older models, why not?[8]

In rather more depth, but for similar reasons, Graham Cray himself argues that distinct 'youth congregations' may be necessary, even as they maintain links with another, more generationally diverse 'sister' church. Like Moynagh, he sees the shift from modernity to postmodernity manifested significantly as a shift from 'neighbourhoods' to 'networks' – that is, as a movement from relating primarily to one's geographical location, and to the inhabitants of that location, to relating primarily to those who share one's basic worldview, experience and lifestyle. This shift has been so momentous, writes Cray, that creative ways must be found to accommodate it before it leaves the church almost wholly behind:

> At a time of changing culture, which … I believe to be the primary reason for a policy of planting youth congregations, the provision of 'space' for people not like 'us' will often, but not always, require the establishing of a new worshipping community, rather than attempts to change the old.[9]

In defence of this approach, Cray adds that it need not be seen as making special provision for a minority: rather, indeed, he points out that the pioneering Christian youth community Soul Survivor in Watford, North London, discovered prior to its foundation that only 700 out of 24,000 fourteen to twenty-four-year-olds in the area had any contact with any church. In other words, Cray contends that as long as they function as missionary congregations oriented to non-members, generation-specific churches may well meet needs that mainline, multigenerational churches are failing to address.

While Moynagh, Buckeridge and Cray's approaches to the 'generation gap problem' are each developed in distinct ways, they may helpfully be set in the wider context of a debate which arose out of the landmark Lausanne Congress on World Evangelization (1974). The debate in question concerns a model of congregational growth developed by a group of North American missiologists – a model which they termed 'The Homogeneous Unit Principle'.

Generations, Church and The Homogeneous Unit Principle

The Homogeneous Unit Principle (HUP) was initially championed in the mid-1970s by members of Fuller Theological Seminary's School of World Mission. Its leading advocates there were Donald McGavran, Charles Kraft, Arthur Glasser and Peter Wagner – men who had pioneered so-called 'church growth theory', and who came present the HUP as a key motor of successful congregational expansion. It is also worth remembering that it was Kraft who around the same time seminally defined the 'generation gap problem' as a crucial issue for the Western church. As this group defined it, a homogeneous unit can be classed as 'a section of society in which all members have some characteristic in common.'[10] These common characteristics were identified typically as geographical, linguistic, ethnic, economic, social or class-based, and the Fuller group began with the widely acknowledged assumption that societies regularly subdivide into groups that are distinguished by such criteria. What made this 'homogeneous unit' thinking into a 'principle', however, was the group's assertion not only that congregations would grow more readily insofar as they observed such distinctions, but that the distinctions themselves were commensurate with the providence and purpose of God for the church.[11]

As McGavran and his colleagues presented it, the primary justification for invoking the HUP is the fact that sociological barriers often inhibit people from conversion to Christ. Given that they have to cross a significant enough threshold in order to embrace the gospel *per se*, the Fuller group held that it would be unhelpful to suggest that they might then have to cross any *further* cultural thresholds to assimilate their newfound faith within the life of a congregation. As McGavran famously expressed it, people 'like to become Christians without crossing racial, linguistic or class barriers'.[12] Thus, whereas many existing churches might be *de facto* homogeneous units, those who adopted the HUP would seek *intentionally* to reach one particular section of society, on the assumption that a mission strategy focused in this way would achieve greater success than one which eschewed the targeting of specific demographic sectors.

The implications of all this for the church's approach to generational groups are clear: no doubt, the HUP could be easily applied to them also, and might well serve as an apologetic for the sort of age- and peer-based specialisation we have mentioned. On the other hand, it is not hard to see how it might be criticised for compromising the counter-cultural vision of inclusiveness promoted in the Gospels and epistles, for too readily conflating the social structures of the church with the divisions of a sinful world, and for ignoring the enmities and injustices which often accompany those divisions.

In 1977, the Lausanne Committee on World Evangelization sponsored a special conference on the HUP at Pasadena, California, to consider these and other pros and cons. Supporters and opponents of the Principle each presented papers. In doing so, they did manage to find some common ground, not least in relation to the contingent nature of the principle as compared with God's ultimate purpose for the church. Thus, one of the conclusions of the report produced from the conference read as follows:

> All of us are agreed that in many situations a homogeneous unit church can be a legitimate and authentic church. Yet we are also agreed that it can never be complete in itself. Indeed, if it remains in isolation, it cannot reflect the universality and diversity of the Body of Christ. Nor can it grow into maturity. Therefore, every [homogeneous unit] church must take active steps to broaden its fellowship in order to demonstrate visibly the unity and variety of Christ's church. This will mean forging with each other and different churches creative relationships which express the reality of Christian love, brotherhood, and interdependence.[13]

On the positive side, the Pasadena report conceded to the Fuller group the point that the New Testament church included relatively monocultural congregations alongside more diverse ones: 'It seems probable', the text ran, 'that, although there were mixed Jewish-Gentile congregations, there were also homogeneous Jewish congregations (who still observed Jewish customs) and homogeneous Gentile congregations (who observed no Jewish customs).'[14] These points are clearly corroborated in contemporary research on Christian origins presented by James Dunn, Christopher Rowland, Tom Wright, Derek Tidball and others.[15] In the same vein, the participants were agreed that although Christ's death on the cross had abolished enmity between races and peoples (Eph. 2:15), 'this did not mean that Jews ceased to be Jews, or Gentiles to be Gentiles'.[16] Furthermore, even when viewed in its *eschatological* dimension, the church as described in the New Testament would, the Pasadena report averred, remain a community in which 'the nations' and national identity would be distinguishable (Rev. 21:26; 22:2).[17] Yet despite these concessions, the critics of the HUP model were insistent that while cultural distinctions were not always bad in themselves, they were prone to sinful distortion and exploitation – not least in respect of racism. As such, they insisted that the HUP must always be subject to self-appraisal and, where necessary, to modification and qualification.

> To acknowledge the fact of homogeneous units is not to acquiesce in the characteristics they possess which are displeasing to Christ. The Christian attitude to homogeneous units is often called the 'realist attitude', because it realistically accepts that homogeneous units exist and will always exist. We would prefer, however, to call this an attitude of 'dynamic realism' because we wish also to affirm that homogeneous units can change and must always change. For Christ the Lord gives to his people new standards. They also receive a new homogeneity which transcends all others, for now they find their essential unity in Christ, rather than in culture.[18]

This tension between 'acquiescence' to a temporal, heterogeneous culture and obedience to the radically inclusive call of Christ goes to the very heart of debate about the church's proper form (ecclesiology) and evangelistic task (missiology). It reflects the tension which lay at the centre of Paul's ministry – the tension between striving to be 'all things to all people' and resisting conformity to the world's 'mould' (1 Cor. 9:20–22; cf. Rom. 12:2). For the church in the postmodern West, this tension becomes especially acute as it relates to the issue of generations.

Throughout our study, we have seen how postmodernity has characteristically refracted society into complex generational groups – groups defined not only demographically as 'cohorts', but also culturally, as discrete subcultures or 'social generational units', delineated by everything from dress codes, musical preferences, sexual behaviour and drug use, to worldview and political allegiance. So while, say, members of 'Generation X' may have been born between 1964 and 1982, as defined by Douglas Coupland's novel of the same name they also typically 'blank out' absolute meanings and values in favour of privatised moralities and contingent rather than grand narratives. So, again, the present 'Chemical Generation' may describe a whole class of 'twenty-somethings', but clearly also indicates a whole *modus vivendi*, defined not only by recreational drug-use but by club culture, consumerism and relative hedonism.

Such examples confirm that when defined in anything other than strictly biological terms, generational distinctions do not come 'value-free'. What is more, they underline that the values implicit within such distinctions may at certain points *diverge* from the values of the Gospel. When such divergence occurs, it is clearly inadvisable for the church simply to accept prevailing generational taxonomies, and to order its life and mission in accordance with them. Rather, it must approach them with discernment, and may even have to reject them as inimical to its own understanding. Thus in regard to generational categorisation, no less than in regard to other 'man-made' structures and perceptions, the church may at times find that it has to be 'counter-cultural' rather than culturally accommodating. As the critics of HUP at Pasadena pointed out, 'in some groups, the common trait of homogeneity which binds them together [may] itself be evil'. And although they cite more obvious and drastic instances such as cannibalism, crime, prostitution and avarice, it is at least important to be aware that ungodliness may also inhere in certain generational self-definitions and traits. In this sense, the warning sounded by another critic of HUP who was *not* at Pasadena – William Abraham – is pertinent:

> the legitimate attempt to respond to the particularity and integrity of cultural diversity becomes, through the use of the homogeneous unit principle, a subtle way of ignoring the radical demands of the gospel with regard to repentance from social and corporate sin; it is also a means of riding roughshod over the

radically inclusive character of the people of God. The way in which church growth theorists introduce and discuss the matter, given the history and continued prevalence of racism in America, is astonishing. They seem to have no sense of how the advocacy of such a principle will almost inevitably be used to keep the social status quo in place, and they make no attempt to explore and explicate other options, which is necessary if the deep problems related to racism and cultural diversity are to be resolved.[19]

Granted, the 'generation gap problem', and the ageism which it can mediate, might not always appear as grave as racism. Yet it still clearly has the potential to divide society in a manner quite incompatible with the demands of Christ, and it would surely be wrong to invoke the HUP if it played down this threat in the way Abraham suggests it might play down the threat of racial prejudice. Indeed, this connection has been made quite explicitly by Mark Ashton and Phil Moon. Reflecting that if Paul were writing Galatians 3:28 today he might add 'youth and age' to his list of distinctions erased in Christ, they advise that 'where a generation barrier appears in congregational life it must be resisted as stoutly as racism or snobbery. The idea of 'youth churches' as a permanent expression of the Christian community's life is highly questionable. Moreover, say Ashton and Moon, 'If we abandon the vision of a church without age barriers, we are discarding a part of the gospel, just as much as if we accepted there should be different churches for different classes, races or skin colours.'[20]

Of course, not all those responsible for 'youth services', or for other intentionally segmented generational church activities, are blind to these problems. In general terms, David Wells is probably right to link the pragmatism of the HUP and the Fuller church growth theorists with the decline in the confessional and theological character of evangelicalism in the 1970s – and there is no doubt that the prioritising of results, numerical growth and short-term 'success' can hamper pursuit of that intergenerational unity which must surely remain the greater goal of the church.[21] Yet Paul's readiness to deploy 'all possible means' to reach the unsaved could be seen as a pragmatic statement which is *at the same time* deeply theological – an exposition, no less, of the Great Commission of Christ (1 Cor. 9:22; cf. Mt. 28:16–20). Indeed, to assume that evangelistic activism, church planting and culturally-engaged witness are somehow 'non-theological' is to suggest a false dichotomy between missiology and theology, as if God were not an intrinsically missional God and the church were not an intrinsically missional church. Or as Graham Cary expresses it: 'the question of unity should never be used to prevent evangelistic initiatives. Rather evangelistic initiatives create a new situation where unity has to be worked out on the ground. At this point missiology takes priority over ecclesiology because the gospel creates the church!'[22]

Moreover, to suggest that contingent, mono-generational tactics cannot form part of a broader multi-generational mission strategy is to risk underplaying the sheer urgency of the evangelistic imperative as it is conveyed in Scripture. To their credit, the delegates at Pasadena realised this well enough:

> In our commitment to evangelism, we all understand the reasons why homogeneous unit churches usually grow faster than heterogeneous or multicultural ones. Some of us, however, do not agree that the rapidity with which churches grow is the only or even always the most important Christian priority. We know that an alien culture is a barrier to faith. But we also know that segregation and strife in the church are barriers to faith. If, then, we have to choose between apparent acquiescence in segregation for the sake of numerical growth and the struggle for reconciliation at the expense of numerical growth, we find ourselves in a dilemma … We recognize that both positions can be defended in terms of obedience – obedience to Christ's commission to evangelize on the one hand, and obedience to live in love and justice on the other. The synthesis between these two still eludes us, although

> we accept our Lord's own words that it is through the brotherly
> love and unity of Christians that the world will come to believe
> him (Jn. 13:35; 17:21, 23).[23]

Clearly, then, while intentional generation-based ministries may
have a role, that role must be seen as at most provisional, and at
best subservient to the essential life of the church – a life which
should be as 'all-age' as possible. In this respect, it is significant that
Peter Wagner has more recently defended the HUP against its
detractors by underlining that it is a '*penultimate* spiritual dynamic'
which should never be thought of as denying the *ultimate*
imperative that 'believers are all one in the body of Christ, and
[that] the more this is manifested in a tangible way, the better'.[24]
Youth congregations, for instance, can hardly expect to assimilate
young people into wider Christian community when they reach
maturity, if they keep them separate from it until that point.
Young people need to experience, benefit from and contribute
to intergenerational groups throughout their development. As
Ashton and Moon observe, 'We cannot treat "youth work" as a
neatly self-contained unit which, with the right resourcing and
servicing, will deliver mature Christian disciples into the adult
congregation of the church on their twentieth birthdays.'[25] In this
regard, Cray's model of a 'partner' youth congregation, linked
organically to a less age-specific church but free to explore new
modes of mission, has a good deal to commend it.

There is, perhaps, an important lesson to be learnt here from
the secular youth work experience. In chapter 3 we mentioned
the Albemarle Report on Youth Work (1959), and recalled its
impact on the shape of Christian youth work, and evangelical
youth in particular, through the ensuing decade. According to
Bob Mayo, however, 'The Albemarle Report left the Youth
Service well intentioned, well financed, but flawed.' One of the
main faults highlighted by Mayo was the fact that the model
commended by Albemarle ultimately 'dealt with young people
in isolation from the rest of the community'.[26] Indeed, within

ten years of the Albemarle Report's publication, thinking on youth work was reacting vigorously against this segregationist approach. As Mayo recalls it, the realisation dawned that 'in making [it] the raison d'être of the Youth Service to deal with disadvantaged young people within the community, the Service ends up enshrining those very differences it was intended to challenge.'[27] These lessons from the secular sphere serve as warnings that 'separatist' solutions to the problems of intergenerational tension within churches may actually result in exacerbating these tensions and ensuring the same problems endure for the future. Although well intentioned, they may inadvertently reinforce the 'generation gap problem'.

In their book *The Family: A Christian Perspective on the Contemporary Home*, Jack and Judith Balswick state that 'God's ideal is that children mature to the point where they and their parents empower each other'.[28] This mutual empowerment must be actively sought in the church as well as the home. John and Olive Drane note that 'A major reason why younger people find relationships difficult is that they have no models to give direction.' They go on to suggest that the only way we will break out of this self-perpetuating cycle of defeat and despair is if we can 'find living examples of people of different dispositions and outlooks being together in harmony, working through their differences in a spirit of mutual respect and humility. The single most valuable thing the church can do for families today is to model life in that sort of community.'[29] And nowhere is this modelling more critically needed than in the arena of worship.

Generations, Church and Worship

True worship is a profoundly unselfish activity. John Drane describes it appropriately as 'all that we are, responding to all that God is'.[30] As such, there is little room within it for self-indulgence or self-absorption. No doubt, as we have said, youth services and youth congregations may perform a positive missionary function, and may help to renew the life of the mainstream church by concentrating the enthusiasm and creativity of the young on new forms of music, liturgy, communication and outreach. Yet if such services are allowed too easily to substitute for multigenerational worship rather than complementing it, the question might well be asked, 'If we can't worship together, what *can* we do together?'

Likewise, given that the gospel has healed the rift between God and humanity, it might be asked what power resides in a church which proclaims that gospel while failing to overcome differences of musical taste and worship 'style'. As Dave Baxter remarks:

> We can become consumeristic about our church services to the point that we come to church choosing which of the three types of service we want. The danger is that we become selfish in our approach to worship and seek out what we want rather than what God wants ... [that] we spend our time trying to please the "consumer" rather than building something reflecting God's heart for "church".[31]

It is apt to recall in this respect the point made at the outset of this report and developed through it – that the increasing refinement of generational distinctions in the West since the 1950s has owed much to the expansion and segmentation of consumer capitalism, and that far from being 'essential' to either church or human existence, they have been constructed largely according to market criteria.

These considerations can be applied similarly to the so-called 'alternative worship movement' – a diverse network of groups and congregations seeking to apply their liturgical and devotional life more appropriately to the postmodern context.[32] In some cases, communities associated with this movement have operated in close conjunction with an existing 'mainstream' congregation, often within the evangelical tradition; in others, they have either broken away and become autonomous, or else have been set up from scratch.[33] As articulated by Michael Riddell, the 'alternativeness' of these communities is most often derived not from a desire to be different for difference's sake, but from a conviction that much of the mainstream church has *itself* become monocultural – wedded to assumptions, forms and practices shaped by modernity, and seemingly unable or unwilling to adapt to the postmodern situation:

> The Western church suffers [from] worship [that] is often routine and cerebral, even in the charismatic churches. Truth tends to be presented as propositional, and fixed immutably by the canon of Scripture. Personal growth seems actively discouraged in some traditions, especially if it conflicts with the teaching of the church. Most damning of all, Christians are regarded as dull people who are lacking in spiritual depth.[34]

In response to all this, alternative worship typically places greater emphasis on non-verbal forms – on images, ambient music, lighting effects, dance and silent meditation – and uses contemporary televisual and computer technology to evoke appropriate atmospheres. Propositionalistic preaching is generally eschewed in favour of narrative, poetry and dialogue, and the setting is often relatively informal, with participants sitting on the floor, or at tables arranged in a 'café'-style layout.[35]

Predictably, such self-conscious distinctions from the majority church community have made the alternative worship movement vulnerable to the same accusations of niche-ministry, elitism and generationism which have been levelled at 'youth churches' and 'youth services'. In this respect, it is salutary to note the response of one the movement's most prominent apologists, Maggi Dawn.[36] In reviewing a TV series on alternative worship communities, Dawn concludes that out of six groups surveyed, only two could be described as truly alternative, 'if by that we mean engaging at depth with cultural change'. Indeed, whereas the other four were essentially standard evangelical youth services, led by adult men from the front even while being dressed up with contemporary Celtic fringe and hip hop music rather than chorus singing, and with 'trendy clothes and jargon', and whereas they duly attracted a 'sector' youth audience, the two meetings in question were quite different. They were, notes Dawn, much less authoritarian, and allowed more time and space for silent prayer, symbolism, and communal action. More significant from our point of view, however, are Dawn's observations on their demographic profile: 'the more truly 'alternative' services', she writes, 'drew widely mixed congregations – from old to very young; fashionable and not. So this is not a phenomenon dreamed up to keep the young people happy.'[37]

No doubt, much 'alternative worship' still functions as a 'Generation X' enclave, or as a pragmatic extension of youth evangelism – but Dawn is suggesting here that to survive authentically, and to enrich the church as fully as possible, it ought typically to be aiming for an ethos of generational diversity. Granted, as Graham Cray suggests, the time it takes to achieve such diversity may vary significantly from one context to another, and in any case so-called mainstream, multigenerational churches may have at least as much to reach out to alternative and youth church communities as those communities have to reintegrate with the mainstream.

To sum up, there is an analogy which might be useful in charting a way forward for various forms of generationally-specific ministry – the analogy between agrarian 'monoculture' and 'mixed' farming. The monocultural approach can undoubtedly serve a useful purpose in the shorter term, and may produce many good harvests. Eventually, however, it is likely to prove unsustainable, and to result in an increasingly barren habitat if not combined with more diverse approaches.

Similarly, in church terms, this report has acknowledged the reality of increasing generational stratification within contemporary Western culture, and has recognised the church's warrant to order in its own life, work and mission in such a way as to take due account of such stratification. In doing so, however, we have also emphasised that such pragmatic accommodation is likely to be subject to the law of diminishing returns. Segmenting congregational life, mission and evangelism along generational lines may be necessary as a 'penultimate' tactic, but it should not be forgotten that the ultimate mandate and destiny of the church is to serve as a foretaste of that heavenly communion in which believers of all tribes, tongues, nations – and ages – will participate together, as the one redeemed community of the one true Lord and Saviour, Jesus Christ.

Conclusions and Recommendations

1. Although generational definitions and distinctions feature widely in Western Christian discourse today, they have been too little related to what the Bible has to say about generations.

2. Considerably more attention needs to be given to the biblical witness on generational differences and intergenerational relationships if current generation-specific mission and church-growth strategies are to have sound theological and hermeneutical foundations.

3. The current lack of biblical and theological reflection on generational issues needs especially to be addressed by evangelicals, because evangelicals have been at the forefront of modern generationally-based mission and church-growth practice, and are distinguished by their high view of biblical authority.

4. 'Generation' in Scripture is a complex concept which has a range of biological, sociological, ethical and ideological dimensions. Christians should therefore beware of too simplistic an interpretation of what generations are, and of how they might bear on gospel witness and outreach in the 21st century.

5. 'Generation' is understood as a similarly complex concept across more general academic disciplines today. A responsible Christian hermeneutics of generations needs to take due account of this complexity.

6. There are suggestive general parallels between the biblical discourse of generations and the various understandings of generations which appear in modern-day scholarship. In particular, both biblical and current scholarly perspectives can be seen to encompass nine basic facets of generational identity, defined according to distinctive criteria:

Genealogical	kinship
Natal	birth year
Periodical	time-span lived through
Epochal	dominant ethos of 'spirit' of the age lived through
Eventual	key historical events
Attitudinal	defining spiritual, philosophical or ideological orientation
Effectual	dominant spiritual, emotional or psychological experience
Actival	dominant activity or behaviour
Functional	social, cultural and institutional significance

More simply, these facets may be reduced to a 'quadrilateral' of kinship, age, social events and worldview. Sometimes, such facets are reduced even further, to a duality between 'generation' as an expression of kinship and genealogy, and 'cohort' as a description of population groups defined by age, events or worldview, or by some combination of the three.

7. While more general parallels can be drawn, it should not be supposed that all specific references to 'generation' in

Scripture can be transferred directly to current contexts and settings. Indeed, within Scripture, as well as beyond it, 'generation' often occurs as a culturally relative term. This point needs to be borne in mind by Christians when using it today in their preaching, teaching, evangelism and social outreach.

8. Just as 'generation' may not have meant the same thing in an ancient Near Eastern situation as it means today, so also, as we have seen, its modern interpretation is frequently different in Third World and developing cultures as compared with the post-industrial West.

9. In order to deal with the complexities mentioned in 7 and 8, Christians focussed on generational issues need, in addition to good biblical exegesis, to formulate a dynamic theology of culture. As far as Western Christianity is concerned, the most relevant focus of such a theology will be on popular culture, since it is within the development of popular culture in America and Europe since the Second World War that the roots of our present generational consciousness, and the increasing generational segmentation that goes with it, are most clearly to be found.

10. Christians should be particularly aware that the sharpening of generational distinctions in the West over the past half-century owes a good deal to the development of specific 'target markets' by advertisers and other opinion-formers. While no less 'real' for this, such distinctions ought thereby to be subject to proper biblical and theological critique.

11. Published Christian work on generation-specific ministry and mission, and evangelical work on the subject in particular, has become overly dependent on the 'Generational Cycle' hypothesised by the popular demographers Neil Howe and William Strauss. While undoubtedly detailed and in many ways impressive and useful, the Howe-Strauss model is not theologically based, and besides that is over-

programmatic, very specific to the United States, too broad in its generalisations and too prone to function as a 'self-fulfilling prophecy' when extrapolated into the future. It also tends to downplay intra-generational sub-divisions and other social variables like class, income, education, race, ethnicity and gender.

12. Despite the consumerist sub-text of much contemporary generational segmentation, the coining of the term 'genera-tion gap' in the mid-late 1960s did indicate a more profound philosophical, ideological and spiritual delineation of 'youth culture' from the culture associated with older generations. To a large degree, this distinction has persisted down to the present, and is reflected in the now familiar division of society into different generational groups, each having been named as they entered early adulthood – specifically, Boomers, Xers and Millennials.

13. Although all age-defined generations merit serious study, social scientists are largely agreed that is it 'youth' and 'rising adult' generations (aged from around 18–43) which most prominently function as agents of change or 'lead cohorts' in Western society.

14. Since even before the 1960s, evangelicals have been espe-cially active within youth ministry and mission. Indeed, work and witness among young people has plausibly been called evangelicals' 'Great Project'. No doubt empirical research bears out the importance of youth generations in the developments of Western society. No doubt, also, statistics on conversion confirm that most people become Christians during youth and early adulthood. This does not mean, however, that mission priorities should be driven purely by numerical or pragmatic imperatives. While cherishing and developing our essential focus on younger generations, Western evangelicals need to be aware of the

dangers of ageism in what is, after all, an increasingly aged society. The Gospel calls us, as the community of Christ's people, to transcend divisions of generation, as well as of gender, class, status, race and culture (Acts 2:5–11; Gal 3:28; Eph. 2:11–22).

15. God has instituted various means of effecting intergenerational co-operation and transition within and alongside the church:

   (i)   The family is a fundamental, divinely–ordained element in human society, and is intended by God to function as a microcosm of the church. At its best, it will be the key training ground of cross-generational understanding and respect.

   (ii) As various parables of Christ demonstrate, forward planning is desirable for God's people (Mt. 7:24–27; Mark 4:30–32; Luke 16:1–12). Effective practice of it in churches and Christian organisations ought normally to include consideration of how leadership will pass from one generation to the next, and appropriate preparation and training for such transition.

   (iii) Cross-generational mentoring is a biblical practice which is enjoying a welcome rediscovery and revival in churches today. While commending it in general terms, we would encourage ongoing theological and empirical assessment of it, so that refinement and modification can be made as appropriate.

16. Despite its advocacy of intergenerational unity, the Word of God in Scripture nonetheless recognises certain distinctive functions and characteristics of childhood, youth and elderhood within the church and the wider world. While not rigid, and while ultimately subservient to faith, anointing and obedience, these functions and characteristics are viewed both as a feature of God's providence and as constitutive of ordered society (Pss. 92:12–14; 128:5–6; Is. 65:20; 2

Cor 4:16; Prov. 1:4; Zec. 9:16–17; 1 Tim. 3:1–12; cf. Is. 3:4–5; Joel 2:28; 1 Tim. 5:1–3).

17. While eschewing ungodly age-prejudice, British churches in particular simply cannot afford to ignore the alarming decline in the proportion of younger people engaged in their life and activities since the 1950s. This decline is in turn related to the serious *overall* drop in church participation through the same period. If we fail to reach younger generations, and to engage the culture or cultures associated with them, the future of the church will be bleak indeed.

18. While basically agreed on the need to reach younger generations with the Gospel, British Christians in general, and British evangelicals in particular, have diverged on the methods to be deployed in achieving this task. Some have argued that overt separation of young people into intentionally distinct youth clubs, Sunday schools, prayer meetings, worship groups and 'youth churches' is ecclesiologically unwarranted, and that every effort should be made, here and now, to model the Bible's ultimate vision of all ages serving and worshipping God together, along with all tribes, tongues and nations (Acts 2:39; cf. Rev. 5:9; 14:6).

Others have taken a more pragmatic view, and have contended that the increasing generational consciousness and stratification of postmodern culture makes such 'age-targeted' strategies necessary. Just as Paul was willing to become 'all things to all people', and to tailor his approach to specific cultural settings (1 Cor. 9:20–22, Acts 17:16–34), most who have adopted this approach have reflected the Homogeneous Unit Principle (HUP) formulated by various missiologists and church growth theorists at Fuller Seminary, California, in the 1970s. Based on the observation that converts to Christianity typically prefer to remain within their own social grouping or 'set', the HUP is readily applied to generation-specific outreach, as much as to class, ethnic and language-specific ministries. It has been criticised, however, on the grounds that it reinforces the very social divisions which are supposed to be overcome in Christ, and in doing so encourages a socio-political conservatism which belies the radical, counter-cultural edge of the Gospel.

19. While recognising these concerns, we note that in response to criticism, proponents of the HUP have more recently emphasised its provisional, 'penultimate' character, and have acknowledged its limited function as a means to an end, rather than an end in itself. We believe that the end in question must remain that of a holistic integration of generational groups within the Christian community. We also believe that this end ought to be worked for diligently within the contemporary church, rather than being complacently deferred to the return of Christ.

20. Having said this, we affirm that intentional, distinct 'youth congregations' may in some contexts offer the best hope of introducing young people to the Gospel, and, in time, to a wider, multi-generational experience of church life. Ideally, we would expect such youth congregations to be linked with more demographically diverse churches – partly for reasons of accountability, but also so that their members have somewhere to move on to as they themselves grow older.

21. We acknowledge that certain churches may *formally* and *theologically* repudiate generational segmentation while *in fact* maintaining negative generational distinctions and hierarchies in their programmes and structures – e.g. by mounting services which actually cater, linguistically, musically and culturally, for one age group only; by barring younger adults from leadership and decision-making processes; by treating youth work as a mere adjunct to the main business of the congregation, and by mistreating youth workers accordingly; by failing to train and mentor young

people for ministry; by ignoring the need for adequate crèche facilities; by undervaluing the prayer and listening ministry of the housebound elderly; by neglecting to provide disabled toilets as used mainly by the aged, and so on. However it is manifested, such inconsistency should be avoided and challenged.

22. Beyond the context of the local church, we recognise and affirm evangelicalism's achievements in various generation-specific para-church ministries, from beach missions and children's homes, through youth evangelism and student work, to sheltered housing, pensioners' lunch clubs and a whole host of other 'targeted' initiatives. Clearly, it would be inappropriate to call for wholesale generational integration in such instances. Even so, we also commend para-church ministries committed to the promotion of intergenerational relationships and mutual generational understanding – e.g. parenting skills programmes, family counselling agencies, visitation schemes for the elderly, etc.

23. As so often in evangelical culture, generational concerns have been addressed through activist schemes and projects rather than by serious biblical and theological analysis. We trust that this report will play some part in bridging the gap between 'theory' and 'practice'. As such, we commend it, within and beyond the evangelical community, for study, discussion and constructive response.

Questions for Further Consideration

These questions are designed to be used individually, or in group discussion. As well as applying them to your own situation, please consider forwarding your responses to the Evangelical Alliance: we would be very glad to receive them.

1. How legitimate is it to 'import' non-theological definitions of generation into our mission and ministry strategies?

2. What degree of overlap do you perceive between biblical and current socio-cultural understandings of 'generation'?

3. What degree of discontinuity do you perceive between biblical and current socio-cultural understandings of 'generation'?

4. It could be said that the Western church did relatively well for centuries without our sophisticated contemporary models of generational segmentation, generational succession, mentoring etc., and that despite their proliferation now, the same church is declining badly. How would you respond to this?

5. What potential dangers does today's complex generational segmentation present to a) society, b) the church? What opportunities does it offer in each case?

6. How far do you perceive ageism to be a problem in a) society in general; b) the church as a whole?

7. How does ageism in the church today affect a) the elderly; b) the younger generation?

8. How, if at all, has your own church sought to overcome ageism a) towards the old; b) towards the young? How might it overcome ageism more effectively in future?

9. Is the Homogeneous Unit Principle a help or a hindrance to the church's life and witness?

10. To what extent do churches in the UK already operate 'unconsciously' as 'Homogeneous Units'? How far do they do so with respect to generational groups in particular?

11. In your view, which para-church organisations operate effective generation-specific ministries? Is generation-specific ministry best confined to the para-church sector?

12. What are the potential dangers of establishing 'intentional' youth congregations? What are the potential advantages?

13. What, if at all, are the key biblical bases for intentional youth congregations?

14. If we promote 'intentional' youth congregations, why not intentional middle-aged churches or old-age churches?

15. To what extent are youth-targeted congregations and ministries expedient and pragmatic, and to what extent might they be a sign of God's coming kingdom?

16. What elements might be essential for effective 'all-age' worship?

17. How can the Evangelical Alliance help to promote better intergenerational relationships a) in the church; b) in society at large?

18. How can your church help to promote better inter-generational relationships a) within the life of its own congregation; b) in society at large?

19. To what extent has your congregation planned ahead for intergenerational leadership succession? What more might it do to ensure that this proceeds effectively?

20. Will generational distinctions be dissolved in heaven, or will they remain, but cease to cause tension? Try to offer biblical grounds for your answer.

21. What key points would you make if you had to talk for 15 minutes to a mixed Christian group on the subject of generations today?

Working Group Biographies

Matt Bird (co-editor) is the founding Director of Joshua Generation, a charity investing in emerging generations of leaders to transform society. He undertakes leadership development mentoring and training across Europe and is author of *Destiny* (2000) and *Manifesto for Life* (2001). He also works as an Organisational Development Consultant to Evangelical Alliance, CARE and other well-known charities. He has a BA in Theology, an MA in Evangelism and is at present studying for an MBA. He lives in West Wimbledon with his wife Esther and enjoys fine wine and socialising with friends.
mattbird@joshgen.org

David Hilborn (co-editor) is Theological Adviser to the Evangelical Alliance (UK); in this capacity, he co-ordinates the Alliance Commission on Unity and Truth among Evangelicals (ACUTE). He edited the ACUTE publications *Faith, Hope and Homosexuality* (1998), *The Nature of Hell* (2000) and *'Toronto' in Perspective* (2001) (all Paternoster Press). Together with Ian Randall, he authored *'One Body in Christ': The History and Significance of the Evangelical Alliance* (2001). He has also published *Picking Up the Pieces: Can Evangelicals Adapt to Contemporary Culture?* (Hodder & Stoughton, 1997). A graduate of Nottingham University (BA, PhD) and Mansfield College, Oxford (MA), he is an ordained Anglican minister and an Associate Research

Fellow of the London Bible College. He is married to Mia, a Hospital Chaplain. They have two children. He suffers chronically from 'vicarious nostalgia' for the 1960s.
dhilborn@eauk.org

Roger Hitchings is a pastor in a pioneering church in a South Nottingham village. He previously worked with older people for a leading national charity in Birmingham, and with people with sensory disabilities in Bristol. He regularly speaks and writes on issues of age and on trends in society.
rjhitchings@aol.com

Mark Knight teaches English Literature at the University of Surrey, Roehampton. He has a BA in English and History from the University of Hull, and a PhD in Literature and Theology from King's College London. He is a member of Raynes Park Community church and does some work for the Salvation Army Mission Team. He is married to Jo and enjoys good food, good coffee and bad films.
jomark@globalnet.co.uk

Amy Orr-Ewing took a First in Theology at Christ Church, Oxford and holds an MA in the History of Christianity from Kings College, London. She has been involved in leading evangelistic missions teams in China, Africa and Central Asia and now works as the Training Director at The Zacharias Trust. She is involved in speaking evangelistically in Universities and teaches apologetics in a variety of settings. She is a member of the executive board of the Evangelical Alliance, and also participates in the Alliance's theological commission, ACUTE. She is married to Frog, who is a curate at St Aldate's, Oxford.
Amy.OrrEwing@btinternet.com

Michael Penrose holds a BA in American Studies from Leicester University and an MA in Philosophy of Religion from

King's College, London. He has worked in the City of London and is currently taking a leadership training course with Ichthus Christian Fellowship, of which he is a member.
michaelpenrose@beeb.net

Steve Spriggs is Research Associate for Joshua Generation, a charity investing in emerging generations of leaders to transform society. He is currently undertaking a PhD at King's College London on leadership succession, which will develop further many of the areas explored in this book. His research has practical application for many organisations and congregations, and has led him to take on an increasing consultancy role. Steve enjoys playing basketball and other sports and lives in Coventry with his wonderful wife, Jenny.
stevespriggs@joshgen.org

Appendix: Generation X Lifestyle Survey

Introduction

The latest English Church Attendance Survey confirmed that those in their twenties and thirties are the least well represented group in the church today. Over the past few years, the Evangelical Alliance has emphasised the desperate need to develop resources which the church can use in reaching and discipling this generational group – a group which, as we have seen, has come most commonly to be called 'Generation X'.

To recap: Xers are those born between around 1964 and 1981. They are sometimes called 'Baby Busters' because, with the advent of the Pill in the early 1960s, this group's 'Baby Boomer' parents produced relatively fewer children than had *their* own Builder Generation parents. In fact, as we noted in chapter 9, the difference in the birth rate was not as great as is often supposed. Canadian writer Douglas Coupland's 1991 novel *Generation X* did much to define the *zeitgeist* of this set, although Coupland in fact borrowed his title from a 1964 paperback on the Mod movement by Charles Hamblett and Jane Deverson, via the seventies punk rock band fronted by Billy Idol.[1] Generation Xers have also been dubbed the 'Friends generation', after the hit TV sitcom which is perceived to represent many of their characteristics, especially as they are manifested in the American context.

God's love for humanity has been supremely manifested in Jesus Christ – the ultimate expression of contextualisation. If the church of the twenty-first century is to reach and disciple Generation X effectively, we must seek to contextualise the gospel of Jesus Christ for them.

With this imperative in mind, in early 2001 the Evangelical Alliance combined with Christian Action Research and Education (CARE), Kingsway publishers, Spring Harvest Conferences and the relief and development agency Tearfund to commission a Generation X Lifestyle Survey. Christian Research used a mix of questionnaires and focus groups, involving 515 Christian and 209 non-Christian young adults, in order to help us understand the distinctive culture, worldview and lifestyle of this generation.

The key findings of the survey are presented here. As we have stressed in the main body of our report, we would encourage every church in the UK to understand, identify and express the good news of Jesus Christ for *every* generational group. The Alliance's particular focus on Generation X at this time, however, reflects both the alarming disenfranchisement of Xers from the church, and the fact that they currently find themselves occupying the role of 'lead cohort' in wider society, and are therefore most likely to shape the form and direction of British society in the early decades of the new millennium.[2]

Community involvement

Christian GenXers appear to be more involved in community service (46%) than their non-Christian counterparts (17%). This is encouraging and affirms the main political parties' recent recognition of the valuable contribution that churches make in delivering community action.

> *Challenge: How can the church support and affirm Generation X in community involvement?*

Political involvement

81% of GenXers vote at general elections, 62% at local elections and 51% are able to name their local MP. Yet only 2% are involved in political organisations.

This may indicate that while GenXers are politically aware and involved, there is apathy towards, or they prefer not to work through, organised political institutions.

Campaigning

64% of GenXers would consider campaigning on an issue of justice. These include:

- world debt 20%
- human rights 20%
- social issues 16%
- environmental issues 9%
- 'whatever I feel strongly about' 9%
- abortion 6%
- children 6%
- animal rights 5%
- homosexual issues 5%
- Christian issues 4%

> *Challenge: How can evangelicalism rediscover its passion and commitment to engage with social issues? Abortion and homosexuality are important, but there are many other issues that Christians have a divine mandate to care about, pray for and act upon with conviction.*

Leisure activities

There is close proximity between Christian and non-Christian GenXers in terms of what leisure activities they enjoy...

- Going to pubs and restaurants: Christians 81%, non-Christians 91%
- Spending time with friends and family: Christians 83%, non-Christians 87%
- Going to cinema and theatre: Christians 82%, non-Christians 85%
- Taking part in health and fitness activities: Christians 46%, non-Christians 57%

(Participation in all these activities declines with age, which is probably due to having children.)

> *Challenge: How can the church make more use of pubs, friendship and cinema in reaching and discipling Generation X?*

Newspaper readership

Non-Christian GenXers take a newspaper twenty-nine days more than Christians, reading a newspaper 163 days a year as opposed to 134 days a year for Christians.

Christian and non-Christian GenXers read:

- free papers 32%
- regional/local papers 31%
- *The Times* 28%

Three times as many non-Christian GenXers read *The Sun* (18%) as Christians (6%), though the figure is low for both.

> *Challenge: How can Christian GenXers be encouraged to read newspapers more, in order to understand what is going on in society and the world around them? How can the church make more use of free and regional/local papers to reach and disciple Generation X?*

Music

Music is the language of Generation X, with 99% listening to music, including:

- pop 77%
- rock 43%
- classical 43%

Christians also listen to contemporary Christian music (45%) and praise and worship music (43%).

> *Challenge: How can the church make more use of music in reaching and discipling Generation X?*

Information Technology

This is a wired generation: 90% have a personal computer, and 96% of those have access to the Internet.

- 31% of men and 14% of women use the Internet more than once a day, for an average of 3.5 hours per week, or half an hour a day overall.
- 83% use the Internet for email, 82% to get general information, and 27% for shopping.

> *Challenge: How can the church make more use of personal computers and the Internet in reaching and discipling Generation X?*

Charitable giving

The average monthly giving to charitable causes amongst Generation X is £40: Christians give £51 (70% give to their church) and non-Christians £14.

- By and large, Christian GenXers give more to people abroad, while non-Christians give more to animal charities.

- 66% of Christian and 44% of non-Christian GenXers believe that rich countries should help poor countries.

> *Challenge: How can the church disciple Generation X in charitable giving, either on a tithe or abundance model? How can the church maximise interest in giving abroad?*

Consumerism

Christians are more likely to buy things because they represent value for money, are good quality or are on special offer (42%) while non-Christians tend to buy things simply because they like them (70%).

Holidays

95% of GenXers take at least one holiday abroad each year (60% use self-catering apartments).

> *Challenge: How can the church make more use of holidays abroad to reach and disciple Generation X? Should the church invest in ethical tourism?*

Values

51% of Christian and 25% of non-Christian GenXers say it is always wrong to tell lies.

How much does belief influence GenX behaviour?

- very much: Christian 60%, non-Christian 28%
- somewhat: Christian 30%, non-Christian 40%

Overall, GenXers say family and friends have the biggest influence on them.

Challenge: How can the church maximise family and friends in reaching and discipling Generation X?

Marriage

18% of Christian and 30% of non-Christian GenXers say being happily married is a priority for them. In relation to specific points, they believe:

- Marriage should be for life: Christian 97%, non-Christian 84%
- Marriage should be for as long as you love each other: Christian 32%, non-Christian 68%
- Separation is all right: Christian 22%, non-Christian 57%
- Divorce is all right: Christian 19%, non-Christian 55%
- Cohabitation before marriage is all right: Christian 33%, non-Christian 83%
- Cohabitation instead of marriage is all right: Christian 12%, non-Christian 59%

Challenge: How can the church prepare and encourage Generation X marriages to work for life? How far is the church willing to renegotiate the Western concept of marriage?

Personal satisfaction

GenXers are generally happy with life, but 73% would change some things if they could, while 20% wouldn't change anything. Only 7% are unhappy or very unhappy and would change their life if they could.

What GenXers would change:

- Finances: Christian 15%, non-Christian 29%
- Spirituality: Christian 18%, non-Christian 6%

> *Challenge: How can the church reach Generation X if they are generally happy with their lives? How can the church tap into their desire for spirituality?*

Spirituality

GenXers encounter God in:

- church meetings 52%
- non–church contexts, including their bedroom, other religious buildings, gigs and nightclubs 35%
- natural environments 13%

> *Challenge: How can the church offer Generation X ways to encounter God wherever they are?*

Church

79% of Christian GenXers attend church on forty-one occasions, or 79% of weeks per year.

In terms of feeling a sense of belonging to their church:

- 52% have a growing sense of belonging
- 25% feel the same sense of belonging as they did last year
- 10% have a sense of belonging but not as strongly as last year

> *Challenge: How can the church help Generation X feel they belong to a community, and develop 'communities of belonging' as a means of discipleship?*

Bible readership

Christian GenXers read their Bible:

- daily 35%
- weekly 31%

- at meetings 13%
- never 9%

On average, Christian GenXers read their Bible 152 days, or 42% of the days of the year.

> *Challenge: How can the church reach Generation X through using the stories of God's relationship with humanity, and relating the story of the Bible to their personal lives?*

The Future

Generation X have differing views on God's role in their lives:

- 'My future is in God's hands': Christian 46%, non-Christian 10%
- 'I have made plans and am putting them into action': Christian 30%, non-Christian 50%

> *Challenge: How can the church help Generation X to trust God for their life plans?*

Produced by Evangelical Alliance in partnership with: CARE, Kingsway, Tearfund, Spring Harvest and Christian Research

Bibliography

Abelove, Henry, *The Evangelist of Desire: Wesley and the Methodists* (California: Stanford University Press, 1990)

Abraham, William J., *The Logic of Evangelism* (London: Hodder & Stoughton, 1989)

Adam, Barbara, *Time and Social Theory* (Cambridge: Polity, 1990)

Age Concern, *The Debate of the Age* (London: Age Concern, 2000)

Alexander, Paul, *Boulevard of Broken Dreams: The Life, Times, and Legend of James Dean* (New York: Viking, 1994)

Annan, Noël Gilroy, *Our Age: The Generation that Made Post-War Britain* (London: Fontana, 1991)

Arminius, Jacobus, 'Declaration of the Sentiments of Arminius, Delivered Before the States of Holland', in *The Works of Jacobus Arminius* Vol. 1 (London Edition, 3 Vols.; trans. James Nichols and William Nichols; Missouri: Beacon Hill Press, 1986), p. 626

Ashford, Faith, *An Estimate of Caravaggio and His Influence on the Succeeding Generation in Italy* (MA dissertation; Courtauld Institute, 1936)

Ashton, Mark and Phil Moon, *Christian Youth Work* (rev'd. edn.; Eastbourne: Kingsway, 1995 [1986])

Ayling, Stanley, *John Wesley* (London: Collins, 1979)

Balswick, Jack O. and Judith K. Balswick, *The Family: a Christian Perspective on the Contemporary Home* (2nd edn.; Grand Rapids: Baker Book House, 1999)

Barker, Nicola (ed.), *Building a Relational Society* (London: Arena, 1996)

Barna, George, *Generation Next: What You Need to Know About Today's Youth* (Ventura: Regal Books, 1995)

——, *Baby Busters: The Disillusioned Generation* (Chicago: Northfield, 1994)

——, *Marketing the Church* (Colorado Springs: NavPress, 1988)

Barrett, David (ed.), *World Christian Encyclopedia* (Nairobi: Oxford University Press, 1982)

Bartholemew, Craig and Thorsten Moritz (eds.), *Christ and Consumerism: A Critical Analysis of the Spirit of the Age* (Carlisle: Paternoster Press, 2000)

Beasley-Murray, G.R., *Baptism in the New Testament* (Carlisle: Paternoster Press, 1972 [1962])

Beaudoin, Tom, *Virtual Faith: The Irreverent Spirituality of Generation X* (San Fransisco: Jossey-Bass, 1998)

Bebbington, David W., *Evangelicalism in Modern Britain: A History from the 1730s to the 1980s* (London: Unwin Hyman, 1989)

Biehl, Bob, *Mentoring: Confidence in Finding and Becoming One* (Nashville: Broadman and Holman, 1996)

Bird, Matt, 'Generation X Lifestyle Survey', in *idea* May 2001.

——, *Manifesto for Life* (London: Hodder & Stoughton, 2001)

Blocher, Henri, *In the Beginning: The Opening Chapters of Genesis* (Leicester: Inter-Varsity Press, 1984)

Bosch, David J., *Transforming Mission: Paradigm Shifts in the Theology of Mission* (New York: Orbis, 1991)

Bradshaw, Peter, 'Over the Moon: Review of 'ET – The Extra Terrestrial, 20th Anniversary Edition', in *Guardian Review*, 29 March 2002, p. 12

Brett, James R., 'The Generations of Americans', at www.csulb.edu/~wwwing/Silents/sgyears.html

——, 'The Silent Generation', at www.csulb.edu/~wwwing/Silents/sgjim.html

Brierley, Peter, *Religious Trends* (London: Christian Research, 2000)

——, *The Tide is Running Out: What the English Church Attendance Survey Reveals* (London: Christian Research, 2000)

Brierley, Peter and Wraight, Heather, *UK Christian Handbook: 1996/7 Edition* (London: Christian Research, 1995)

Brower, Stephen, Paul Gifford and Susan Rose (eds.), *Exporting the American Gospel: Global Christian Fundamentalism* (New York/London: Routledge, 1996)

Brown, Callum, *The Death of Christian Britain* (London: Routledge, 2001)

Brown, Colin, 'Generation', in Colin Brown, (ed.), *New International Dictionary of the New Testament* Vol. 2 (4 Vols.; rev'd. edn.; Carlisle: Paternoster Press, 1986), pp. 35–9

Bruner, Dale, *Matthew: A Commentary: Volume 1 – The Christbook, Matthew 1–12* (Dallas/London: Word, 1987)

Buchanan, Colin, *A Case for Infant Baptism* (Grove Booklet on Ministry and Worship, No. 20; Bramcote: Grove Books, 1973)

Buchanan, Patrick J., *The Death of the West: How Dying Populations and Immigrant Invasions Imperil our Country and Civilization* (New York: Thomas Dunne Books, 2002)

Buckeridge, John, 'Editorial', in *Youthwork*, July 2000, p. 1

Burton, Richard, 'Effective Ministry to Baby Busters' at www.epbd.edu/burt94.html

Butler, R.N., 'Ageism', in *The Encyclopedia of Aging* (New York: Springer, 1987), pp. 22–3

Calver, Clive & Rob Warner, *Together We Stand: Evangelical Convictions, Unity and Vision* (London: Hodder & Stoughton, 1996)

Calvin, John, *Institutes of the Christian Religion* (1559) (trans. Henry Beveridge; Grand Rapids: Eerdmans, 1989)

Carlton, Paul, *Death of the Woodstock Generation* (Bethesda: Van Cortlandt Books, 1994)

Carson, D.A., *Divine Sovereignty and Human Responsibility: Biblical Perspectives in Tension* (London: Marshall, Morgan & Scott, 1981)

Carvalho, George, 'Employee X: What Companies Need to Know About Recruiting, Motivating, Retaining and Promoting Generation X Workers', at www.rushmoreau.com

Celek, Tim and Dieter Zander, *Inside the Soul of New Generation* (Grand Rapids: Zondervan, 1996)

Chaney, Charles L., *The Birth of Missions in America* (Pasadena: William Carey Library, 1976)

Chowdhury, V., *Management 21C* (London: Financial Times, 2000)

Christian Publicity Organisation, *Faith in Life: A Snapshot of Church Life in England at the Beginning of the 21st Century* (London: CPO, 2001)

Clements, Keith W., *Lovers of Discord: Twentieth Century Theological Controversies in England* (London: SPCK, 1988)

Coates, Gerald (ed.), *Breaking the Mould* (Eastbourne: Kingsway, 1993)

Codrington, Graeme, 'Understanding Multi-Generational Ministry: Lessons from the Life of Joshua and the Age of Transition in South

Africa' (paper presented to the Fourth Conference on Youth Ministry, Mansfield College, Oxford, January 2001), at www.youth. co.za/minresource001.html

——, '25 Sentences that Define a Generation', at www.youth.co.za/ xpaper1010.html

——, 'Generation X: Who, What, Why and Where To?', at www. youth.co.za/genthesis/toc.html

Coleman, R.J., *Issues of Theological Conflict: Liberals and Evangelicals* (Grand Rapids: Eerdmans, 1972)

Collier, Jane, 'Contemporary Culture and the Role of Economics', in Hugh Montefiore (ed.), *The Gospel and Contemporary Culture* (London: Mowbray, 1992), pp. 103–28

Corsten, Michael, 'The Time of Generations', in *Time and Society* 8.2 (1999), 251–3

Côté, James A., *Adolescent Storm and Stress: A Evaluation of the Mead/ Freeman Controversy* (Hillsdale, NJ: Lawrence Erlbaum, 1994)

Côté, James A. and Anton L. Allahar, *Generation on Hold: Coming of Age in the Late Twentieth Century* (New York/London: New York University Press, 1996)

Coupland, Douglas, *Life After God* (London: Touchstone Books, 1994)

——, *Generation X* (London: Abacus, 1992 [originally published in the USA by St. Martin's Press, 1991])

Courtauld Institute of Art, *Five French Painters of the Second Generation of Post-Impressionism* (London: Roland, Browse & Delbraco, 1954)

Cray, Graham, *Youth Congregations and the Emerging Church* (Cambridge: Grove Books, 2002)

——, 'Postmodernism: Mutual Society in Crisis', in Nicola Barker (ed.), *Building a Relational Society* (London: Arena, 1996)

——, *From Here to Where? – The Culture of the Nineties* (Occasional Paper No. 3; London: Board of Mission, 1992)

Currie, R., Gilbert A. and Horsely, L., *Churches and Churchgoers: Patterns of Church Growth in the British Isles Since 1700* (Oxford, Oxford University Press, 1977)

Dalby, Mark, *Open Baptism* (London: SPCK, 1989)

Dawn, Maggi, 'You have to Change to Stay the Same', in *The Post-Evangelical Debate* (London: SPCK, 1997), pp. 35–56

DeVries, Mark, *Family-Based Youth Ministry: Reaching the Been-There, Done-That Generation* (Downers Grove: InterVarsity Press, 1994)

Dilthey, Wilhelm, 'Types of World-View and their Development in the Metaphysical Systems' (1911), in David Klemm (ed.), *Hermeneutical Enquiry* Vol. 2 (Atlanta: Scholars Press, 1986)

Diocese of Southwark, *The Chemical Generation: Understanding Young People and Drug Use: A Review of Issues and Options* (London: Southwark Diocesan Board for Church and Society/National Council for Social Concern, 1998)

Dolan, Marc, *Modern Lives: A Cultural Re-Reading of the 'Lost Generation'* (West Lafayette, Ind.: Purdue University Press, 1996)

Drane, John and Olive, *Happy Families* (London: HarperCollins, 1995)

Draper, Brian and Kevin Draper, *Refreshing Worship* (Oxford: Bible Reading Fellowship, 2001)

Dunn, James G.D., *Unity and Diversity in the New Testament* (London: SCM Press, 1977)

Dylan, Bob, *Lyrics, 1962–1985* (London: Jonathan Cape, 1985)

Edwards, David L., *Christian England* (London: Fount, 1989)

Edwards, Joel, 'The Evangelical Alliance: A National Phenomenon', in Steve Brady and Harold Rowdon (eds), *For Such a Time as This: Perspectives on Evangelicalism, Past, Present and Future* (Milton Keynes/London: Scripture Union/Evangelical Alliance, 1996)

Ellis, Joseph J., *Founding Brothers: The Revolutionary Generation* (London: Faber & Faber, 2002)

Ellis, Roger and Roger Mitchell, *Radical Church Planting* (Cambridge: Crossway, 1992)

Emmott, Bill and Clive Cook, *Globalisation* (London: Economist Books, 2002)

Engstrom, Ted and Rohrer, *The Fine Art of Mentoring* (Brentwood, TN: Wolgemuth and Hyatt, 1989)

Enroth, R.M., E.E. Ericson and C.B. Peters, *The Story of the Jesus People: A Factual Survey* (Exeter: Paternoster Press, 1972)

Erickson, Millard J., *A Basic Guide to Eschatology* (Grand Rapids: Baker Book House, 1998)

Erikson, Erik H., *Identity: Youth and Crisis* (New York: Newton, 1968)

Esler, P.F, (ed.), *Modelling Early Christianity: Social-Scientific Studies of the New Testament in its Context* (London: Routledge, 1995)

Estes, Daniel J., *Hear, My Son: Teaching and Learning in Proverbs 1–9* (Leicester: Apollos, 1997)

Evangelical Alliance, *Evangelical Alliance Commission on Strategic Evangelism* (Inaugural Report; London: Evangelical Alliance, 1998)

Feuer, Lewis S., *The Conflict of Generations: the Character and Significance of Student Movements* (New York, Basic Books, 1969)

Finch, J., *Family Obligations and Social Change* (Cambridge: Polity, 1989)

Ford, Kevin, *Jesus for a New Generation* (London: Hodder & Stoughton, 1996)

Franklin, Annie and Bob Franklin, 'Age and Power', in Tony Jeffs and Mark Smith (eds), *Young People: Inequality and Youth Work* (Basingstoke: MacMillan, 1990), pp. 1–27

Friedman, Milton and Rose Friedman, *Free to Choose: A Personal Statement* (London: Secker & Warburg, 1980)

Frith, Simon, *The Sociology of Youth* (Lancashire: Causeway, 1984)

Fulcher, James and John Scott, *Sociology* (Oxford: Oxford University Press, 1999)

Gadamer, Hans-Georg, *Truth and Method* (2nd rev'd edn; trans. Joel Weinsheimer and Donald G. Marshall; London: Sheed & Ward, 1989 [originally published as *Warheit und Methode. Grundzüge einer philosophischen Hermeneutik*. Mohr, Tübingen, 1965])

Gallatin, Judith, 'Political Thinking in Adolescence', in Joseph Adelson (ed.), *Handbook of Adolescent Psychology* (New York: Wiley, 1980), pp. 344–82

Gay, Craig M., *With Liberty and Justice for Whom? The Recent Evangelical Debate Over Capitalism* (Grand Rapids: Eerdmans, 1991)

Gergen, Kenneth, *An Invitation to Social Construction* (London: Sage Publications, 1999)

Gibbs, Eddie, *I Believe in Church Growth* (London: Hodder & Stoughton, 1981)

Gibbs, Eddie and Ian Coffey, *Church Next* (Leicester: Inter-Varsity Press, 2001)

Gilbert, Eugene, *Advertising and Marketing to Young People* (Scranton: Printer's Ink Publishing Company, Inc., 1957)

Goetzmann, J., '*Oikos*' in Colin Brown (ed.), *Dictionary of New Testament Theology* Vol. 2 (Carlisle: Paternoster Press, 1986), pp. 247–51

Gomes, Alan W., *Unmasking the Cults* (Carlisle: OM Publishing, 1995)

Gorg, Alan Kent, *The Sixties:Biographies of the Love Generation* (Marina Del Ray, CA.: Media Associates, 1995)

Goudzwaard, Bob, *Globalization and the Kingdom of God* (Grand Rapids: Baker Book House/Center for Public Justice, 2001)

Graham, Billy, *Just As I Am: The Autobiography of Billy Graham* (London: HarperCollins, 1997)

Green, Joel, Scott McKnight and I. Howard Marshall (eds), *Dictionary of Jesus and the Gospels* (Leicester: Inter-Varsity Press, 1992)

Green, Jonathon, *All Dressed Up: The Sixties and the Counterculture* (London: Pimlico, 1999)

Green, Jonathon, *Days in the Life* (London: Heinemann, 1988)

Green, Michael, *Evangelism Through the Local Church* (London: Hodder & Stoughton, 1990)

Green, V.H.H., *John Wesley* (London: Thomas Nelson and Sons, 1964)

Greenslade, S.L., *Schism in the Early Church* (London: SCM, 1953)

Grenz, Stanley, *Theology for the Community of God* (Carlisle: Paternoster Press, 1994)

Griffiths, Brian, 'Christianizing the Market', in John Atherton (ed.), *Social Christianity: A Reader* (London: SPCK, 1994), pp. 355–71

Grigsby, Jill S., 'Paths for Future Population Aging', in Julia Johnson and Robert Slater (eds), *Ageing and Later Life* (London: Sage/Open University, 1993), pp.344–51

Grudem, Wayne, *Systematic Theology: An Introduction to Biblical Doctrine* (Leicester: Inter-Varsity Press, 1994)

Guinness, Os, *The Dust of Death: A Critique of the Establishment and the Counter Culture – and a Proposal for a Third Way* (London: Inter-Varsity Press, 1973)

Gunton, Colin, 'God, Grace and Freedom', in C. Gunton, (ed.), *God and Freedom: Essays in Historical and Systematic Theology* (Edinburgh: T. & T. Clark, 1995).

Hahn, Todd and David Verhaagen, *Genxers After God* (Grand Rapids: Baker Book House, 1998)

Hall, G. Stanley, *Adolescence* (New York: Appleton, 1904)

Hamblett, Charles and Jane Deverson, *Generation X* (London: Tandem, 1964)

Hammersley, Richard, Furzana Khan and Jason Ditton (eds), *Ecstasy and the Rise of the Chemical Generation* (New York: Routledge, 2002)

Handy, Charles, *The Hungry Spirit: Beyond Capitalism – A Quest for Purpose in the Modern World* (London: Arrow, 1998)

Harvey, David, *The Condition of Postmodernity* (Oxford: Blackwell, 1990)

Hayes, Carlton, *A Generation of Materialism: 1871–1900* (New York: London: Harper Row, 1941)

Hebidge, Dick, 'Banalarama, or Can Pop Save Us All?', in *New Statesman and Society*, 9 December 1988.

Heitzenrater, Richard P., *Wesley and the People Called Methodists* (Nashville: Abingdon Press, 1995)

Helm, Paul, *The Providence of God* (Leicester: Inter-Varsity Press, 1993)

Henderson, Stewart, *Since the Beginning: Greenbelt* (London: Greenbelt, 1984)

Hesselgrave, David J., *Communicating Christ Cross-Culturally* (2nd edn; Grand Rapids: Zondervan, 1991)

——, *Planting Churches Cross-Culturally* (Grand Rapids: Baker Book House, 1980)

Hilborn, David (ed.), *'Toronto' in Perspective: Papers on the New Charismatic Wave of the Mid-1990s* (Carlisle: Paternoster Press, 2001)

——, *Picking Up the Pieces: Can Evangelicals Adapt to Contemporary Culture?* (London: Hodder & Stoughton, 1997)

HMSO, *Social Trends* (London: HMSO, 1996)

Hopkins, Bob and Tim Anderson (eds), *Planting New Churches* (Guildford: Eagle, 1992)

Horne, A.D., *The Wounded Generation: America After Vietnam* (Eaglewood Cliffs, NJ.: Prentice Hall Trade, 1981)

Horrobin, Peter, 'Claiming the Ground', Ellel Ministries Teaching Series (Cassette Tapes, 1990)

Horton, Douglas, *Congregationalism: A Study in Church Polity* (London: Independent Press, 1952)

Howe, Neil & William Strauss, *Millennials Rising: The Next Great Generation* (New York: Vintage, 2000)

——, *The Fourth Turning: An American Prophecy* (New York: Broadway Books, 1993)

——, *13th Gen: Abort, Retry, Ignore, Fail?* (New York: Vintage, 1993)

——, *Generations: The History of America's Future, 1584–2069* (New York: William Morrow/Quill, 1991 [credited to 'William Strauss and Neil Howe'])

Hutchinson, Roger, *High Sixties: The Summers of Riot and Love* (Edinburgh: Mainstream, 1992)

Hylson-Smith, Ken, 'Roots of Pan-Evangelicalism 1735–1835', in Steve Brady and Harold Rowdon (eds), *For Such a Time as This:*

Perspectives on Evangelicalism, Past, Present and Future (London/Milton Keynes, Evangelical Alliance/Scripture Union, 1996), pp. 137–47

Inhelder, Bärbel and Jean Piaget, *The Growth of Logical Thinking from Childhood to Adolescence* (New York: Basic Books, 1958)

Jackson, Bill, *The Quest for the Radical Middle* (USA: Vineyard International Publishing, n.d.)

Jasper, Tony, *Jesus and the Christian in a Pop Culture* (London: Robert Royce, 1984)

Johnson, Julia and Bill Bytheway, 'Ageism: Concept and Definition', in Julia Johnson and Robert Slater (eds), *Ageing and Later Life* (Open University/Sage: London, 1993), pp. 200–6

Johnson, Julia and Robert Slater (eds), *Ageing and Later Life* (London: Sage/Open University, 1993)

Johnstone, Patrick, *Operation World* (Carlisle: Operation Mobilisation, 1993)

Jones, Pennant, *What Parents Should Know About Generational Sin* (Tonbridge: Sovereign World, 1999)

Kaiser, Otto, *Isaiah 1–12* (London: SCM, 1972)

Kalache, Alex, 'Ageing in Developing Countries: Has It Got Anything to Do With Us?', in Julia Johnson and Robert Slater (eds), *Ageing and Later Life* (London: Sage/Open University, 1993), pp. 339–43

Kelly, Gerard, *Get a Grip on the Future: Without Losing Your Hold on the Past* (Monarch: London, 1999)

Kendrick, Graham, Gerald Coates, Roger Forster and Lynn Green, *March For Jesus* (Eastbourne: Kingsway Publications, 1992)

Kennedy, John F., 'The Torch Has Been Passed to a New Generation', in Brian McArthur (ed.), *The Penguin Book of Twentieth Century Speeches* (London: Penguin, 1993), p. 301

Klein, Alexander (ed.), *Natural Enemies? Youth and the Clash of Generations* (Philadelphia: Lippincott, 1969)

Kohn, Marek, *The Chemical Generation and Its Ancestors: Dance Crazes and Drug Panics Across Eight Decades*, available at www.drugtext.org/articles/97833.html

Kraft, Charles, *Christianity in Culture* (New York: Orbis, 1979)

Krallmann, Günter, *Mentoring for Mission: A Handbook on Leadership Principles Exemplified by Jesus Christ* (2nd edn; Hong Kong: Jensco, 1992)

Kuhrt, Gordon, *An Introduction to Christian Ministry: Following Your Vocation in the Church of England* (London: Church House Publishing, 2000)

Küng, Hans, *Christianity* (London: SCM Press, 1995)

Lacey, T.A., *Unity and Schism* (London: Mowbray, 1917)

Lambert, Frank. *'Pedlar in Divinity': George Whitefield and the Transatlantic Revivals, 1737–1770* (New Jersey: Princeton University Press, 1994)

Lane, Vann, *Children of Revival* (Shippensburg: Revival Press, 1998)

Leaming, Barbara, *Marilyn Monroe* (New York: Crown, 1998)

Lee, Robert A., *The Beat Generation Writers* (London: Pluto, 1995)

Leech, Kenneth, *Youthquake: Spirituality and the Growth of the Counter-Culture* (London: Abacus, 1973)

Leith, John H., *Introduction to the Reformed Tradition* (Atlanta: John Knox Press, 1981)

Lewis, Peter, 'Renewal, Recovery and Growth: 1966 Onwards', in Steve Brady and Harold Rowdon (eds), *For Such a Time as This: Perspectives on Evangelicalism, Past, Present and Future* (Milton Keynes/London: Scripture Union/Evangelical Alliance, 1996)

Long, Jimmy, *Generating Hope* (Downers Grove: InterVarsity Press, 1997)

Lyons, John, *Semantics* Vol. 1 (Cambridge: Cambridge University Press, 1977)

Lyotard, Jean-François, *The Postmodern Condition: A Report on Knowledge* (Manchester: Manchester University Press, 1979)

MacDonald, Ian, *Revolution in the Head: The Beatles' Records and the Sixties* (London: Fourth Estate, 1994)

MacPherson, Myra, *The Hurting Generation* (Indiana: Indiana University Press, 2002)

Mahedy, William and Janet Bernardi, *A Generation Alone: Xers Making a Place in the World* (Downers Grove: InterVarsity Press, 1994)

Makkreel, Rudolf A., 'Dilthey, Wilhelm', in Robert Audi (ed.), *The Cambridge Dictionary of Philosophy* (2nd edn; Cambridge: Cambridge University Press, 1999), pp. 235–6

Maltby, Richard (ed.), *Dreams for Sale: Popular Culture in the 20th Century* (London: Harrap, 1989)

Mannheim, Karl, 'The Problem of Generations', in Paul Kecskemeti (ed.), *Essays on the Sociology of Knowledge* (London: Routledge &

Kegan Paul, 1952 [first published in German in 1928 in *Kölne Vierjahreshaufte für Soziologie*, pp. 157–85, 309–30]), pp. 276–322

Marsh, Dave, *Before I Get Old: The Story of The Who* (London: Plexus, 1983)

Marsh, John, 'Time' in Richardson, Alan (ed.), *A Theological Word Book of the Bible* (London: SCM, 1950), pp. 258–9

Marshall, I. Howard, *The Gospel of Luke: A Commentary in the Greek Text* (Exeter: Paternoster Press, 1978)

Martin, Bernice, *A Sociology of Contemporary Cultural Change* (Oxford: Blackwell, 1981)

Marty, Martin, 'The Spirit's Holy Errand: The Search for a Style in Secular America', in *Daedalus* 96.1 (Winter, 1967), pp. 99–115

Marwick, Arthur, *The Sixties: Cultural Revolution in Britain, France, Italy and the United States, c. 1958 – c. 1974* (Oxford: Oxford University Press, 1998)

Maslow, Abraham, *The Farther Reaches of Human Nature* (New York: Viking Press, 1971)

——, *Motivation and Personality* (2nd edn; New York, Harper & Row, 1970)

Mayo, B. and D. Baxter, 'Is History Repeating Itself?', in *Youthwork*, October 1998

McAllister, Dawson, *Saving the Millennial Generation* (Eugene, Or.: Authentic Publishing, 1999)

McBain, Douglas, *Fire Over the Waters: Renewal Among the Baptists and Others from the 1960s to the 1990s* (London: Darton, Longman & Todd, 1997)

McGavran, Donald, *Understanding Church Growth* (Grand Rapids: Eerdmans, 1970)

McIntosh, Gary, *Three Generations* (Michigan: Flewing Revell, 1995)

Mead, Margaret, *Culture and Commitment* (New York: Natural History Press/Doubleday, 1970)

——, *Coming of Age in Samoa: A Psychological Study of Primitive Youth for Western Civilization* (New York: Morrow Quill Paperbacks, 1928)

Ministry of Education, *The Youth Service in England and Wales* (The Albermarle Report), Cmnd. 929 (1960)

Mitchell, T.C., 'Generation' in J.D. Douglas (ed.), *The Illustrated Bible Dictionary* Vol. 1 (Leicester: Inter-Varsity Press, 1980), p. 549

Moberg, David O., *The Church as a Social Institution* (2nd edn; Grand Rapids: Baker Book House, 1984)

Monk, Janice and Cindi Katz, 'When in the World are Women?', in Cindi Katz and Janice Monk (eds), *Full Circles: Geographies of Women Over the Life Course* (London: Routledge, 1993)

Montgomery, Jim, *DAWN 2000* (Crowborough, Highland, 1990)

Moxnes, Halvor (ed.), *Constructing Early Christian Families: Family as Social Reality and Metaphor* (New York: Routledge, 1997)

Moynagh, Michael, 'The Tailor-Made church?', in *Christian Herald*, 23 October 1999, p. 9

Moynagh, Michael and R. Worsley, *Tomorrow* (London: Lexicon, 2000)

Murray, D. Gow, *The Book of Ruth: Its Structure, Theme and Purpose* (Leicester: Appollos, 1992)

Murray, Iain D., *Martyn Lloyd-Jones: The Fight of Faith 1939–1981* (Edinburgh: Banner of Truth, 1990)

Nelson, R. and J. Cowan, *Revolution X: A Survival Guide for Our Generation* (New York, Penguin, 1994)

Noll, Mark, David W. Bebbington and George A. Rawlyk (eds), *Evangelicalism: Comparative Studies of Popular Protestantism in North America, the British Isles, and Beyond, 1700–1990* (New York/Oxford: Oxford University Press, 1994)

Oakes, Philip, *Tony Hancock* (London: Woburn Press, 1975)

Oates, S.B., *Let the Trumpet Sound: A Life of Martin Luther King Jr.* (New York: New American Library, 1985)

Osiek, Carolyn and David Balch, *Families in the New Testament World: Households and House Churches* (Louisville: Westminster John Knox Press, 1997)

Overton, J.H., *John Wesley* (London: Methuen & Co, 1891)

Palmer, F.H., 'Adoption', in J.D. Douglas (ed.), *The Illustrated Bible Dictionary* Part 1 (Leicester: Inter-Varsity Press, 1980), p. 17

Pannenberg, Wolfhart, *Systematic Theology – Volume 1* (trans. Geoffrey Bromiley, Edinburgh: T. &T. Clark, 1991 [1988])

Parker, Russ, *Healing Wounded History* (London: SPCK, 2001)

Pawson, David and Colin Buchanan, *Infant Baptism Under Cross-Examination* (Grove Booklet on Ministry and Worship, No. 24; Bramcote: Grove Books, 1976)

Pearsall, Judy and Trumble, Bill (eds), *The Oxford English Reference Dictionary* (2nd edn; New York: Oxford University Press, 1996)

Pilcher, Jane, *Age and Generation in Modern Britain* (Oxford: Oxford University Press, 1995)

Pilcher, Jane and Stephen Wagg, *Thatcher's Children? Politics, Childhood and Society in the 1980s and 1990s* (London/Washington DC: Falmer Press, 1996)

Pirie, Madsen and Robert M. Worcester, *The Millennial Generation* (London: Adam Smith Institute, 1998)

Pollock, John, *John Wesley* (Oxford: Lion Publishing, 1989)

——, *George Whitefield* (Oxford: Lion Publishing, 1986)

Postman, Neil, *Amusing Ourselves to Death* (Reading: Cox & Wyman, 1995)

Pott, David, 'The Drifting Generation', in *Crusade*, March 1967, pp.16–8, 27–8

Rabey, Steve, *In Search of Authentic Faith: How Emerging Generations are Transforming the Church* (Colorado Springs: Waterbrook Press, 2001)

Rack, Henry, *Reasonable Enthusiast: John Wesley and the Rise of Methodism* (London: Epworth Press, 1989)

Randall, Ian and David Hilborn, *One Body in Christ: The History and Significance of the Evangelical Alliance* (Carlisle: Paternoster Press, 2001)

Riddell, Michael, *Threshold of the Future: Reforming the Church in the Postmodern West* (London: SPCK, London, 1998)

Riddell, Mike, Mark Pierson and Cathy Kirkpatrick, *The Prodigal Project: Journey into the Emerging Church* (London: SPCK, 2000)

Rinaldi, Sue, *Trend: A Pattern of Life* (London: Hodder & Stoughton, 1999)

Robinson, John A.T., *Honest to God* (London: SCM Press, 1963)

Robinson, John A.T. and David L. Edwards, *The Honest to God Debate* (London: SCM Press, 1963)

Robinson, Martin, 'The Mission Church in Revival' in *Church Growth Digest: Year 21 Issue 2, Winter 1999/2000.*

——, *The Faith of the Unbeliever* (East Sussex: Monarch, 1994)

Rogerson, John, 'The Family and Structures of Grace in the Old Testament', in Stephen C. Barton (ed.), *The Family in Theological Perspective* (Edinburgh: T. &T. Clark, 1996), pp. 25–42

Roof, Wade Clark, *Spiritual Marketplace: Baby Boomers and the Remaking of American Religion* (Princeton, NJ: Prineton University Press, 1999)

——, *A Generation of Seekers: The Spiritual Journeys of the Baby Boom Generation* (London/New York: Hodder & Stoughton, 1993)

Roof, Wade Clark, Jackson Carroll and David A. Roozen (eds), *The Post-War Generation and Establishment Religion: Cross-Cultural Perspectives* (Boulder, CO: Westview Press, 1995)

Ross, Andrew, *No Respect: Intellectuals and Popular Culture* (London: Routledge, 1989)

Rushkoff, Douglas, 'Introduction: Us, By Us', in Douglas Rushkoff (ed.), *The GenX Reader* (New York: Ballantine Books, 1994), pp. 3–8

—— (ed.), *The GenX Reader* (New York: Ballantine Books, 1994)

Ryder, Norman B., 'The Cohort as a Concept in the Study of Social Change', in *American Sociological Review* 30 (Dec 1965), pp. 843–61

Sabin, Roger, 'Generation X' in Jonathan Buckley, Orla Duane, Mark Ellingham and Al Spicer, *Rock: The Rough Guide* (rev'd edn; London: Rough Guides, 1999), pp. 403–4

Sanders, J. Oswald, *Spiritual Leadership* (London: Lakeland/STL, 1981 [1967])

Savage, John, *England's Dreaming: The Sex Pistols and Punk Rock* (London: Faber, 2001)

Schaeffer, Francis, *The God Who Is There* (London: Hodder & Stoughton, 1968)

Schuman, Howard and Jaqueline Scott, 'Generations and Collective Memories', *American Sociological Review* 54.3 (June 1989), pp. 359–81

Schwarz, Charles, *Natural Church Development: A Practical Guide to a New Approach* (Moggerhanger: British Church Growth Association, 1996)

Scotland, Nigel, *Charismatics and the New Millennium* (2nd edn; Guildford: Eagle, 2000)

Sheppard, David, *Parson's Pitch* (London: Hodder & Stoughton, 1964)

Siegel, Roberta S. and Hoskin, Marilyn Brooks, 'Perspectives on Adult Political Socialization', in Stanley Allen Renshon (ed.), *Handbook of Adolescent Psychology* (New York: Free Press, 1977), pp. 259–93

Sine, Tom, *Mustard Seed Versus McWorld* (London: Monarch, 1999)

Sire, James, *The Universe Next Door* (2nd edn; Downers Grove: InterVarsity Press, 1988)

Speiser, E.A., *Genesis* (New York: Doubleday, 1969)

Springhall, John, *Coming of Age: Adolescence in Britain, 1860–1960* (Dublin: Gill & MacMillan, 1986)

Stanley, Brian, *The Bible and the Flag: Protestant Missions and British Imperialism in the Nineteenth and Twentieth Centuries* (Leicester: Apollos, 1990)

Stanley, Paul, *Connecting: The Mentoring Relationships You Need to Succeed in Life* (Colorado: NavPress, 1992)

Starkey, Mike, *God, Sex and Generation X: A Search for Lost Wonder* (London: Triangle, 1997)

Storey, John, 'Postmodernism and Popular Culture', in Stuart Sim (ed.), *The Routledge Companion to Postmodernism* (London: Routledge, 2001), pp. 147–57

——, *An Introduction to Cultural Theory and Popular Culture* (2nd edn; London: Prentice Hall, 1997 [1993])

Stott, John, *Issues Facing Christians Today* (London: Marshall Pickering, 1990)

—— (ed.), *The Pasadena Consultation: Homogeneous Unit* (Lausanne Occasional Papers No. 1; Wheaton: Lausanne Committee for World Evangelization, 1977)

Stout, Harry S., *The Divine Dramatist: George Whitefield and the Rise of Modern Evangelicalism* (Grand Rapids: Eerdmans, 1991)

Summerton, Neil, *A Noble Task: Eldership and Ministry in the Local Church* (Exeter: Paternoster Press, 1987)

Tapia, Andres, 'Reaching the First Post-Christian Generation', at users.vnet/rdavis/CTXer.html

Tapscott, Don, *Growing up Digital* (New York: McGraw-Hill, 1998)

Tasker, R.V.G., *James* (Leicester: Inter-Varsity Press, 1957)

Thiselton, Anthony C., *The Two Horizons: New Testament Hermeneutics and Philosophical Description with Special Reference to Heidegger, Bultmann, Gadamer and Wittgenstein* (Exeter: Paternoster Press, 1980)

Thwaites, James, *The Church Beyond the Congregation* (Carlisle: Paternoster Press, 1999)

Tidball, Derek, *The Social Context of the New Testament* (Carlisle: Paternoster Press, 1997 [1983])

US Bureau of the Census, *Ageing in the Third World* (International Population Reports, Series P. 95, No. 79; Washington DC: US Government Printing Office, 1987)

Verner, D.C., *The Household of God: The Social World of the Pastoral Epistles* (SBLDS 71; Chico: Scholar's Press, 1983)

Viall, Amanda, *Everybody Was So Young: Gerald and Sara Murphy, a Lost Generation Love Story* (New York: Broadway Books, 1999)

Von Balthasar, Hans Urs, *Theo-Drama — Vol. 1: Prolegomena* (trans. Graham Harrison; San Francisco: Ignatius Press, 1988 [1983])

Wagner, Peter, *Church Growth and the Whole Gospel: A Biblical Mandate* (Eugene: Wipf & Stock, 1998)

Walker, Andrew, *Restoring the Kingdom: The Radical Christianity of the House Church Movement* (rev'd edn; Guildford: Eagle, 1998)

Wall, Phil, *I'll Fight …: Holiness at War* (Tonbridge: Sovereign World, 1998)

Walsh, Brian J. and J. Richard Middleton, *The Transforming Vision: Shaping a Christian World View* (Downers Grove: InterVarsity Press, 1984)

Ward, Pete (ed.), *Mass Culture: Eucharist and Mission in a Post-Modern World* (Oxford: Bible Reading Fellowship, 1999)

——, *Growing Up Evangelical: Youthwork and the Making of a Subculture* (London: SPCK, 1996)

Warner, Rob, *21ˢᵗ Century Church* (London: Hodder & Stoughton, 1994)

Watson, Francis, *Text and Truth: Rethinking Biblical Theology* (Edinburgh: T. & T. Clark, 1997)

Watson, Owen, *Longman Modern English Dictionary* (London: Longman, 1968)

Watson, Steven, *The Birth of the Beat Generation: Visionaries, Rebels and Hipsters, 1944–1960* (New York: Pantheon Books, 1995)

Watts, Michael R., *The Dissenters: From the Reformation to the French Revolution* (Oxford: Clarendon Press, 1978)

Weiner, Paul, *Woodstock Census: The Nationwide Cultural Survey of the Sixties Generation* (New York: Viking, 1979)

Wells, David M., *God in the Wasteland: The Reality of Truth in a World of Fading Dreams* (Leicester: Inter-Varsity Press, 1990)

Wendel, François, *Calvin* (London: Fontana, 1965)

Wesley, John, *The Journal of The Rev. John Wesley* Vol. 1 (London: Robert Culley, 1909)

Whalen, Jack and Richard Flacks, *Beyond the Barricades: The Sixties Generation Grows Up* (Philadelphia: Temple University Press, 1990)

Wice, Nathaniel, 'Generalization X', in Douglas Rushkoff (ed.), *The GenX Reader* (New York: Ballantine Books, 1994).

Williams, C.P., 'The Recruitment and Training of Overseas Missionaries in England Between 1850 and 1900' (M. Litt. Thesis, University of Bristol, 1976)

Williams, D., *One in a Million: Billy Graham with Mission England* (Berkhamstead: Word Books, 1984)

Wilson, R.R., *Genealogy and History in the Biblical World* (New Haven: Yale University Press, 1977)

Wolde, Ellen Van, *Ruth and Naomi* (London: SCM Press, 1997)

Wright, David F. (ed.), *Essays in Evangelical Social Ethics* (Wilton, Conn.: Morehouse-Barlow, 1979)

Wright, Eric E., *Strange Fire? Assessing the Vineyard Movement and the Toronto Blessing* (Darlington: Evangelical Press, 1996)

Wright, N.T., *Jesus and the Victory of God* (Minneapolis: Fortress Press, 1996)

——, *The New Testament and the People of God* (London: SPCK, 1992)

Wright, Nigel G., *The Radical Evangelical: Seeking a Place to Stand* (London: SPCK, 1996)

Wyatt, David, *Out of the Sixties: Storytelling and the Vietnam Generation* (Cambridge/New York: Cambridge University Press, 1993)

Zoba, Wendy Murray, *Generation 2K: What Parents and Others Need to Know About the Millennials* (Grand Rapids: Zondervan, 1999)

Notes

Chapter 1

[1] For a summary of this work, see C. Kraft, *Christianity in Culture* (New York: Orbis, 1979), pp. 378–9. See also D. McGavran, *Understanding Church Growth* (Grand Rapids: Eerdmans, 1970).

[2] D. Pott, 'The Drifting Generation' in *Crusade*, March 1967, pp. 16–18, 27–28.

[3] O. Guinness, *The Dust of Death: A Critique of the Establishment and the Counter Culture – and a Proposal for a Third Way* (London: Inter-Varsity Press, 1973). F. Schaeffer, *The God Who Is There* (London: Hodder & Stoughton, 1968).

[4] Guinness, *Dust of Death*, p. 319.

[5] Ibid., p. 327.

[6] C. Brown, *The Death of Christian Britain* (London: Routledge, 2001), pp. 178–9.

[7] 'Eleanor Rigby', Northerm Songs, 1966.

[8] J. Green, *All Dressed Up: The Sixties and the Counterculture* (London: Pimlico, 1999), p. x.

[9] Cit.; J. Côté and A.L. Allahar, *Generation on Hold: Coming of Age in the Late Twentieth Century* (New York/London: New York University Press, 1996), p. xi; J. Springhall, *Coming of Age: Adolescence in Britain, 1860–1960* (Dublin: Gill & MacMillan, 1986).

[10] Green, *All Dressed Up*, p. x.

[11] Ibid., pp. x–xi.

[12] This period of social history is discussed more fully in the next chapter, but for a summary of its development, see A. Marwick, *The Sixties: Cultural Revolution in Britain, France, Italy and the United States, c. 1958 – c. 1974* (Oxford: Oxford University Press, 1998), pp. 489–98. Green, *All Dressed Up*, pp. 212–33.

[13] P. Ward, *Growing Up Evangelical: Youthwork and the Making of a Subculture* (London: SPCK, 1996), pp. 80–104. For a first-hand account, see R.M. Enroth, E.E. Ericson and C.B. Peters, *The Story of the Jesus People: A Factual Survey* (Exeter: Paternoster Press, 1972). See also Guinness, *Dust of Death*, pp. 325–31.

[14] S. Henderson, *Since the Beginning: Greenbelt* (London: Greenbelt, 1984); K. Leech, *Youthquake: Spirituality and the Growth of the Counter-Culture* (London: Abacus, 1973); A. Walker, *Restoring the Kingdom: The Radical Christianity of the House Church Movement* (Guidford: Eagle, 1998); T. Jasper, *Jesus and the Christian in a Pop Culture* (London: Robert Royce, 1984); B. Draper and K. Draper, *Refreshing Worship* (Oxford: Bible Reading Fellowship, 2001); M. Riddell, M. Pierson and C. Kirkpatrick, *The Prodigal Project: Journey into the Emerging Church* (London: SPCK, 2000).

[15] E.g. N.B. Ryder, 'The Cohort as a Concept in the Study of Social Change', in *American Sociological Review* 30 (Dec 1965), p. 845; L.S. Feuer, *The Conflict of Generations: the Character and Significance of Student Movements* (New York, Basic Books, 1969); A. Klein (ed.), *Natural Enemies? Youth and the Clash of Generations* (Philadelphia: Lippincott, 1969); J. Pilcher, *Age and Generation in Modern Britain* (Oxford: Oxford University Press, 1995), pp. 66–72; Marwick, *The Sixties*, pp. 97–8.

[16] N. Howe and W. Strauss, *Generations: The History of America's Future, 1584–2069* (New York: Quill/William Morrow, 1991), pp. 261–94.

[17] G. Barna, *Baby Busters: The Disillusioned Generation* (Chicago: Northfield, 1994); D. Coupland, *Generation X: Tales for an Accelerated Culture* (London: Abacus, 1992 [1991]); D. Rushkoff (ed.), *The GenX Reader* (New York: Ballantine Books, 1994); N. Howe and W. Strauss, *13th Gen: Abort, Retry, Ignore, Fail?* (New York: Vintage, 1993), pp. 12ff.

[18] M. Pirie and R.M. Worcester, *The Millennial Generation* (London: Adam Smith Institute, 1998); N. Howe, Neil and W. Strauss, *Millennials Rising: The Next Great Generation* (New York: Vintage, 2000).

[19] W.C. Roof, *A Generation of Seekers: The Spiritual Journeys of the Baby Boom Generation* (London/New York: Hodder & Stoughton, 1993); Barna, *Baby Busters*; W. Mahedy and J. Bernardi, *A Generation Alone: Xers Making a Place in the World* (Downers Grove: InterVarsity Press, 1994); M. DeVries, *Family-Based Youth Ministry: Reaching the Been-There, Done-That Generation* (Downers Grove: InterVarsity Press, 1994); G. Barna, *Generation Next: What You Need to Know About Today's Youth* (Ventura: Regal Books, 1995); K. Ford, *Jesus for a New Generation* (London: Hodder & Stoughton, 1996); T. Celek

and D. Zander, *Inside the Soul of New Generation* (Grand Rapids: Zondervan, 1996); J. Long, *Generating Hope* (Downers Grove: InterVarsity Press, 1997); M. Starkey, *God, Sex and Generation X: A Search for Lost Wonder* (London: Triangle, 1997); T. Beaudoin, *Virtual Faith: The Irreverent Spirituality of Generation X* (San Fransisco: Jossey-Bass, 1998); T. Hahn and D. Verhaagen, *Genxers After God* (Grand Rapids: Baker Book House, 1998); W.C. Roof, *Spiritual Marketplace: Baby Boomers and the Remaking of American Religion* (Princeton, NJ: Prineton University Press, 1999); W.M. Zoba, *Generation 2K: What Parents and Others Need to Know About the Millennials* (Grand Rapids: Zondervan, 1999); D. McAllister, *Saving the Millennial Generation* (Eugene, Or.: Authentic Publishing, 1999); Rabey, *In Search of Authentic Faith*.

[20] G. Codrington, 'Generation X: Who, What, Why and Where To?' at www.youth.co.za/genthesis/toc.html; G. Codrington, 'Understanding Multi-Generational Ministry: Lessons from the Life of Joshua and the Age of Transition in South Africa' (paper presented to the Fourth Conference on Youth Ministry, Mansfield College, Oxford, January 2001), www.youth.co.za/minresource001.html; A. Tapia, 'Reaching the First Post-Christian Generation', at users.vnet/rdavis/CTXer.html. Each of Codrington's artcles has useful details on other Internet resources.

[21] Howe and Strauss, *Generations*; Howe and Strauss, *13th Gen*; N Howe and W. Srauss, *The Fourth Turning: An American Prophecy* (New York: Broadway Books, 1997); Howe and Strauss, *Millennials Rising*.

[22] Fishman's company's web site is at www.annfishman.com/800/nlet01-4.html. Howe is quoted there as having worked and written newspaper articles with her.

[23] E.g. Maslow's 'Hierarchy of Needs', ch. 1, p. 26; Rick Warren's 'Purpose Driven Church Model', ch. 4, pp. 1–3, and Mark Tittley's 'Commitment Level' model of religious affiliation, ch. 4, pp. 4–16.

[24] Codrington, 'Generation X', ch. 4, pp. 17–22.

[25] Rabey, *In Search of Authentic Faith*, pp. 17–18.

[26] Ibid.

[27] Mahedy and Bernardi, *A Generation Alone*, pp. 38–40.

[28] Beaudoin, *Virtual Faith*.

[29] Howe and Strauss, *Generations*, p. 34.

[30] Codrington is heavily dependent on Howe and Strauss, but does at least summarise the development of generational study in various fields in his paper 'Understanding Multi-Generational Ministry', pp. 3–5.

[31] E.g., Beaudoin, *Virtual Faith*, pp. 23–24, 44; Rabey, *In Search of Authentic Faith*, p. 119, Codrington, 'Generation X', p. 1.

[32] G. Barna, *Marketing the Church* (Colorado Springs: NavPress, 1988), pp. 23, 26–37, 78. Cit. Rabey, *In Search of Authentic Faith*, pp. 168–9.

[33] H-G. Gadamer, *Truth and Method* (2nd rev'd edn.; trans. J. Weinsheimer and D.G. Marshall; London: Sheed & Ward, 1989), pp. 306–7, 374–5. See also A.C. Thiselton, *The Two Horizons: New Testament Hermeneutics and Philosophical Description with Special Reference to Heidegger, Bultmann, Gadamer and Wittgenstein* (Exeter: Paternoster Press, 1980), pp. 15–17.

Chapter 2

[1] J. Lyons, *Semantics* Vol. 1 (Cambridge: Cambridge University Press, 1977), p. 244.

[2] E.A. Speiser, *Genesis* (New York: Doubleday, 1969), pp. 93–4.

[3] D. Brunner, *Matthew: A Commentary: Volume 1 – The Christbook, Matthew 1–12* (Dallas/London: Word, 1987), pp. 5–8.

[4] G.R Beasley-Murray, *Baptism in the New Testament* (Carlisle: Paternoster Press, 1972 [1962]); C. Buchcanan, *A Case for Infant Baptism* (Grove Booklet on Ministry and Worship, No. 20; Bramcote: Grove Books, 1973); D. Pawson and C. Buchanan, *Infant Baptism Under Cross-Examination* (Grove Booklet on Ministry and Worship, No. 24; Bramcote: Grove Books, 1976); M. Dalby, *Open Baptism* (London: SPCK, 1989).

[5] As in 'pertaining to events' rather than as in 'final' or 'ultimate'. Cf. the French term *éventuel*.

[6] For further discussion of this point, see C. Brown, 'Generation', in Colin Brown, (ed.), *New International Dictionary of the New Testament* Vol. 2 (4 Vols.; rev'd. edn; Carlisle: Paternoster Press, 1986), pp. 38–9. *Genea* here may also refer to those people of Israel who might be preserved in some distinct way through the *eschaton* (Rom. 11:25–32).

[7] R.R. Wilson, *Genealogy and History in the Biblical World* (New Haven: Yale University Press, 1977), pp. 158–9; T.C. Mitchell, 'Generation' in J.D. Douglas (ed.), *The Illustrated Bible Dictionary* Vol. 1 (Leicester: Inter-Varsity Press, 1980), p. 549.

[8] For a survey of the various eschatological positions on Israel see M.J. Erickson, *A Basic Guide to Eschatology* (Grand Rapids: Baker Book House, 1998).

[9] P. Jones, *What Parents Should Know About Generational Sin* (Tonbridge: Sovereign World, 1999), pp. 10–15.

[10] Ibid., pp. 27–44; P. Horrobin, 'Claiming the Ground', Ellel Ministries Teaching Series (Cassette Tapes, 1990). For a more moderate approach to retrospective healing of 'generational sin', see R. Parker, *Healing Wounded History* (London: SPCK, 2001), pp. 122–33.

[11] For more detail see J. Rogerson, 'The Family and Structures of Grace in the Old Testament', in S.C. Barton (ed.), *The Family in Theological Perspective* (Edinburgh: T. & T. Clark, 1996), pp. 25–42.

[12] D.J. Estes, *Hear, My Son* (Leicester: Apollos, 1997).

[13] N. Summerton, *A Noble Task: Eldership and Ministry in the Local Church* (Exeter: Paternoster Press, 1987).

Chapter 3

[1] Pilcher, *Age and Generation*, p. 66.

[2] Ibid., pp. 66–71.

[3] Ryder, 'The Cohort', p. 843.

[4] Ibid.

[5] Pilcher, *Age and Generation*, p. 6. See also J. Fulcher and J. Scott, *Sociology* (Oxford: Oxford University Press, 1999), pp. 369–73.

[6] M. Corsten, 'The Time of Generations', in *Time and Society* 8.2 (1999), pp. 251–3.

[7] Pilcher, *Age and Generation*, pp. 151–60.

[8] Ibid., p. 6.

[9] H. Schuman and J. Scott, 'Generations and Collective Memories', in *American Sociological Review* 54.3 (June 1989), p. 360.

[10] 'Biosphere', in *Encyclopedia Britannica: Macropedia* (London, 1993), p. 1139.

[11] HMSO, *Social Trends* (London: HMSO, 1996), p. 60.

[12] For statistics and analysis on this contrast see US Bureau of the Census, *Ageing in the Third World* (International Population Reports, Series P. 95, No. 79, Washington DC: US Government Printing Office, 1987). See also J.S. Grigsby, 'Paths for Future Population Ageing', in J. Johnson and R. Slater (eds), *Ageing and Later Life* (London: Sage/Open University, 1993), pp. 344–51; and A. Kalache, 'Ageing in Developing Countries: Has It Got Anything to Do With Us?'; also in J. Johnson and R. Slater (eds), *Ageing and Later Life* (London: Sage/Open University, 1993), pp. 339–43.

[13] J. Monk and C. Katz, 'When in the World are Women?', in C. Katz and J. Monk (eds.), *Full Circles: Geographies of Women Over the Life Course* (London: Routledge, 1993).

[14] For a summary of ancient and modern understandings of this text see R.V.G. Tasker, *James* (Leicester: Inter-Varsity Press, 1957), p. 76.

[15] For a detailed exposition of this principle from an evangelical perspective see S. Grenz, *Theology for the Community of God* (Carlisle: Paternoster Press, 1994).

[16] For a digest of evangelical understandings of this point see D.F. Wright (ed.), *Essays in Evangelical Social Ethics* (Wilton, Conn.: Morehouse-Barlow, 1979).

[17] For more on this, see Pilcher, *Age and Generation*, pp. 66–72.

[18] G.S. Hall, *Adolescence* (New York: Appleton, 1904); R.E. Muuss, *Theories of Adolescence* (New York: McGraw-Hill, 1988). For a summary of the arguments, see Côté and Allahar, *Generation on Hold*, pp. xii–xiv.

[19] Hall, *Adolescence*; J.A. Côté, *Adolescent Storm and Stress: A Evaluation of the Mead/Freeman Controversy* (Hillsdale, NJ: Lawrence Erlbaum, 1994).

[20] M. Mead, *Coming of Age in Samoa: A Psychological Study of Primitive Youth for Western Civilization* (New York: Morrow Quill Paperbacks, 1928).

[21] Green, *All Dressed Up*, p. x.

[22] Ibid.

[23] Ibid.

[24] Marwick, *The Sixties*, pp. 49–50.

[25] For excellent analysis of these more radical developments, see Green, *All Dressed Up*, and Marwick, *The Sixties*, especially pp. 584–678.

[26] E. Gilbert, *Advertising and Marketing to Young People* (Scranton: Printer's Ink Publishing Company, Inc., 1957).

[27] *Harpers Magazine*, November 1958, Cit. Marwick, *The Sixties*, p. 46.

[28] Marwick, *The Sixties*, pp. 46–7. See also S. Frith, *The Sociology of Youth* (Lancashire: Causeway, 1984), p. 9.

[29] Frith, *The Sociology of Youth*, p. 9.

[30] Marwick, *The Sixties*, p. 45.

[31] Roof, *A Generation of Seekers*, p. 1. See also Pepsi web site at www.pepsi.com.

[32] www.luxurycorner.com.

[33] C.M. Gay, *With Liberty and Justice for Whom? The Recent Evangelical Debate over Capitalism* (Grand Rapids: Eerdmans, 1991); C. Bartholemew and T. Moritz (eds), *Christ and Consumerism: A Critical Analysis of the Spirit of the Age* (Carlisle: Paternoster Press, 2000).

[34] Ministry of Education, *The Youth Service in England and Wales* (the Albermarle Report), Cmnd. 929 (1960), pp. 33–4.

[35] Ward, *Growing Up Evangelical*, p. 68.

[36] B. Mayo and D. Baxter, 'Is History Repeating Itself?', in *Youthwork*, October 1998.

[37] D. Sheppard, *Parson's Pitch* (London: Hodder & Stoughton, 1964), p. 160.

[38] Marwick, *The Sixties*, pp. 62–3.

[39] D. Marsh, *Before I Get Old: The Story of The Who* (London: Plexus, 1983), p. 4.

[40] C. Hamblett and J. Deverson, *Generation X* (London: Tandem, 1964).

[41] Idol and James read Hamblett and Deverson's book in the late seventies and named their own band after it, following the break-up of their previous group, Chelsea. In 1991, the novelist Douglas Coupland in turn borrowed the phrase 'Generation X' for the title of his own best-selling analysis of the then rising generation of youth: Coupland, *Generation X*. For more on the etymology and usage of the term, see Rushkoff (ed.), *The GenX Reader*.

[42] Townshend, Pete, © TRO-Devon [BMI], 1965.

[43] Ward, *Growing Up Evangelical*, p. 92.

[44] On the rising profile of Mannheim's work during this period, see Pilcher, *Age and Generation*, pp. 139–41.

[45] Ryder, 'The Cohort', pp. 843–61.

[46] K. Mannheim, 'The Problem of Generations', in Paul Kecskemeti (ed.), *Essays on the Sociology of Knowledge* (London: Routledge & Kegan Paul, 1952), p. 300.

[47] Ibid., p. 309.

[48] Roof, *A Generation of Seekers*, p. 2.

[49] Mannheim, 'The Problem of Generations', pp. 300–1.

[50] Ibid., p. 301.

[51] Ibid., p. 301.

[52] D.O. Moberg, *The Church as a Social Institution* (2nd edn; Grand Rapids: Baker Book House, 1984).

[53] M. Mead, *Culture and Commitment: A Study of the Generation Gap* (New York: Doubleday/Natural History Press, 1970).

[54] Ryder, 'The Cohort', p. 851.

[55] Liefeld, Walter L., 'Luke', in Kenneth L Barker and John R Kohlenberger III (eds), *Zondervan NIV Bible Commentary: Volume 2 – New Testament*, Grand Rapids: Zondervan, 1994, p. 223.

[56] O. Kaiser, *Isaiah 1–12* (London: SCM, 1972), p. 162.

[57] R.N. Butler, 'Ageism', in *The Encyclopedia of Ageing* (New York: Springer, 1987), pp. 22–3.

[58] J. Johnson and B. Bytheway, 'Ageism: Concept and Definition', in Julia Johnson and Robert Slater (eds), *Ageing and Later Life* (Open University/Sage: London, 1993), pp. 200–6.

[59] A. Franklin and B. Franklin, 'Age and Power', in T. Jeffs and M. Smith (eds), *Young People: Inequality and Youth Work* (Basingstoke: MacMillan, 1990), pp. 1–27.

[60] P. Brierley, *The Tide is Running Out: What the English Church Attendance Survey Reveals* (London: Christian Research, 2000), p. 170.

[61] D. Bebbington, *Evangelicalism in Modern Britain: A History from the 1730s to the 1980s* (London: Unwin Hyman 1989), p. 225; Ward, *Growing Up Evangelical*, pp. 45–62.

Chapter 4

[1] Mannheim, 'The Problem of Generations'.

[2] Ibid., p. 276.

[3] Pilcher, *Age and Generation*, p. 6.

[4] Mannheim, 'The Problem of Generations', p. 309.

[5] Ibid., pp. 278–9.

[6] J. Pilcher and S. Wagg, *Thatcher's Children? Politics, Childhood and Society in the 1980s and 1990s* (London/Washington DC: Falmer Press, 1996).

[7] M. Friedman and R. Friedman, *Free to Choose: A Personal Statement* (London: Secker & Warburg, 1980); B. Griffiths, 'Christianizing the Market', in J. Atherton (ed.), *Social Christianity: A Reader* (London: SPCK, 1994), pp. 355–71; Gay, *With Liberty and Justice for Whom?*.

[8] For a more detailed assessment of this distinction, see B. Adam, *Time and Social Theory* (Cambridge: Polity, 1990), pp. 11ff.

[9] Mannheim, 'The Problem of Generations', pp. 281–4.

[10] W. Dilthey, 'Types of World-View and their Development in the Metaphysical Systems' (1911), in D. Klemm (ed.), *Hermeneutical Enquiry* (Atlanta: Scholars Press, 1986), Vol. 2.

[11] See, for example, B.J. Walsh and J.R. Middleton, *The Transforming Vision: Shaping a Christian World View* (Downers Grove: InterVarsity Press, 1984); J. Sire, *The Universe Next Door* (2nd edn; Downers Grove: InterVarsity Press,

1988); D.J. Hesselgrave, *Communicating Christ Cross-Culturally* (2nd edn; Grand Rapids: Zondervan, 1991), pp. 193–285. For a more detailed assessment of worldview in relation to epistemology and biblical interpretation, see Thiselton, *Two Horizons*, pp. 133–9, 252–68.

12 R.A. Makkreel, 'Dilthey, Wilhelm', in R. Audi (ed.), *The Cambridge Dictionary of Philosophy* (2nd edn; Cambridge: Cambridge University Press, 1999), p. 236.

13 Walsh and Middleton, *Transforming Vision*, p. 32.

14 Mannheim, 'The Problem of Generations', p. 282.

15 This point is well made by N. Wice, 'Generalization X', in Rushkoff (ed.), *The GenX Reader*, p. 280.

16 Pilcher and Wagg, *Thatcher's Children?*.

17 C. Hayes, *A Generation of Materialism: 1871–1900* (New York: London: Harper Row, 1941).

18 Green, *All Dressed Up*, pp. x–xii.

19 Diocese of Southwark, *The Chemical Generation: Understanding Young People and Drug Use: A Review of Issues and Options* (London: Southwark Diocesan Board for Church and Society/National Council for Social Concern, 1998); R. Hammersley, F. Khan and J. Ditton (eds), *Ecstasy and the Rise of the Chemical Generation* (Springfield, Ill.: Harwood, 2002); M. Kohn, *The Chemical Generation and Its Ancestors: Dance Crazes and Drug Panics Across Eight Decades*, available at www.drugtext.org/articles/97833.html.

20 Corsten, 'The Time of Generations', pp. 258–62.

21 J. Storey, 'Postmodernism and Popular Culture', in S. Sim (ed.), *The Routledge Companion to Postmodernism* (London: Routledge, 2001), p. 148.

22 D. Hebidge, 'Banalarama, or Can Pop Save Us All?', in *New Statesman and Society*, 9 December 1988.

23 J.F. Lyotard, *The Postmodern Condition: A Report on Knowledge* (Manchester: Manchester University Press, 1979), p. xiv.

24 Mannheim, 'The Problem of Generations', p. 286.

25 George Barna most recently suggests 1946–64 (Barna Research Online, www.barna.org/cgi-bin/PageCategory.asp?Category; Howe and Strauss, by contrast, suggest 1943–60, *Generations*, pp. 299–316.

26 W.C. Roof, J. Carroll and D.A. Roozen (eds) *The Post-War Generation and Establishment Religion: Cross-Cultural Perspectives* (Boulder, CO: Westview Press, 1995); cf. N.G. Annan, *Our Age: The Generation that Made Post-War Britain* (London: Fontana, 1991).

[27] A.K. Gorg, *The Sixties:Biographies of the Love Generation* (Marina Del Ray, CA.: Media Associates, 1995); K–Tel (CD), *Flower Power: 14 Songs from the Peace and Love Generation*, NU–666-8, USA 1987. The manager of the West Coast rock band The Grateful Dead, Rock Scully, once referred to the fateful Altamont Festival of December 1969, at which Hell's Angels stabbed a young black spectator to death, as 'the end of the peace-love generation for sure' (Blues in Technicolour web site, www.pbs.org/wgbh/pages/rocknroll/mrttechnicolor.html); Cecil, Brian Slade's first manager in the film *Velvet Goldmine*, says of Slade at one point, 'He despised the Peace and Love Generation and felt his music spoke more to its orphans and outcasts'. On the term 'Woodstock Generation', see P. Carlton, *Death of the Woodstock Generation* (Bethesda: Van Cortlandt Books, 1994); UPC (CD), *The Woodstock Generation: Everything is Beautiful*, CD UPC 72438952022, 2001; Britannica.com, 'The Woodstock Generation', www.britannica.com.

[28] Copyright © Siquomb Publishing Company.

[29] D. Wyatt, *Out of the Sixties: Storytelling and the Vietnam Generation* (Cambridge/ New York: Cambridge University Press, 1993); Schuman and Scott, 'Generations and Collective Memories', 374.

[30] J. Marsh, 'Time' in A. Richardson (ed.), *A Theological Word Book of the Bible* (London: SCM, 1950), pp. 258–9.

[31] B. Inhelder and J. Piaget, *The Growth of Logical Thinking from Childhood to Adolescence* (New York: Basic Books, 1958); E.E. Erikson, *Identity: Youth and Crisis* (New York: Newton, 1968); R.S. Siegel and M.B. Hoskin, 'Perspectives on Adult Political Socialization', in S.A. Renshon (ed.), *Handbook of Adolescent Psychology* (New York: Free Press, 1977), pp. 259–93; J. Gallatin, 'Political Thinking in Adolescence', in J. Adelson (ed.), *Handbook of Adolescent Psychology* (New York: Wiley, 1980), pp. 344–82.

[32] Ryder, 'The Cohort', p. 853.

[33] Marwick, *The Sixties*, p. 751.

[34] Mannheim, 'The Problem of Generations', p. 304.

[35] Ibid., p. 304.

[36] Pilcher, *Age and Generation*, p. 140.

[37] J.J. Ellis, *Founding Brothers: The Revolutionary Generation* (London: Faber & Faber, 2002).

[38] F. Ashford, *An Estimate of Caravaggio and His Influence on the Succeeding Generation in Italy* (MA dissertation; Courtauld Institute, 1936); Courtauld Institute of Art, *Five French Painters of the Second Generation of Post-Impressionism* (London: Roland, Browse & Delbraco, 1954).

[39] R.A. Lee, *The Beat Generation Writers* (London: Pluto, 1995); S. Watson, *The Birth of the Beat Generation: Visionaries, Rebels and Hipsters, 1944–1960* (New York: Pantheon Books, 1995).

[40] For more on such sub-cultures see Rabey, *In Search of Authentic Faith*, pp. 49–67.

[41] Cf. D. Hilborn, *Picking Up the Pieces: Can Evangelicals Adapt to Contemporary Culture?* (London: Hodder & Stoughton, 1997), pp. 74–8.

[42] J.D.G. Dunn, *Unity and Diversity in the New Testament* (London: SCM Press, 1977); D. Tidball, *The Social Context of the New Testament* (Carlisle: Paternoster Press, 1997 [1983]).

[43] C. Calver and R. Warner, *Together We Stand: Evangelical Convictions, Unity and Vision* (London: Hodder & Stoughton, 1996), pp. 128–30.

[44] J. Finch, *Family Obligations and Social Change* (Cambridge: Polity, 1989), p. 3; F.H. Palmer, 'Adoption', in J.D. Douglas (ed.), *The Illustrated Bible Dictionary* Part 1 (Leicester: Inter-Varsity Press, 1980), p. 17.

[45] P. Weiner, *Woodstock Census: The Nationwide Cultural Survey of the Sixties Generation* (New York: Viking, 1979); J. Whalen and R. Flacks, *Beyond the Barricades: The Sixties Generation Grows Up* (Philadelphia: Temple University Press, 1990). Pirie and Worcester, *Millennial Generation*; Howe and Strauss, *Millennials Rising*.

[46] On the age of Jesus at this point, see I.H. Marshall, *The Gospel of Luke: A Commentary in the Greek Text* (Exeter: Paternoster Press, 1978), p. 162.

[47] Howe and Strauss, *Generations*, pp. 299–316; Roof, *A Generation of Seekers*.

[48] The French word 'éventuel' still carries that sense of 'pertaining to events' which an older usage of this word carried in English. See O. Watson, *Longman Modern English Dictionary* (London: Longman, 1968), p. 362.

[49] Schuman and Scott, 'Generations and Collective Memories', pp. 359–81.

[50] Ibid.

[51] Howe and Strauss, *Generations*, pp. 261–78; Wyatt, *Out of the Sixties*; Schuman and Scott, 'Generations and Collective Memories', p. 374.

[52] Schuman and Scott, 'Generations and Collective Memories', p. 374.

[53] Marwick, *The Sixties*, pp. 3–22.

[54] D. Hilborn (ed.), *'Toronto' in Perspective: Papers on the New Charismatic Wave of the Mid-1990s* (Carlisle: Paternoster Press, 2001).

[55] 'Lost Generation', in J. Pearsall and B. Trumble (eds), *The Oxford English Reference Dictionary* (2nd edn; New York: Oxford University Press, 1996), p. 849; Strauss, Howe and Strauss, *Generations*, pp. 247–60.

[56] M. Dolan, *Modern Lives: A Cultural Re-Reading of the 'Lost Generation'* (West Lafayette, Ind.: Purdue University Press, 1996); A. Viall, *Everybody Was So*

Young: Gerald and Sara Murphy, a Lost Generation Love Story (New York: Broadway Books, 1999); and 'Lost Generation', in Pearsall and Trumble (eds), *Oxford English Reference Dictionary*, p. 849.

[57] M. MacPherson, *The Hurting Generation* (Indiana: Indiana University Press, 2002); A.D. Horne, *The Wounded Generation: America After Vietnam* (Eaglewood Cliffs, NJ: Prentice Hall Trade, 1981).

[58] J.R. Brett, 'The Generations of Americans', at www.csulb.edu/~wwwing/ Silents/sgyears.html; Diocese of Southwark, *The Chemical Generation*; Hammersley et al (eds), *Ecstasy*; Kohn, *The Chemical Generation and Its Ancestors.*

[59] Pilcher, *Age and Generation*, p. 25.

Chapter 5

[1] Generational phases in the life course (Strauss and Howe 1991), pp. 43–57.

[2] Howe and Strauss, *Generations*, p. 519.

[3] Ibid., p. 32.

[4] Ibid., pp. 34–5.

[5] Ibid..

[6] Developed from ibid., p. 34.

[7] Ibid., p. 35.

[8] Ibid.

[9] Ibid., pp. 80–96.

[10] Cf. ibid., p. 87.

[11] Ibid., pp. 80–96.

[12] Cf. ibid., p. 35.

[13] Cf. ibid., pp. 84–7, 2000:41; * This final, additional level of the model is suggested by James R. Brett, 2002, 'The Generations of Americans', at www.csulb.edu/~wwwing/Silents/sgyears.html

[14] Howe and Strauss, *Generations*, pp. 433–519.

[15] Ibid., pp. 36–7.

[16] R. Maltby, 'Introduction' in R. Maltby (ed.), *Dreams for Sale: Popular Culture in the 20th Century* (London: Harrap, 1989), p. 11; J. Storey, *An Introduction to Cultural Theory and Popular Culture* (2nd edn; London: Prentice Hall, 1997 [1993]), pp. 11–12.

[17] Howe and Strauss, *Generations*, p. 37. For a helpful analysis of these trends, and of globalisation in particular, see B. Emmott and C. Cook, *Globalisation* (London: Economist Books, 2002). For a Christian interpretation, see

B. Goudzwaard, *Globalization and the Kingdom of God* (Grand Rapids: Baker/Center for Public Justice, 2001).

[18] For an illuminating survey of this transatlantic interaction, see M. Noll, D.W. Bebbington and G.A. Rawlyk (eds), *Evangelicalism: Comparative Studies of Popular Protestantism in North America, the British Isles, and Beyond, 1700–1990* (New York/Oxford: Oxford University Press, 1994).

[19] S. Brower, P. Gifford and S. Rose (eds), *Exporting the American Gospel: Global Christian Fundamentalism* (New York/London: Routledge, 1996).

[20] Howe and Strauss, *Generations*, pp. 90–2.

[21] C.L. Chaney, *The Birth of Missions in America* (Pasadena: William Carey Library, 1976), p. 1.

[22] D.J. Bosch, *Transforming Mission: Paradigm Shifts in the Theology of Mission* (New York: Orbis, 1991), pp. 281–2.

[23] Howe and Strauss, *Generations*, pp. 232–46.

[24] M. Marty, 'The Spirit's Holy Errand: The Search for a Style in Secular America', in *Daedalus* 96.1 (Winter 1967), pp. 99–115.

[25] Green, *All Dressed Up*, p. 230.

[26] B. Martin, *A Sociology of Contemporary Cultural Change* (Oxford: Blackwell, 1981), p. 217.

[27] I. MacDonald, *Revolution in the Head: The Beatles' Records and the Sixties* (London: Fourth Estate, 1994).

[28] Marwick, *The Sixties*, pp. 533–83.

[29] Ibid., pp. 288–358.

[30] Ibid., pp. 543–5.

[31] Ibid., pp. 750–1.

[32] J.R. Brett, 'The Silent Generation', at www.csulb.edu/~wwwing/Silents/sgjim.html.

[33] Schuman and Scott, 'Generations and Collective Memories', pp. 365–6.

[34] Howe and Strauss, *Generations*, p. 93.

[35] J. Collier, 'Contemporary Culture and the Role of Economics', in H. Montefiore (ed.), *The Gospel and Contemporary Culture* (London: Mowbray, 1992), p. 104.

[36] Howe and Strauss, *13th Gen*, p. 163.

[37] Ibid., p. 61.

[38] Ibid., p. 196.

[39] Ibid., p. 180.

[40] Ibid., pp. 218–25.

[41] Schuman and Scott, 'Generations and Collective Memories', pp. 359–381 (italics our emphasis).

[42] E.g., P.J. Buchanan, *The Death of the West: How Dying Populations and Immigrant Invasions Imperil our Country and Civilization* (New York: Thomas Dunne Books, 2002); American Reformation Project, 'Woodstock Values v. "God's Country"', at www.americanreformation.org/culturewar/woodstock.html.

[43] G. Carvalho, 'Employee X: What Companies Need to Know About Recruiting, Motivating, Retaining, and Promoting Generation X Workers', at www.rushmoreau.com.

[44] Howe and Strauss, *Generations*, p. 302.

[45] Howe and Strauss, *Millennials Rising*.

[46] Codrington, 'Generation X', p. 27.

[47] A. Maslow, *Motivation and Personality* (2nd edn; New York, Harper & Row, 1970); A. Maslow, *The Farther Reaches of Human Nature* (New York: Viking Press, 1971).

Chapter 6

[1] For more on these developments, see D. Harvey, *The Condition of Postmodernity* (Oxford: Blackwell, 1990), pp. 10–38.

[2] Howe and Strauss, *Generations*, pp. 261–6.

[3] J.F. Kennedy, 'The Torch Has Been Passed to a New Generation', in B. McArthur (ed.), *The Penguin Book of Twentieth Century Speeches* (London: Penguin, 1993), p. 301.

[4] Howe and Strauss, *Generations*, p. 263.

[5] Ibid.

[6] Ibid.

[7] Ibid., p. 265.

[8] Ibid., p. 264.

[9] B. Graham, *Just As I Am: The Autobiography of Billy Graham* (London: HarperCollins, 1997).

[10] Howe and Strauss, *Generations*, p. 365.

[11] Green, *All Dressed Up*, pp. 51–4.

[12] Marwick, *The Sixties*, p. 41.

[13] R. Hutchinson, *High Sixties: The Summers of Riot and Love* (Edinburgh: Mainstream, 1992), pp. 15–18.

[14] Brown, *Death of Christian Britain*, pp. 164–75, esp. pp. 172–3.

[15] Ibid.

[16] D. Williams, *One in a Million: Billy Graham with Mission England* (Berkhamstead: Word Books, 1984), p. 184; Brown, *Death of Christian Britain*, p. 173; I. Randall and D. Hilborn, *One Body in Christ: The History and Significance of the Evangelical Alliance* (Carlisle: Paternoster Press, 2001), pp. 220–31.

[17] Randall and Hilborn, *One Body in Christ*, pp. 220–31.

Chapter 7

[1] Howe and Strauss, *Generations*, pp. 279–81.

[2] Ibid., p. 285.

[3] Cit. ibid., p. 281.

[4] Howe and Strauss, *Fourth Turning*, p. 39.

[5] Howe and Strauss, *Generations*, p. 284.

[6] Ibid., pp. 284–5.

[7] B. Leaming, *Marilyn Monroe* (New York: Crown, 1998).

[8] P. Alexander, *Boulevard of Broken Dreams: The Life, Times, and Legend of James Dean* (New York: Viking, 1994).

[9] S.B. Oates, *Let the Trumpet Sound: A Life of Martin Luther King Jr* (New York: New American Library, 1985).

[10] Pilcher, *Age and Generation*, p. 7.

[11] Marwick, *The Sixties*, pp. 118–28.

[12] Green, *All Dressed Up*, p. 19.

[13] David Widgery, *The Left in Britain*, Cit. Green, *All Dressed Up*, p. 24.

[14] Green, *All Dressed Up*, pp. 13–25.

[15] P. Oakes, *Tony Hancock* (London: Woburn Press, 1975). See especially Hancock's 1960 film *The Rebel*.

[16] J.A.T. Robinson, *Honest to God* (London: SCM Press, 1963); J.A.T. Robinson and D.L. Edwards, *The Honest to God Debate* (London: SCM Press, 1963); K.W. Clements, *Lovers of Discord: Twentieth Century Theological Controversies in England* (London: SPCK, 1988), pp. 178–217.

[17] Brown, *Death of Christian Britain*, pp. 173–4.

[18] Brierley, *The Tide Is Running Out*.

[19] www.barna.org/cgi-bin/PageCategory.asp?CategoryID=22.

Chapter 8

1   Howe and Strauss, *Generations*, pp. 299–316.
2   Ibid., p. 305.
3   Ibid., p. 299.
4   Ibid., p. 301.
5   Pilcher, *Age and Generation*, p. 9.
6   Larkin, Philip, 'Annus Mirabilis' (1974).
7   J. Green, *Days in the Life* (London: Heinemann, 1988), p. 344.
8   MacDonald, *Revolution in the Head*, p. 12.
9   Ibid., p. 13.
10 Bob Dylan, 'The Times They Are A Changin', *The Times They Are A Changin'* (CBS CD, 1992 [1964]). Lyrics in B. Dylan, *Lyrics, 1962–1985* (© 1963, 1964 Warner Bros. Inc.; London: Jonathan Cape, 1985), p. 91.
11 MacDonald, *Revolution in the Head*, p. 19.
12 R. Currie, A. Gilbert and L. Horsely, *Churches and Churchgoers: Patterns of Church Growth in the British Isles since 1700* (Oxford, Oxford University Press, 1977), pp. 167–8; Church of England, *Yearbook of the Church of England, 1974, 1980–2000* and *1984*, Statistical Supplement, p. 41. Total confirmations in the Church of England fell from 190,713 in 1960 to 113, 005 in 1970. For males aged twelve to twenty years old, the fall in the same period was from 27.6% of the population to 15.3%; for women in the same age-bracket it was from 40.9% down to 24.2%.
13 N. Scotland, *Charismatics and the New Millennium* (2nd edn; Guildford: Eagle, 2000), pp. 36–7.

Chapter 9

1   Coupland, *Generation X*, pp. 25–6.
2   R. Sabin, 'Generation X' in J. Buckley, O. Duane, M. Ellingham and A. Spicer, *Rock: The Rough Guide* (rev'd edn; London: Rough Guides, 1999), pp. 403–4.
3   D. Rushkoff, 'Introduction: Us, By Us', in Rushkoff (ed.), *The GenX Reader*, p. 7. cf. Starkey, *God, Sex and Generation X*.
4   Howe and Strauss, *13th Gen*, p. 7; Pilcher, *Age and Generation*, p. 7.
5   Ibid., p. 7; Pilcher, *Age and Generation*, 1995.
6   Ford, *Jesus for a New Generation*, p. 9.

[7] 'Revolution' (single) © Northern Songs, 1968.

[8] Marwick, Arthur, *The Sixties*, Oxford: Oxford University Press, 1998, pp. 536–46.

[9] John Lennon, 'God', *John Lennon Plastic Ono Band*, (Apple CD) 1970; Pete Townshend, 'Won't Get Fooled Again', *Who's Next* (Polydor CD), 1971. Beaudoin, *Virtual Faith*, pp. 3–7.

[10] Rushkoff, 'Introduction', p. 7.

[11] R. Nelson and J. Cowan, *Revolution X: A Survival Guide for Our Generation* (New York: Penguin, 1994), pp. 209–21.

[12] Pete Townshend, 'Lifehouse Chronicles', London: Eelpie, 2000, p. 7.

[13] J. Savage, *England's Dreaming: The Sex Pistols and Punk Rock* (London: Faber. 2001).

[14] Howe and Strauss, *13th Gen*, p. 61.

[15] Starkey, *God, Sex and Generation X*, p. 28.

[16] Beaudoin, *Virtual Faith*, pp. 51–72, 122.

[17] G. Codrington, '25 Sentences that Define a Generation', at www.youth. co.za/xpaper1010.html.

[18] Rushkoff, 'Introduction', p. 7.

[19] D. Coupland, *Life After God* (London: Touchstone Books, 1994), pp. 273–4.

[20] P. Bradshaw, 'Over the Moon: Review of 'ET – The Extra Terrestrial, 20th Anniversary Edition', in *Guardian Review*, 29 March 2002, p. 12.

[21] Beaudoin, *Virtual Faith*, pp. 159–80.

[22] Codrington, 'Generation X', ch. 5; Ford, *Jesus for a New Generation*, pp. 227–50; R. Burton, 'Effective Ministry to Baby Busters', at www.epbd.edu/burt94.html.

Chapter 10

[1] Howe and Strauss, *Millennials Rising*, p. 6.

[2] Ibid., p. 14.

[3] Ibid., p. 110.

[4] Ibid., p. 365.

[5] Pirie and Worcester, *Millennial Generation*.

[6] Ibid., p. 21.

[7] Ibid., pp. 10–11.

[8] HMSO, *Social Trends*.

[9] Pirie and Worcester, *Millennial Generation*, p. 12.

[10] On singleness, with projections for Millennials, see HMSO, *Social Trends*, pp. 50–1; on singleness and family aspirations, see Pirie and Worcester, *Millennial Generation*, p. 16.

[11] Pirie and Worcester, *Millennial Generation*, p. 11.

[12] Ibid., p. 15.

[13] Ibid., p. 8.

[14] Ibid., pp. 13–14: 'A breakdown of the answers shows a huge gain in respect for teachers by eighteen to twenty-year-olds. Compared with their counterparts twelve years ago, 47 %of these young people list teachers as against the 32 percent who did so in 1986, nearly half as many again.' See also p. 17.

[15] Brierley, *The Tide Is Running Out*.

[16] Pirie and Worcester, *Millennial Generation*, p. 17.

[17] Ibid., p. 19.

[18] Ibid., pp. 18–19.

[19] Ibid., pp. 8, 21.

Chapter 11

[1] Finch, *Family Obligations*, p. 53.

[2] While the 'typical' nuclear family of contemporary society may be made up of two parents and their children this is increasingly not the case. A survey published in *The Daily Telegraph*, 30 September 1998, shows that 23% or nearly one in four families with dependent children is headed by a single parent. This excludes cohabiting couples and couples who married after the birth of their children. The number of single parent families has almost doubled over the last thirteen years.

[3] Rogerson, 'Family Structures of Grace', pp. 25–42.

[4] It is not good for Adam to be alone (Gen 2:18), while it is God who sets the lonely in families (Ps. 68:6).

[5] For more detail see J. Goetzmann, 'Oikos' in Colin Brown (ed.), *Dictionary of New Testament Theology* Vol. 2 (Carlisle: Paternoster Press, 1986), pp. 247–51.

[6] Philo: *Legatio*, pp. 115, 210.

[7] Ibid. and Josephus: *Contra Apionem* 2.178.

[8] 'Children, obey your parents in everything, for this pleases the Lord.' (Col. 3:20). This passage deals in sequence with wives, husbands and

children: each group is addressed directly, with their place in the body of Christ being affirmed.

[9] D.C. Verner, *The Household of God: The Social World of the Pastoral Epistles.* (SBLDS 71; Chicago: Scholar's Press, 1983).

[10] On the close relationship between leadership development and succession planning in the wider sphere, see e.g. v. Chowdhury, *Management 21C* (London: *Financial Times*, 2000), p. 181.

[11] G. Kuhrt, *An Introduction to Christian Ministry: Following Your Vocation in the Church of England* (London: Church House Publishing, 2000), pp. 83–92.

[12] D. Horton, *Congregationalism: A Study in Church Polity* (London: Independent Press, 1952), pp. 17–51.

[13] J.H. Leith, *Introduction to the Reformed Tradition* (Atlanta: John Knox Press, 1981), pp. 155–64.

[14] W. Grudem, *Systematic Theology: An Introduction to Biblical Doctrine* (Leicester: Inter-Varsity Press, 1994), p. 935.

[15] Walker, *Restoring the Kingdom*.

[16] Bebbington, *Evangelicalism in Modern Britain*, pp. 201–53; N.G. Wright, *The Radical Evangelical: Seeking a Place to Stand* (London: SPCK, 1996), pp. 73–86; R.J. Coleman, *Issues of Theological Conflict: Liberals and Evangelicals* (Grand Rapids: Eerdmans, 1972).

[17] Source: P. Brierley and H. Wraight, *UK Christian Handbook: 1996/7 Edition* (London: Christian Research, 1995), p. 673.

[18] H.S. Stout, *The Divine Dramatist: George Whitefield and the Rise of Modern Evangelism* (Grand Rapids: Eerdmans, 1991).

[19] C.P. Williams, 'The Recruitment and Training of Overseas Missionaries in England Between 1850 and 1900' (M. Litt. Thesis; University of Bristol, 1976), pp. 17–22, 311, Appendix A. Cit. B. Stanley, *The Bible and the Flag: Protestant Missions and British Imperialism in the Nineteenth and Twentieth Centuries* (Leicester: Apollos, 1990), p. 83.

[20] Randall and Hilborn, *One Body in Christ*, pp. 283–308; P. Lewis, 'Renewal, Recovery and Growth: 1966 Onwards', in Steve Brady and Harold Rowdon (eds.), *For Such a Time as This: Perspectives on Evangelicalism, Past, Present and Future* (Milton Keynes/London: Scripture Union/Evangelical Alliance, 1996), p. 187; J. Edwards, 'The Evangelical Alliance: A National Phenomenon', in Brady and Rowdon (eds.), *For Such a Time as This*, pp. 51–9.

[21] For an account of Phil Wall's vision and approach see his *I'll Fight ...: Holiness at War* (Tonbridge: Sovereign World, 1998).

[22] D. McBain, *Fire Over the Waters: Renewal Among the Baptists and Others from the 1960s to the 1990s* (London: Darton, Longman & Todd, 1997), pp. 64ff.; Scotland, *Charismatics and the New Millennium*, p. 16.

[23] These details are based on an interview with Erica Youngman-Butler, former MFJ International Co-ordinator. The early story of MFJ is recorded in: G. Kendrick, G. Coates, R. Forster and L. Green, *March For Jesus* (Eastbourne: Kingsway Publications, 1992). See also Scotland, *Charismatics and the New Millennium*, pp. 319–20.

[24] M.R. Watts, *The Dissenters: From the Reformation to the French Revolution* (Oxford: Clarendon Press, 1978), pp. 212–20; D.L. Edwards, *Christian England* (London: Fount, 1989), p. 301.

[25] These observations are based on an interview with Jason Clark, a leader in the Sutton Vineyard in Surrey. On the Vineyard ministry in general, see McBain, *Fire Over the Waters*, pp. 91–107; Scotland, *Charismatics and the New Millennium*, pp. 27–9; E.E. Wright, *Strange Fire? Assessing the Vineyard Movement and the Toronto Blessing* (Darlington: Evangelical Press, 1996).

[26] On the statistical decline in ministers, and people offering for ministry, see P. Brierley (ed.), *Religious Trends 2000/2001 No. 2* (London: Christian Research/Harper Collins, 1999), p. 2.12.

[27] Brierley, *The Tide Is Running Out*, p. 4.9

[28] Evangelical Alliance, *Evangelical Alliance Commission on Strategic Evangelism* (Inaugural Report; London: Evangelical Alliance, 1998), p. 21.

[29] M. Bird, 'Generation X Lifestyle Survey', insert in *idea*, May 2001.

[30] Christian Publicity Organisation, *Faith in Life: A Snapshot of Church Life in England at the Beginning of the 21st Century* (London: CPO, 2001), p. 8.

[31] For such examples, see T.A. Lacey, *Unity and Schism* (London: Mowbray, 1917); S.L. Greenslade, *Schism in the Early Church* (London: SCM, 1953).

[32] Walker, *Restoring the Kingdom*, pp. 51–64.

[33] Ibid.

[34] Bebbington, *Evangelicalism in Modern Britain*, p. 275.

[35] K. Hylson-Smith, 'Roots of Pan-Evangelicalism 1735–1835', in Brady and Rowdon (eds.), *For Such a Time as This*, p. 137.

[36] M. Robinson, *The Faith of the Unbeliever* (East Sussex: Monarch, 1994), pp. 147–8.

[37] J. Wesley, *The Journal of The Rev. John Wesley* Volume 1 (London: Robert Culley, 1909), pp. 475–6.

[38] R.P. Heitzenrater, *Wesley and the People Called Methodists* (Nashville: Abingdon Press, 1995).

[39] A.W. Gomes, *Unmasking the Cults* (Carlisle: OM Publishing, 1995), pp. 62–80.

[40] For the implications of this, and other biblical models of effective leadership succession, see O.J. Sanders, *Spiritual Leadership* (London: Lakeland/STL, 1981 [1967]), pp. 137–41.

[41] F. Wendel, *Calvin* (London: Fontana, 1965), p. 106.

[42] Interview with Steve Double, leader of St. Austell Church.

[43] *Christianity Today* 45.1 (8 January 2001), p. 20.

[44] Among the many evangelical books published on the subject in the last few years see: T. and R. Engstrom, *The Fine Art of Mentoring* (Brentwood, TN: Wolgemuth and Hyatt, 1989); G. Krallmann, *Mentoring for Mission: A Handbook on Leadership Principles Exemplified by Jesus Christ* (2nd edn; Hong Kong: Jensco, 1992); P. Stanley, *Connecting: The Mentoring Relationships You Need to Succeed in Life* (Colorado: Navpress, 1992); B. Biehl, *Mentoring: Confidence in Finding and Becoming One* (Nashville: Broadman & Holman, 1996).

[45] Stanley, *Connecting*, p. 33.

[46] Biehl, *Mentoring*, p. 19.

[47] J. Green, S. McKnight, I.H. Marshall (eds), *Dictionary of Jesus and the Gospels* (Leicester: Inter-Varsity Press, 1992), pp. 176–82.

[48] Krallmann, *Mentoring for Mission*, p. 33.

[49] Stanley, *Connecting*, p. 41.

[50] Ibid., p. 162.

[51] *The NIV Study Bible* (Great Britain: The Zondervan Corporation, 1987), p. 1786.

[52] Krallmann, *Mentoring for Mission*, p. 130.

[53] Ibid., p. 125.

[54] Ibid., p. 124.

Chapter 12

[1] GrahamCray, 'Postmodernism: Mutual Society in Crisis', in N. Barker (ed.), *Building a Relational Society* (London: Arena, 1996), p. 69.

[2] M. Moynagh and R. Worsley, *Tomorrow* (London: Lexicon, 2000), p. 85.

[3] Ibid., p. 94.

[4] Ibid., p. 94.

[5] Age Concern, *The Debate of the Age* (London: Age Concern, 2000).

[6] M. Moynagh, 'The Tailor-Made Church?', in *Christian Herald*, 23 October 1999, p. 9.

[7] Ibid.

[8] J. Buckeridge, 'Editorial', in *Youthwork*, July 2000, p. 1.

[9] GrahamCray, *Youth Congregations and the Emerging Church* (Cambridge: Grove Books, 2002), p. 18.

[10] J. Stott (ed.), *The Pasadena Consultation: Homogeneous Unit* (Lausanne Occasional Papers No. 1; Wheaton, Ill.: Lausanne Committee for World Evangelization, 1977), p. 3.

[11] Ibid., p. 3.

[12] Ibid.

[13] Ibid., p. 4.

[14] Ibid., p. 4.

[15] Dunn, *Unity and Diversity*, pp. 235–308; Christopher Rowland, *Christian Origins*, London: SPCK, 1985, pp. 109ff.; N.T. Wright, *The New Testament and the People of God* (London: SPCK, 1992), pp. 118–20, 341–58, 444–64; Tidball, *Social Context of the New Testament*, pp. 41–75.

[16] Stott (ed.), *Pasadena Consultation*, p. 4.

[17] Ibid., p. 7.

[18] Ibid., p. 6.

[19] W.J. Abraham, *The Logic of Evangelism* (London: Hodder & Stoughton, 1989).

[20] M. Ashton and P. Moon, *Christian Youth Work* (Eastbourne: Kingsway, 1986), p. 147.

[21] D.M. Wells, *God in the Wasteland: The Reality of Truth in a World of Fading Dreams* (Leicester: Inter-Varsity Press, 1990), p. 71.

[22] Cray, *Youth Congregations*, p. 15.

[23] Stott (ed.), *Pasadena Consultation*, 1977, p. 5.

[24] P. Wagner, *Church Growth and the Whole Gospel: A Biblical Mandate* (Eugene: Wipf & Stock, 1998), p. 168.

[25] Ashton and Moon, *Christian Youth Work*, p. 153.

[26] Mayo and Baxter, 'Is History Repeating Itself?'.

[27] Ibid.

[28] J.O. Balswick and J.K. Balswick, *The Family: a Christian Perspective on the Contemporary Home* (2nd edn.; Grand Rapids: Baker Book House, 1999).

[29] John and Olive Drane, *Happy Families* (London: HarperColins, 1995), p. 92.

[30] Ibid., p. 93.

[31] Mayo and Baxter, 'Is History Repeating Itself?'.

[32] For a survey of the movement see Draper and Draper, *Refreshing Worship*. Also P. Ward (ed.), *Mass Culture: Eucharist and Mission in a Post-Modern World* (Oxford: Bible Reading Fellowship, 1999).

[33] For case studies see M. Riddell, *Threshold of the Future: Reforming the Church in the Postmodern West* (London: SPCK, London, 1998), pp. 157–75; Draper and Draper, *Refreshing Worship*.

[34] Riddell, *Threshold of the Future*, p. 11.

[35] For further descriptions see Hilborn, *Picking Up the Pieces*, pp. 119–62.

[36] M. Dawn, 'You have to Change to Stay the Same', in *The Post-Evangelical Debate* (London: SPCK, 1997), pp. 35–56.

[37] Ibid., p. 49.

Appendices

[1] Coupland, *Generation X*; Hamblett and Deverson, *Generation X*.

[2] For more on the notion of youth generations as 'led cohorts', see the main body of our report.

Index

Useful Contacts on Generational Issues

Crusaders: Equipping, empowering and encouraging leaders to reach young people for Jesus Christ and engage them in effective Christian living with a passion to connect with unchurched youth and children.

Tel.:   01727 855422
E-mail: email@crusaders.org.uk
Web: www.crusaders.org.uk www.life2themax.net

European Evangelical Alliance (EEA): Encouraging national youth networks across Europe. Nurturing a new generation of Europeans who want to help build God's Kingdom in public life.

Tel.:   020 7582 7276
E-mail: EEAoffice@aol.com
Web: www.european.org www.nesfor.org

Fusion: Working strategically with churches and students to plant and multiply student cells and see students equipped to impact and transform their universities and future workplaces.

Tel.:   01243 531898 #307
E-mail: admin@fusion.uk.com
Web: www.fusioncells.net

Graduate Impact: Helping people in the transition from university into the workplace. Operating as a joint venture between UCCF and the London Institute for Contemporary Christianity to train final year students to see the role they can carry out for Christ in their working life and to see recent graduates well supported by their churches as they move into this new phase of life.

Tel.:   020 7399 9564
E-mail: tim@graduateimpact.com
Web: www.graduateimpact.com

Joshua Generation: Investing in emerging generations of leaders to transform society. Supporting young people in the transition to university, students through university and young adults in their workplace.

Tel.:   020 8947 1313
E-mail: admin@joshgen.org
Web: www.joshgen.org

Oasis Trust: Providing mentored work placements for 18–25 year olds across a broad range of vocations, coupled with weekly training on the intrinsic links between faith and work through the Oasis Youth Vocation Programme.

Tel.:   020 7450 9022
E-mail: laura.bagley@oasistrust.org
Web: www.oasistrust.org/youthvocationprogramme

Soul Survivor: Longing to see young people grow in relationship with God and equipped to go. Intimate worship, passionate about his word and open to all the Holy Spirit wants to do.

Tel.:   01923 333331
E-mail: info@soulsurvivor.com
Web: www.soulsurvivor.com

Spring Harvest: Equipping young adults through evolution and student evolution – the next step for those aged 17–25. Annual events and ongoing resources to help you engage with God, with each other, with your culture.

Tel.:   01825 769111
E-mail: info@springharvest.org
Web: www.springharvest.org

Steward's Trust: Offering Teaching Weekends Away for young adults, seeking to refresh, nourish and encourage those embarking on their working lives and equipping them as Christians in the workplace, complementing their regular church life.

Tel.:   0870 241 3567
E-mail: finolastack@easel.fsworld.co.uk